The Dream of Human Life. *This is a reproduction of one of Michaelangelo's drawings made by a member of one of Mrs. Pogson's groups in 1961. See page 410.*

THE WORK LIFE

Based on Teachings of G. I. Gurdjieff,
P. D. Ouspensky and Maurice Nicoll

Beryl Pogson

SAMUEL WEISER, INC.

York Beach, Maine

First published in 1994 by
Samuel Weiser, Inc.
P.O. Box 612
York Beach, ME 03910-0612

Library of Congress Cataloging-in-Publication Data

Pogson, Beryl
    The work life : based on the teachings of G. I. Gurdjieff, P. D.
  Ouspensky, and Maurice Nicoll / by Beryl Pogson.
        p.   cm.
    Includes bibliographical references and index.
    1. Fourth Way (Occultism)   2. Gurdjieff, Georges Ivanovitch,
  1872–1949.   3. Uspenkii, P. D. (Petr Dem 'Ianovich), 1878–1947.
  4. Nicoll, Maurice, 1884–1953. I. Title.
  BP605.G92P64   1994
  197—dc20   93–45899
                                                            CIP

ISBN 0–87728–809–7
EB
Printed in the United States of America

99   98   97   96   95   94
10   9   8   7   6   5   4   3   2   1

Table of Contents

As with men, it has always seemed to me that books have their own peculiar destinies. They go towards the people who are waiting for them, and reach them at the right moment. They are made of living material and continue to cast light through the darkness long after the death of their authors.

—Miguel Serrano
C. G. Jung and Herman Hesse

Foreword

The esoteric teaching known to those who try to follow it as "the Work" was introduced to the West by G. I. Gurdjieff in the first quarter of the 20th century. Beryl Pogson studied the Work for many years under one of Mr. Gurdjieff's pupils, Dr. Maurice Nicoll.[1] Before his death in 1953, Dr. Nicoll had authorized Mrs. Pogson to teach, and by 1955 she had groups in Sussex and London, where meetings were held at her Nutley Terrace flat in Hampstead. However, these groups lacked scope for the experience of practical group work with other people, known in this teaching as the second line of work.

At Easter 1956, Mrs. Pogson took a number of her group to Dorton House in Buckinghamshire for the first time. For the next six years at Christmas, Easter, and in the summer, she conducted residential sessions of intensive group work there. At these times Mrs. Pogson held meetings daily. Those who were present had ample opportunity in the varied activities between the meetings to put into practice what they heard.

The meetings were not formal lectures followed by questions. Frequently Mrs. Pogson would ask for a question at the beginning, and would allow the discussion to take its course from the question asked. It was her objective to bring everyone into a quiet, inward place in themselves. Drawing together this very ordinary group of people—all from different backgrounds, and at different stages in the Work—into a unity of purpose was possible partly to the special circumstances of the session, to the common aim shared by those who had made the effort and sacrifices to attend, and most of all because of the leadership and inspired teaching of Mrs. Pogson, herself. It was she who "held the level," as she expressed it, enabling others to see truths and experience states of consciousness they might never glimpse in the ordinary course of their lives.

---

[1]For her detailed life of Dr. Nicoll see Beryl Pogson's *Maurice Nicoll: A Portrait* (London: Vincent Stuart, 1961; reprinted New York: Fourth Way Books, 1987).

In the varied activities undertaken at Dorton, people could make practical use of the energy and new understanding created at the meetings. The activities included major projects that demanded the skills of all those present, like the series of mural paintings depicting the Labors of Hercules, building a summer house, and making a glass mosaic representing the twelve signs of the zodiac. These projects were often intentionally ambitious, and there was an element of the miraculous in getting each completed in the strictly limited time of the session. On the other hand, people also worked more at their own pace and according to their ability when making pottery and painting. Each session included a hastily rehearsed production of a drama, usually by Shakespeare or one of the Greek tragedians.[2]

The excellence of the result was never the most important consideration in these activities. The first purpose was that people through doing things fresh to them should have the opportunity to develop their inner potential. Secondly, that in taking part in work together as a group, they should begin to see how all things can be performed with more awareness.

In between these sessions at Dorton, Mrs. Pogson held meetings every fortnight at her Hampstead flat. Over this time an annual pattern was established, and this plan included intensive work at certain times, and periods when people were more or less on their own, when they could attempt to practice in everyday life something of what they had learned. This pattern continued when Mrs. Pogson moved to Upper Dicker in Sussex in 1961, giving her group a residential center. From that time the sessions, alternating with regular meetings, went on uninterrupted until Mrs. Pogson's death in 1967.

It was only in 1958 that Mrs. Pogson began to ask people to keep a record of these discussions, and as this volume shows, the earlier attempts were often sketchy personal summaries rather than a verbatim report. However, later records were more accurate, and were corrected by Mrs. Pogson, herself. The editors have made many minor alterations to the wording in the interests of clarity, but without altering the meaning. In arriving at an arrangement of the extracts chosen, the editors decided against either a strictly chrono-

---

[2]Mrs. Pogson had made a deep study of Shakespearean drama and published a book of commentaries on certain plays: *In the East My Pleasure Lies* (London: Stuart and Richards, 1950).

logical sequence or an arrangement according to subject. Instead, in view of the importance Mrs. Pogson attached to the year as a recurring pattern consciously devised to assist men and women in their efforts to awaken, the records of meetings for three years (1958 to 1961) have been treated as a single year by bringing together into each chapter the meetings held in successive years at the same season or festival. The single exception to this practice is the series of talks on cosmology (see chapter 4). When various discussions of a subject are scattered in different contexts in the book, the reader will be able to bring them together with the help of the index. Footnotes have been used sparingly for the same purpose. Other footnotes refer the reader to comparable discussions in other volumes of Work Talks by Mrs. Pogson and in other Work books. See bibliography for a complete list of other titles written by Mrs. Pogson.

CHAPTER 1

NUTLEY TERRACE, ADVENT

On the Year
December 1, 1959

(2) Jesus said: Let him who seeks, not cease seeking until he finds, and when he finds, he will be troubled, and when he has been troubled, he will marvel and he will reign over the All.[1]

MRS. POGSON: I want to consider the second of these sayings of Jesus from the *Gospel of Thomas*. It has some interesting connections. It was among the fragments found in 1897 or 1903. . . . It appears that it is pre-Christian and very old, and can be traced back to the Egyptian Mysteries.

You see what is written? These refer to the five stages of development which can be traced through all the great religions, and we find them not only there but in nature as well. It is marvelous to think that organic life, in which man is placed and which is a background for man, contains these correspondences. These stages—which belong to the year and are stages in the progression of the sun through the year—are also stages in initiation.

You begin in the winter solstice with the *finding*, with the birth. The God has to be found—also in oneself. Then comes spring, the time for work and the doing of miracles. Then comes summer, when the sun, when Christ, is at the height of his power. Then comes a curious time, when the sun begins to descend. Then comes the end of the year, when the sun has to depart.

You see, first the new thing has to be found. I think this refers to Christ; the newborn has to be found in oneself. Then he does wonders, and is troubled, and has new experiences. Then he has power.

---

[1]A. Guillaumont, H.-CH. Puech, G. Quispel, W. Till, Yassah 'Abd Al Masih, *The Gospel According to Thomas* (Leiden: E. J. Brill, 1959), section 2. All other references to the Gospels are from the same volume.

Then come the last two stages which are the times of death and regeneration. If we follow the course of Hercules, this is the time when he goes down into the Underworld. . . . This is a period when work has to be done, when you are shocked, when you meet with difficulties. Then there comes a time when Christ is powerful in a man; and after that the test of death, when it becomes possible to die to oneself.

Robert Graves equates these stages with trees (see *The White Goddess*). There are five trees. The tree of birth he calls the silver fir, the pine, which has become our Christmas tree. The palm tree plays a similar role in some legends. Apollo was born under a palm. In European countries we have the Christmas tree to celebrate the first stage.

The tree connected with spring is the gorse. Is it not nearly always in flower? Yet there is a time when the prickles have to go so that the new can come. The wonder is that the old can be stripped away and burned by the power of the sun; and then the new can come. The next is the heather, which is connected with summer. It is sacred to Venus and Isis and signifies the mystic marriage. The tree connected with autumn is the white poplar or aspen. When Hercules conquered death, so the legend goes, he bound his head with aspen, which explains why their leaves are white on one side. The last one is the yew. It belongs to the end, to death. The other was the mystical death. The yew is dangerous to animals; it is a tree that can kill. I just present this for you to think about. It is an interesting correspondence. (Our "tree" discussion appears on page 4.)

We think at Christmas about the birth of the New Man. This is in all the great religions. The infant Bacchus came in a basket, floating on the water. There is the story of Moses, and a similar story in other legends. The point is that the child is found, and he has to be found in a *container*. It is always something simple, an ordinary container in which the infant can float until it is found. We talk about this in the Work, that there must be a container to protect the child until it is found and received.

Then, after it is found, comes the stage of work when there are shocks. And then the stage when one's being begins to have some unity and power.

X: Does this mean that at certain times of year there is more force than at others?

MRS. POGSON: There is a certain rhythm in the year. All through the ages, influences have been directed at specific times of year, and there are correspondences between the religions. The Celtic New Year corresponds to All Saints Day; 2nd February is celebrated in the Christian religion as Candlemas or the Feast of St. Bridget. The birth of a solar God is always celebrated at the winter solstice.

X: So we must learn how to work with these influences—go with the stream?

MRS. POGSON: Yes. We have to see what the influences are and do what is possible. Don't start making something quite new at the beginning of November because it is the time for throwing away. As it is said in Ecclesiastes: There is a time for building and a time for throwing down. These are cosmic influences. There are certain nodes in the year, just as we have tides in our lives.

[The following sayings from the *Gospel of Thomas* were read:]

(3) Jesus said: If those who lead you say to you: "See, the Kingdom is in heaven," then the birds of the heaven will precede you. If they say to you: "It is in the sea," then the fish will precede you. But the Kingdom is within you and it is without you. If you will know yourselves, then you will be known and you will know that you are the sons of the Living Father. But if you do not know yourselves, then you are in poverty and you are poverty.

(4) Jesus said: The man old in days will not hesitate to ask a little child of seven days about the place of Life, and he will live. For many who are first shall become last and they shall become a single one.

(5) Jesus said: Know what is in thy sight, and what is Hidden from thee will be revealed to thee. For there is nothing hidden which will not be manifest.

(6) His disciples asked Him, they said to Him: Wouldst thou that we fast, and how should we pray, and should we give alms, and what diet should we observe? Jesus said: Do not lie; and do not do what you hate, for all things are manifest before Heaven. For there is nothing hidden that shall not be revealed and there is nothing covered that shall remain without being uncovered.

The Twelve Trees.

Astrological Sign	Element	Tree	Significance
Capricorn	Earth	Birch	Beating the "bounds."
Aquarius	Air	Rowan	Quickbeam. "Tree of Life."
Pisces	Water	Ash	The tree of sea power; sacred to Poseidon.
Aries	Fire	Alder	Three dyes: *Red* bark, *green* leaves, *brown* bark.
Taurus	Earth	Willow	Witch. Wicker for baskets.
Gemini	Air	Hawthorn	Unlucky tree; enforced chastity.
Cancer	Water	Oak	Royalty of oak; tree of Zeus, Jupiter, and Hercules.
Leo	Fire	Holly	Means "holy." Barley harvest.
Virgo	Earth	Hazel	Divining hidden water. Tree of wisdom.
Libra	Air	Vine	Tree of joy, exhilaration.
Scorpio	Water	Ivy	Month of Bacchanal revels. Ivy bush. Ivy ale at Trinity college.
Sagittarius	Fire	Dwarf Elder	Arrows are made. Elder is unlucky. King William Rufus killed by archer posted under elder tree. Crucifixion tree.

MRS. POGSON: This saying about the birds, when it occurred in the earlier fragment, was quite muddled. Now we can understand it. All these sayings are about self-knowledge and about the necessity for knowing yourselves first. Only when we know ourselves will we be known. What does this mean? Is this what you want? *How many of you really want to be known?* When we know ourselves, there is something in us that we can be connected with. Then it is possible to know where we belong. The only real poverty is lack of self-knowledge.

X: What do you think is meant by the man old in days asking a little child of seven days about the place of Life?

MRS. POGSON: What do *you* think?

X: I thought it referred to someone fully developed.

MRS. POGSON: Don't you think it refers to the Essence in him? To the new birth? The old man is the unregenerate man. We all have this old man in us when we come into the Work. But the old man has no life in him except by virtue of this child, this Essence, this spark in him. All real knowledge will come from what is newborn; it is intuitive knowledge. Whoever has this always has a connection. For the child is connected with higher centers. So the old man can ask the child about the place of Life, and he will live.

It is interesting that the Greek word for truth means "not-forgetting." This child in us can give us real truth, because it remembers.

X: It is interesting that although we have this connection in us, we have to be taught from without.

MRS. POGSON: Yes. First we have to be taught from without because Essence has been smothered by life. A system has been specially devised to teach people. But you find in the Work that you gradually begin to remember things and make inner connections. The deepest parts in us are always connected with this truth. Some mystics, like Jacob Boehme, could be taught from within. Education and the stress of life take us away from what we know. But then you find in the Work that you begin to recognize things; you remember. One of the most important things in the Work is to feed Essence.

X: Do you think that if one goes through a period when Essence is being fed, one has intuitive knowledge, and then when it is not being fed, one loses it?

MRS. POGSON: Yes. The literal mind would say nonsense to the intuitive knowledge. In the sixth saying the disciples ask Christ about fasting and praying and giving alms. But you see, Christ does not answer directly. He says: Do not lie! Dr. Nicoll used to answer formatory questions like this. In esoteric teaching a formatory question is not answered directly.

What is meant by Christ's answer: Do not lie, and do not do what you hate?

X: From a higher level in ourselves we would hate these things in us. But as we are, we can only see what we hate in other people, and we can only try not to do what we hate in other people.

And it means, don't go against real conscience. But until we are linked with real conscience, it can mean don't go against the instructions of the Work.

X: If we've done something, we can see it and hate it afterwards.

X: I thought of it in connection with what the Work says, that lying kills Essence.

MRS. POGSON: Yes, this is what it means. *Lying is the chief obstacle to seeing oneself.* Don't lie to yourself. Then you come to see yourself. And when you no longer lie to yourself, you won't lie to others. The instructions are so simple. If we could follow them, everything would be changed. They are school instructions which are only given to disciples. How much of the Work is in them!

The Meaning of Christmas
December 20, 1960

MRS. POGSON: In speaking about Christmas we have to realize that before there can be any new truth, there has to be some kind of conjunction, just as there must be in order to have a physical birth. There has to be some conjunction with the

Work. If you can conjoin with certain ideas and see the good of them, something may happen. You begin perhaps by being in love with some of the ideas of the Work or with an example from one of the teachers of the Work; but then you have to conjoin with some of the ideas of the Work yourself.

[There was a reading from Nicoll, *Psychological Commentaries,* Vol. V, p. 1631, "Conjunction with the Work."]

Mrs. Pogson: Now, there are two kinds of people here. There are people still in self-love, even in the Work. They seem to love the Work although really they love themselves in the Work. And then there are others who are beginning to love the Work. If you begin to have conjunction with the Work, it is like someone speaking in you, like the herald. If you have affection for it, you can conjoin with the Work, and something new can begin to be born. This is, in one way, the meaning of Christmas.

Christmas is also a time for expanding our relationships. This is represented externally as going shopping and buying things for people, but internally it means opening our hearts to people.

We will speak about diagram 1 below. If you're looking on your life in horizontal time, you see Christmas—Christmas—Christmas, one after the other. When you were in Essence, as a small child, you had lovely impressions of Christmas. Then the Christmases go on, and people get quite old and look back on past Christmases and

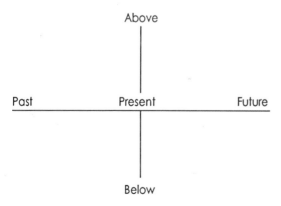

Diagram 1. Passing Time and Eternity.

compare, thinking of the Christmases they used to have. This is mechanical man. Back they go, always comparing. Do you see how negative emotion comes in here? It always does when you compare. But this is only along the horizontal line. When you compare, imagination comes in. "That was a wonderful Christmas," you say. But was it really? You think only of the lovely Christmases in the past, the nice party, the nice dress. But something was wrong somewhere. Now do you see where this person is who wrote: "I'll be thankful when Christmas is over?"

The Work teaches something different—that Christmas is NOW. I've spoken before of the Aeon of our real destiny, where the Real I is. At the nodes, at special times of the year, in particular the winter solstice when the sun is reborn, we can be connected with this. And here it is possible to experience the joy of a connection with higher influences. Here all our Christmases come together. This is true of our Dorton Christmases, isn't it? That they are all, in a sense, one. From the logical mind we can recall different Christmases at Dorton, but it's all one Christmas, simply this experience of everyone being together, because people no longer in the body are present at these times. They're in the Aeon.

CHAPTER 2

CHRISTMAS AT DORTON

Fear and Faith
December 24, 1959

MRS. POGSON: The first sentence of the angels' message at Christmas was "Be not afraid." Why was this?

X: Might it not be in contrast to the fears so often referred to in the Old Testament?

MRS. POGSON: Fear here is better described as awe, the awe that should be felt by the lower level toward the higher. People have not enough awe.

Then there are the other kinds of fear we suffer from—material fears, fears of the future and destiny, fears for health—which underlie the Christmas festivities, but which can be absorbed if, like the Shepherds, we had what is called "the Great Fear," the fear of the revelation of God. It was this fear to which the angels' message referred. The angels can really speak to them if they have the fear of God. Faith and fear are closely connected, because fear can only be dispelled by faith.[1] In St. Paul's Epistle to the Philippians he says:

> Be careful for nothing; but in every thing by prayer and supplication with thanksgiving let your requests be made known unto God (4:6).[2]

The meaning of the Greek word used for "being careful" or "being anxious" is having a divided mind; and this clearly illustrates how in anxiety we are at the mercy of small "I's" dragging us in different

---

[1]For teaching on fear, see Beryl Pogson: *Work Talks at the Dicker*, 1966, pp. 86–92.
[2]References to the bible are from the King James version.

directions. . . . When we are divided we become glued to something and hear nothing else. Drag yourself away and you hear again. When we are divided by the small fears of Christmas we cannot hear the angels. We shall not be open to the message.

One of the material fears mentioned was of our destiny, but in the Work we know that our destiny is cared for; our greatest concern is to be able to fulfill it.

In the grip of small "I's" we have fears at every moment but they disappear when we can look out from a higher place.

We are told that Koestler had a wonderful vision in self-remembering and while he was returning from it he became aware of a small nagging thought on the fringe of his mind reminding him of some tiresome requirement of ordinary life. He then remembered that he was to be executed next day; but something else in him knew that it was his destiny, seen perhaps in relation to a long series of lives, although the small "I's" in him where he then was would be very frightened. When St. Paul wrote the passage which I quoted previously in his Epistle to the Philippians about being anxious for nothing, he also was awaiting trial and execution.

It is the purpose of the Work to help us to remember that the two levels are there, and that the higher level which we do occasionally contact *is* accessible.

X: I have wondered why I can't get back after a wonderful experience.

MRS. POGSON: The Work memory is not strong enough to register it and say, "We must have this in our memory."

Dame Julian, in a revelation, was told repeatedly that "All manner of things shall be well." This memory remained with her for the rest of her life. It is an example of a deeply felt shock accompanied by self-remembering.

With the Shepherds, the same angel commanded and also comforted in freeing them from the Great Fear which, when felt, swallows up all lesser fears.

December 26, 1959

MRS. POGSON: The question is, how to remember the higher Work experiences when the feeling of "I" is in small "I's." This requires faith. We all have to do something to preserve our memory of these moments of certainty; when one has need of them, they are there. Asking is need.

We have to have need of these moments; but we also have to assemble the moments of certainty we have had, so that they are accessible to us.

We were speaking yesterday of two kinds of fear. One kind of fear belongs to small "I's" and the outer divisions of the mind. Another fear is the fear of God—awe. Thoughts of anxiety are one of the most frequent causes of negative emotions—small fears about something that may never happen.

We also talked about destiny, but man does not want to know about his or her real destiny. In deeper "I's," all you want is to fulfill your higher destiny, for when you were conscious you chose that destiny, and saw the pattern of life, and knew what it was possible to do.

Do you sometimes try to see in directed imagination what this vision might have been, what you were able to see before you returned to this body? Then you knew it was possible, that you had enough gifts and strength for what was intended, *as long as the pattern was followed. . . .* The thing is to follow the pattern and not to break it. It becomes a wasted life if the pattern is broken. Then the life has to be lived over again . . .

For years Essence is smothered and we forget the pattern. Then there is a vague feeling that there was something, and we seek meaning. All the great religions have instructions, and people go to one of these religions for teaching. The Work has these instructions. So for a long time you have to follow the instructions of the Work; then the child in you will show the way and take you in the right direction, although you may not know where it is taking you. When people have gone in one way for a long time, things become more simple. Then you begin to see.

From our parents—and the environment they have given us— we get certain characteristics to work against. They help in the development of personality—what we can use in life—and of false personality. This is the enemy for Essence to work against, and which it needs in order to become strong. When you think of choosing your parents, do you think of it in this way? From the point of view of parents, you have to develop your children and equip them as well as possible for the world.

December 28, 1959

MRS. POGSON: What general questions have people got?

X: Can faith be connected with knowing what is possible for one at any time?

MRS. POGSON: Why, yes. We call faith an *awareness of levels*. This is what Dr. Nicoll told us it could be called. Faith shows us levels in ourselves and what is possible at any one time, although to small "I's" the same thing might appear as impossible. No one need ever be discouraged who understands levels in man. For whenever anything seems difficult, psychologically difficult, you know that at a higher level it will not seem so. The way of the Work stretching before you may seem difficult to a lower level. Yet you know that at your level, as you are, you do not have to meet these difficulties; there is something at a higher level that can take over.

X: There is a world of difference between feeling you are nothing and feeling too feeble to cope.

MRS. POGSON: Yes. These are negative "I's." Isn't that an expression of their's? "Too feeble to cope!" In an inner place there are "I's" that can act for you. You must discriminate between what the small "I's" say and what the deeper "I's" say.

X: One set of "I's" may be very active, and the deeper "I's" more passive. You can also tell the difference by the smaller "I's" that want to do something, and the bigger "I's" that know they can't.

MRS. POGSON: Yes. They know that something else will do it, if you can step out of the way of the clamouring "I's," and let it act for you.

X: Why can't we do this?

MRS. POGSON: Because we do not discriminate levels enough. You have to be able to distinguish all levels, so that you know where you are all the time.

[A diagram of the emotional center was put on the board (see diagram 2 on p. 14).[3]]

X: Isn't it true that it's very difficult to be sincere with oneself when one is identified with negative "I's"?"

MRS. POGSON: Any thought will lie when you are in a negative state. It is good to have seen this and to remember afterward what you have seen. Now let us look at the list on the board (see page 189). In the outer division of the negative part of the emotional center are the small negative "I's" that can come at any time of the day. We can work on these at the time. Here are small irritations which can be worked on each day.

In the middle division of the negative part of the center are self-emotions. These are emotions which have become habitual, like self-pity, resentment, regret, melancholy, nostalgia, which is a kind of self-pity. These negative emotions have been with you for such a long time that you can't work on them directly or at the time. They have to be worked on indirectly—through the mind—by *metanoia*. For example, with regret, you have to see that it is a negative emotion, and cancel it. So also with self-pity. It takes time. It can be done by thinking differently about it. Through the power of this new thinking which the Work gives us, these emotions can be changed. Self-pity is due to a feeling of being owed. Through the thinking of the Work, you see you have what is needed or what you have attracted. Or disappointment. When you were a child you expected the weather to be fine for a picnic, and you were disappointed when it was not. Later it's like that in bigger things. You become disappointed in people or things. In the Work, we know this is silly because we know that anything can happen. The deeper negative emotions, in the inner part of the center, are a different matter. People should know their own deeper negative emotions. Someone may have resentment, envy, or jealousy. You should try to name it.

X: Is this the sort that can only be transformed by prayer?

---

[3]Cf. the lists of negative emotions in the outer, middle and inner divisions of the center on p. 242.

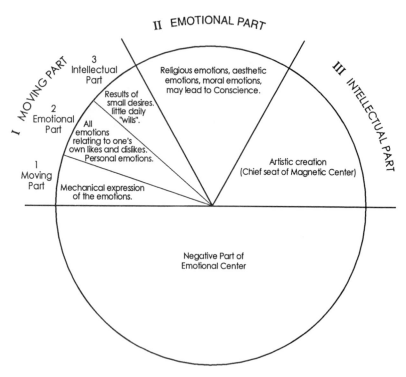

Diagram 2. Emotional Center.

MRS. POGSON: Yes.

X: What about the denying "I's"?

MRS. POGSON: They are partly in the intellectual center. But all these negative "I's" deny the Work. Hatred comes in here, and suspicion. These deep-standing negative emotions are shown very well in novels and plays. The deepest emotions of all are probably connected with the chief feature in some way. One has to learn to live with them and realize that one cannot transform them oneself. And then only a deep wish to be free from them, which is prayer, can help. If there is this desire, then whatever is working for one can lessen them in time. . . .

X: What gives one the strength to accept one's deep negative emotions?

MRS. POGSON: Understanding of the Work, understanding that this is how man is, that we may have one or two of these deep negative emotions. This is self-knowledge. You see, one has to discriminate between these different kinds of negative emotions and how to work on them. In the middle part of the emotional center is a feeling of delight in higher things. Love is an energy of different qualities, working in different parts of the centers. In the outer parts of the centers, the energy of love is coarse. In the middle parts, the energy of love is more fine, and can be directed toward beauty. In the inner part, it is a different kind of love that can become, for example, love of one's neighbor.

December 29, 1959

MRS. POGSON: Someone has sent me a thought about the saying, "He that is not for me is against me," which the person has suddenly understood. [She reads from Matthew 12:30, 31]:

> He that is not with me is against me; and he that gathereth not with me scattereth abroad. Wherefore I say unto you, All manner of sin and blasphemy shall be forgiven unto men: but the blasphemy against the Holy Ghost shall not be forgiven unto men.

The meaning of this verse has to be seen against the Ray of Creation. It means that you cannot stand still. You must be contributing either to the descending or ascending forces. You cannot be neutral. For a long time people think this is possible. They think they are in a middle position looking here and there. But they are not. The sin against the Holy Ghost is the denial of a higher level. The greatest sin is to prevent the Work, the ascent, which the great teachers have come into the world to make possible. The downward forces scatter everything into multiplicity, into ultimate meaninglessness and entropy. Can everyone accept this great truth? It is something that people hear and then forget, as they do with other truths.

Some people may have the shock of hearing this, others hear with the formatory mind and do not hear at all. It was a revelation to this person to see that one *cannot* be neutral. There is a movement always in one direction or another. And so it is also in a group. Some people like to think they are neutral. There are "I's" which want to preserve the *status quo*. From time to time people have a shock and see how many "I's" in them are really against the Work.

X: It is easy to confuse the idea of being passive with that of being neutral.

MRS. POGSON: Yes. Being passive is really a very active state, the activity of waiting. People who have been coming to Dorton many times see Dorton as continuous. They see that something invisible goes on all the time connecting all the Dortons together, so that it is possible to inhabit, in between Dortons, the "I's" they inhabit at Dorton.

From the passage of Plutarch read at lunch, we learned that those among men who had lived many lives and developed the fullness of their being were able to return and become intermediaries, messengers, and to help those who had come to the point of awakening and wished to return. They were not interested in helping those who were still enmeshed in life, but only those who were seeking meaning and rebirth. This describes part of the work of Conscious Humanity. This is the work Dr. Nicoll wanted to be able to do, to help invisibly through the mind.

In Ouspensky's novel, *The Strange Life of Ivan Osokin*, you find the idea that once you have found the Work, the chances are limited. In the novel, it was suggested that after that, there were only three chances. If you have found the Work and you turn away from it, then the higher level is not interested in helping you. If your flame becomes dull and goes out, they won't help. The principle of economy is at work in the whole universe. You don't waste your energy on people who don't want to or can't respond.

In connection with what we have been talking about, do you realize what the ultimate aim of the teaching is? The aim is to have all experiences necessary on Earth and be free from coming back so that one is able to live a much fuller life. To live at the level of the sun means to have ascended the ladder of the side octave. Do people really want this? Some don't, so it is well to think from time to time about this also, this aim. We say that we want to come under fewer laws, which means eventually escaping from the laws of life and death on this planet. People have to think whether they really want this, and whether they can feel it or not; people have to be aware that this is the aim of the teaching, in the light of the Ray of Creation. Think about what you want. This is a serious matter and requires that you think about it.

Fear of the unknown can prevent accepting this; a sign of higher being is to welcome the unknown. People want to stay in their own psychology and don't want to risk things, or go to another place, or meet new people. The Work is to give us courage to have new experiences.

So people might be afraid of awakening for fear of what they might see or what their destiny might be. But you don't need to have this fear; you are provided with the necessary armor to meet it. The only fear we need have is the fear not to have awakened in this life, not to have really lived. That is a holy fear.

New Birth at Christmas
December 23, 1960

MRS. POGSON: When you feel you can do nothing, then something can be born. This is the keynote of Christmas. Something is born from above, nothing to do with you. There is an empty space or cave where one knows one cannot do and in this place something new is born.

X: How can we make greater effort?

MRS. POGSON: Only by repeated failure. You have really to see many times that you cannot "do" with your own strength, and then something else may "do" through you. I had a dream once where a man was walking on a strange structure of wires; he was carrying planks and he fell down on the wires, face forward. But higher up there was still another man who walked on the wires, and he came along carrying planks quite easily and walked on top of the first man. This dream shows that when the lower man falls down, there is another man higher up who can walk and carry planks. We have to do what we can and find that we cannot do. The only thing we can do is to remember ourselves. It would be no use to give up at the beginning and say "I cannot do." Does everyone know what is meant by "Man Cannot Do"?

X: He has no power to stay awake when he wants to.

MRS. POGSON: Yes. If a man could stay awake all the time, just think what could happen! Also a man has not the power to change himself. He cannot do what he would like to do, even from the inner man. He cannot change other people. Quite simply he cannot do what he would like to do from the Work because nothing can happen until the energy is coming through from within, and then he can do the impossible. Something else does it through him. Something else can take over and do the impossible through you, but do you want this? Would you like your life to be directed by something within, whether you willed it or not? Do people want this? You do not know in what direction you might be led. You might just have to do the job you are doing but to do it in a different way. You might have to give up some things. Would you be willing for some new understanding to take over your life?

December 24, 1960

[Diagram 3 on page 20 illustrates the first conscious shock.]

MRS. POGSON: Have you thought for yourselves how the birth of Christ is described in the different Gospels? It is sometimes spoken of as "the Word made flesh"; or Christ may be spoken of as the "light" or the "Son." But the one we are most familiar with is the birth of a child, as recorded by St. Luke.

The Greek word *logos* means more than "word." It means the fullest expression of a creative idea in outer manifestation. God is described as creating the Aeons (all levels, all times) which come out into expression. I will read the start of the Epistle to the Hebrews in Dr. Schonfield's version:

> At varying intervals and in varied fashions God spoke of old to our fathers by the Prophets; but at the close of these times he has spoken to us by a Son, whom he appointed heir to everything. By him also he instituted

the Aeons. He, being the reflection of God's glory and the exact expression of his nature, bringing everything into being by the exercise of God's power, when he had effected an expiation for sins, sat down at the right hand of the Majesty in the heavenly heights. In this respect he is superior to the angels, in so far as he has obtained a more exalted status than theirs. For to which of the angels did God ever say, "You are my son, today I have begotten you," or again, "I will be a father to him, and he shall be a son to me?" Or again, when he introduced the Firstborn to his world estate he says, "And let all God's angels pay him homage."[4]

MRS. POGSON: Think of the Word here as the complete expression of the creative idea; and think of this against the background of the Ray of Creation and the background of the sun octave. Think of the force coming down in order to make possible the return. Christ is spoken of as the reconciling force making the way open for the return of man. Man was created from the level of the sun; we are created with free will and the issue was not certain; we are between two forces. But if a manifestation of the higher is sent down to express all the possibilities once and for all in their fullness—and He returns again—the way is opened for man to return. Christ shows what everyone can do. (That is how we think of the Word; and the symbol of the son returning to the father is clearly shown in the story of the Prodigal Son.) We have the Word described as light descending as far as it can, illuminating everything, and we have the symbolism of the child which describes in more detail what can happen in man as we follow the way that has been set out for us. The whole life of Christ can be seen as a conscious drama showing what can happen in everyone. We think of Christmas as a manifestation of what the Work teaches psychologically, that whenever it is possible to have a conjunction between Good and Truth—to accept and love the ideas of the Work and die to what the outer man wants—then it is possible for new understanding to be born. Dr. Nicoll used to speak of *Mi 12*, which we show in diagram 3 (page 20), as the place in us where something

[4]Hugh J. Schonfield, *The Authentic New Testament* (London: Dobson, 1956), p. 399.

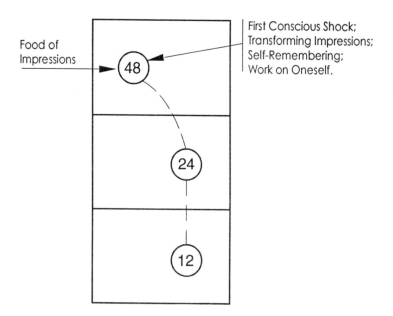

Food of
Impressions

First Conscious Shock;
Transforming Impressions;
Self-Remembering;
Work on Oneself.

Diagram 3. First Conscious Shock. This happens where DO 48 *enters the upper story of the "factory," where* Hydrogen Mi 48 *is present (from the beginning of the air octave).*

new can be born. There can be a miniature birth in us, a smaller birth heralding the final birth of what is Christ in us which can grow and grow, leading us to our Creator and helping us to follow our destiny.

The first conscious shock on a small scale is remembering an idea of the Work and acting from it, instead of reacting in the usual way. Perhaps you can take disappointments in the same way every time but your reaction can be transformed and you can receive the event as material to be transformed; you can remember that you have lost force in the past; you can remember the first conscious shock and that it is possible to make a new relation with the event. As shown in diagram 3, the impression of the event can be received in the emotional center and the energy transformed to hydrogen 24 and then to hydrogen 12, which is a very fine creative energy, and then something new may be born. Dr. Nicoll used to speak of the necessity of caring for this new birth as if it were a child. You have dreams sometimes about a child that you have to look after, and this is an indication that you have to cherish and not neglect this new thing. If ever you have new understanding it is very important to keep it and relate it to *Mi 12*, which heralds the birth of Christ in you.

This is comparable with the birth of a physical child; all the processes of a physical birth go on without your knowing it. The physical child is hidden during this period and develops while being looked after by something other than you. The same is true with new understanding. The child which is in you has the power to lead you all the way. This child knows the way but cannot speak and tell you about it. It does not use words.

Do you see why the first conscious shock is made so important in the Work? If you can see that the central event in Christianity is the birth of Christ, you can see the importance of the first conscious shock in the Work, but the whole thing is expressed in different language because sometimes people rest on symbols and are so used to the pictorial representation that they forget the meaning of the symbols. Many think of Christmas only as an historical birth of a child, and find it difficult to relate to it. Some people, having been taught through the language of the Work, are astonished to find that it was all there already in the Scriptures. There has to be reformulation at the end of every age.

This new understanding we talk about is a tiny birth; but when the event really happens it is a new being within you, a spiritual being which can grow and lead your life for you. After long work and many stages there is this small new being. . . . You cannot force this new birth because it is done for you, but in order for it to happen, much work has to be done; we have many instructions of what to do. The work of Conscious Humanity is to send down reminders to those who are half awake; the calendar is marvelously devised to remind us.

Enough instructions are given but people do not follow them. We do not need more instructions than we are given in the Work. Although it is described as "fragments of an unknown teaching," we are told these contain enough material for us to build up a system; certain work has to be done by us in using the fragments, thinking about the ideas and acting on them. The instructions which were given at the beginning were: "Observe yourself, remember yourself, externally consider." Then, "Do not express negative emotions, do not internally consider, do not justify, observe wrong imagination and do not identify." The Buddhist precepts cover the same ground.

It is said that there are three types of people in the Work whose work can be described very roughly as work against negative emotions, work against imagination, and work against sensual thinking. You will find that your work lies on one of these lines. When I was with Dr. Nicoll, it was interesting to see how people did fall into these categories. Some people would change completely when they became free from wrong imagination which was the most important thing for them to work on. Some people stick and do not change their thinking for a long time. Do not be too quick in deciding into what category you fall and do not instantly put others into a category. We have to work on all three things.

X: While you were talking about this, I was putting myself into one of the categories but an "I" can do this, thinking it knows.

MRS. POGSON: Just put the matter right away from you now and a little later on you may see. The Work is taught in hints.

We will read some examples of stillness. [Mrs. Pogson read the following passage from *Myth and Ritual in Christianity* by Alan Watts.]

> Precisely at midnight there occurred the event which, for Christendom, marks the very centre of time. . . . The Virgin gave birth to the Child who is true God and true man, in whom time and eternity are one.
>
> While all things were in quiet silence, and night was in the midst of her course, thine almighty Word, O Lord, came down from thy royal throne: alleluia!
>
> In the middle of the centuries, at the depth of the year—the Winter Solstice, in the midst of the night, and in the cave—the depth of the earth, the King of kings and Light of lights was born in circumstances of the most extreme humility.
>
> The Virgin today brings forth the Superessential, and the earth offers a cave to the Unapproachable. . . . I behold a

Mystery strange and wondrous (*paradoxon*): the cave is Heaven, and the Virgin is the throne of the Cherubim; in the confines of the manger is laid the Infinite.

The tradition holds that at the moment of the Lord's birth all Nature was still as if time itself had missed a beat. . . . According to the *Golden Legend*, "it was revealed to every class of creatures. . . ." It was made known to stone by the sudden crumbling of the "Eternal Temple of Peace" in Rome, concerning which the oracle of Apollo had prophesied that it would stand until the day when a virgin gave birth to a child. It was made known to water, for in the same night a spring that flowed in Rome was changed into a fountain of oil. . . . to plants, for the vines of Cades suddenly flowered, bore grapes, and produced their wine. . . . to animals, to the ox and ass present at the manger. . . . to the birds, for at midnight the cock crew as at dawn. . . . to the angels, for the whole Host of Heaven had come down to earth and shone around the cave with a brilliance that turned night into day. Hardly had that intense throb of silence passed when all the nine choirs of heaven cried out, singing—

> *Gloria in excelsis Deo*—Glory be to God on high,
> and on earth peace to men of good will!

And, by the angels, it was made known also to men through the shepherds of Bethlehem, to whom the Messenger of God came as they watched their sheep, saying: "Fear not: for, behold, I bring you good tidings of great joy, which shall be to all people. For unto you is born this day in the city of David a Saviour, who is Christ the Lord."[5]

[Then the following was read from the Book of James in the Apocryphal New Testament.]

And leaving her and his sons in the cave, Joseph went forth to seek a Hebrew midwife in the village of Bethle-

---

[5] Alan Watts, *Myth and Ritual in Christianity* (London & New York: Thames & Hudson, 1959), pp. 119–122.

hem. But as I was going (said Joseph) I looked up into the air, and I saw the clouds astonished, and the fowls of the air stopping in the midst of their flight. And I looked down towards the earth, and saw a table spread, and working people sitting around it, but their hands were upon the table, and they did not move to eat. They who had meat in their mouths did not eat. They who lifted their hands up to their heads did not draw them back: And they who lifted them up to their mouths did not put anything in; But all their faces were fixed upwards. And I beheld the sheep dispersed, and yet the sheep stood still. And the Shepherd lifted up his hand to smite them, and his hand continued up. And I looked unto a river, and saw the kids with their mouths close to the water, and touching it, but they did not drink.[6]

External Considering
December 25, 1966

MRS. POGSON: We have been asked the question that leads us into what we want to talk about: "Is it a case of wrong imagination when I think I am externally considering and may be merely a nuisance?"

You probably were a nuisance. . . . The kind of help you may have been giving was doing something for the person's good. Think how we ourselves would feel if someone did the same to us; see how many people have tried to help *you* in the wrong way. If someone is trying to change you, you immediately become worse—young children do this—it sets up resistance. There must be no question of doing anything. This is one of the most important laws, and some people will recall that Mr. Gurdjieff's early tutor told him that until real conscience was developed in him the best he could do was not to do to anyone what he would not like done to him.

Is everybody clear about internal considering and what it is? Can you recognize the taste of it? How can you recognize internal

---

[6]*The Lost Books of the Bible and the Forgotten Books of Eden.* This is from "The Protevangelion," chapter 13, p. 33.

considering? You are always concerned about yourself. You are identified with yourself. It goes on after the event: "Did he agree with me, did he think I was a fool?," and so on.

X: If you have a feeling that you have hurt someone, this can be internal considering, too.

MRS. POGSON: Yes. In order to reverse the whole situation, you have to direct your attention to the other person; you cannot externally consider unless you are using a very fine energy of attention. Here is where the diagram of the emotional center (see diagram 2 on p. 14) comes in, where the deeper "I's" can begin to receive the energy with which they can give attention to somebody. The small "I's" which hate, like, and so on, are always serving the self; but if you direct your attention to the other person, it may be that gradually you will have an intuition of what the real needs of the person are. The needs of the external man differ. Some people need health, some need money, and some need physical rest, but the needs of the inner man are nearly the same for everybody. What sort of thing does the inner man want?

X: He needs recognition.

MRS. POGSON: Suppose we are acting or doing something for other people, the outer man needs some reassurance but the inner man does not want quite the same thing. He only wants his existence accepted by another person, and if this happens there can be a relation with that person . . .

X: Would it be true to say that the inner man needs beauty?

MRS. POGSON: Yes.

X: Would you say he needs opportunity?

MRS. POGSON: He needs opportunity to grow, to manifest.

X: He needs good impressions.

MRS. POGSON: I was given a book with charming illustrations of the inner and outer man. The inner man was illustrated in radiant white with wings. It is not necessarily one's guardian angel, for the inner man is winged, he can rise. He has incipient wings. He is close to Essence.

You are not likely to be able to externally consider in the person's presence unless you have thought about him for a long time when he is not there. This is how things go wrong sometimes. How can you know how to connect with a person in his presence unless you have held him in your consciousness when he is not there? You visualize him, and the next time you meet, your relationship is different. . . . The inner man of each person needs freedom; he does not need to be coerced in any way. You must not coerce anyone. I do not mean physical force; you must not think a person should behave in a certain way. We sometimes have these thoughts. We will read a few things that Dr. Nicoll says about this. It is a question of seeing a person objectively without bringing yourself into it.

[She reads from *Commentary*, Vol. 1, p. 265, "Internal Considering and External Considering"].

MRS. POGSON: You have no right to expect other people to put up with certain conditions that you yourself would not put up with. It is not right to think, "He is tough."

X: Nor does it seem right to think, "I can do that, so anybody else can do it, too."

MRS. POGSON: You must not say that, because everyone must be thought of separately. But if you have experienced something you can think of the other person in relation to it. I remember an example of wrong helping when a person first came into the group at Amwell. Mrs. Nicoll was gardening. She was probably the best gardener we had, and this person came along and took the fork, roughly in a way, from Mrs. Nicoll, saying, "I will do that," and commenced digging. You can see how Mrs. Nicoll would have felt, but she did not say anything. About ten years later the same person came to me and said, "I have had a very strange experience. I was digging in the garden and somebody came along and took the fork out of my hand and said, 'Let me do that,' and commenced to dig." She saw the whole thing from the other point of view.

X: It shows how events recur.

MRS. POGSON: If you are in the Work, events come round again and you see the other side.

X: If you really realized this and remembered that what you do to other people will be done to yourself, it would give you a shock and make you treat people more kindly.

MRS. POGSON: It would not be a sufficient shock, and it is not quite the reason for not acting in a certain way. You may have certain reasons in life events; that is different.

Dr. Nicoll warned us not to let external considering change into internal considering. Suddenly a person rejects your help and you get angry and are offended and you care only about yourself again. The possibility of developing "I's" in the inner part of a center that can externally consider is there, only we have to do a lot of work first, and here again centers have to work together. You will have to act emotionally when the time comes and you will have to act from *wanting to*. It is really from the emotional center. But when you are assembling all you know about the person, the intellectual center does it.

X: Does the intellectual center work for results, and the emotional center for love?

MRS. POGSON: Outer "I's" serve the self-will. Inner "I's" can work from love. The only way we can make conscious love possible is to understand people. We can begin to understand people whom we may even mechanically dislike, because the person's inner man may be quite different from the outer man. Does everyone accept this? When I first came into the Work, we were told we would probably dislike certain people in the group, and we were told that probably these were the people with whom we would eventually have a conscious relationship. If you relate to a person you mechanically dislike, it will have to be a conscious relationship.

X: In trying to visualize another person, you can be made aware of something about yourself, because you see your relationship with the other person.

MRS. POGSON: Yes, the effort of doing this puts you into a more essential part of yourself. This is connected with "love of neighbor," which is only possible with the "I's" in the inner part of centers. It is an effort, and can only follow the development of "I's" which have "love of God," or love of something higher, or love of the Work. Otherwise there is no reason for "love of neighbor." Sometimes people say, "love of neighbor" is easier than "love of God." They may mean they feel themselves through liking other people. If you begin to have love for the Work it brings you to love of God in yourself, your own "Real I."

If the innermost part of the center is inhabited, a door is open and the higher emotional center will come through. You may have a vision of another person. We have at the same time to have an almost conscious love for ourselves, for a part of ourselves. It is the outer man which gives us trouble; you have to hate your outer man in a way and then have compassion for him. First there must be a division; then there is a uniting. First, you must hate the outer man who becomes your enemy, interfering with everything you try to do, interfering with the Work. When you have overcome your enemy, he becomes your servant, and the two men are one.

X: What about the part of you which has to go, the false personality?

MRS. POGSON: "I's" don't die. They are sent out to the periphery of your being, but if the occasion is suitable, you can hear them speak. I warn you that this can happen.

X: Does the inner man ever use the outer man to communicate?

MRS. POGSON: Yes, he does this on purpose. You behave in a certain way if it is expedient. Mr. Gurdjieff showed initiative on every occasion; he used "I's" as he wanted to use them. He knew his "I's" and had control over them. It becomes more and more necessary. It has to do with playing a part in life. You have to go through life as though playing a part.

X: Are you obliged to feel guilty when you are seeing the outer man?

MRS. POGSON: You should never feel guilty. The Work frees you from the past. You do not have to feel guilty, but you must see that your outer man is like that. You are responsible now.

X: You are made to feel uncomfortable.

MRS. POGSON: Dr. Nicoll liked the word, "uncomfortable." You do not come into the Work to be more comfortable.

CHAPTER 3

Nutley Terrace, New Year

The Day as a Unit for Work
January 13, 1959[1]

MRS. POGSON: A day in which we are unaware of the existence of help or on which we fail to make inner contact, this is a day of sleep. Let us take any day of our choice, during which we shall try to keep awake. We cannot choose a longer period with any hope of success. Here the most important beginning is the night before, or the day before. On this previous day we must be careful not to lose energy; rather we must seal ourselves and remember our aim. "The organism usually produces in the course of one day all the substances necessary for the following day" (*In Search of the Miraculous*, p. 198). But this energy can be dissipated by some unpleasant mood. We must remember, too, that certain events or people are, as it were, landmarks during the day, for which we must prepare.

We should observe how we attract the same sort of events continually—being late, being early, losing things. "Here I am, attracting the same sort of thing again." But we should look for the reason, and watch for the second force. It would also be useful to note the things we don't attract, but would like to.

An untoward day could be described as a good day for the Work. We should choose our day and record accurately and objectively—the duration of our recording is not so important. We should be clever, and arrange our alarm clocks well.

---

[1]See Nicoll: *Psychological Commentaries*, Vol. I, "On Work on Oneself" (London: Vincent Stuart, 1964), pp. 25–28.

Sources of Christianity
January 3, 1961

Feast of the Aeon: January 5th

If they are asked the meaning of the mystery, they answer and say: Today at this hour the maiden (Kore), that is the virgin, has given birth to the Aeon.

MRS. POGSON: The Feast of the Aeon was held in Alexandria. This was really the Christmas date and another representation of the birth. It corresponds with our Epiphany, for when the date of Christmas was altered, Epiphany remained on the date of the old Christmas.

At Dorton, in speaking about the visit of the Magi, we spoke of Dr. Nicoll's interpretation. Dr. Nicoll liked to think of the three wise men as representing three streams of the three teachings: the Jewish, the Hermetic and the Greek (or Chaldean), from which Christianity derived so much—each of these streams giving what it could to Christianity.

X: Evidence of this is in the passage, "Certain Greeks came. . . ."

MRS. POGSON: Yes. Dr. Nicoll made this very clear in *The Mark* (pp. 62–63), where he spoke of the connection with the Greek mysteries as revealed in this passage in John's Gospel: "Except a corn of wheat fall into the ground and die, it abideth alone: but if it die, it bringeth forth much fruit . . ." (12:24). The whole Gospel shows the influence of the Greek mysteries; and so also in the Passion, if you take Judas as the hierophant who hands over the candidate. . . . Now where do we find evidence of the Jewish teaching?

X: The first commandment.

MRS. POGSON: Yes, in the twentieth chapter of Exodus and in Leviticus, in the teaching of Moses.

X: It is the same teaching which is given in the Gospels, then Christ adds: "But I say this," which is an extension of the teaching.

MRS. POGSON: Yes. So often the quotation from the older teaching is given and then Christ says: "I say this."

X: Christ shows how to live from the inner meaning of the Jewish instructions.

MRS. POGSON: Yes. At the end of the age the inner meaning of the old religion has to be shown. The Jewish teaching contributed the framework of Christianity. Wherever Christ says that he did this in order that the teaching might be fulfilled, it is related to the earlier teaching. First it is necessary to fulfill the commandments of Moses; but Christ is continuing the teaching, he is fulfilling the prophecy, only enlightening people more about it.

Next, there is the Hermetic or Egyptian stream of teaching. Hermes, if he lived, was contemporaneous with Moses. Both give the shepherd teaching. Here, in this teaching, the Logos is spoken of. The Gospel of John is closer to this teaching, whereas other Gospels are closer to the Jewish teaching. The Hermetic teaching is supposed to derive from the Egyptian in unbroken tradition. The Hermetic teaching, which was about 1500 B.C., speaks of the Logos, and the feminine principle is spoken of as Wisdom, Sophia.

And he, the Logos, is represented as the author of speech, sacred speech and writing, and is said to have taught the arts and sciences. When he speaks of the invisible world, he calls it the "land of the living."

An important symbol in this teaching is the net. The soul is bound on earth by "ropes and cords and pulleys and hooks." You can link with this the painting done at Dorton of man asleep; the cords are really there, holding the man who is asleep. This person is spoken of as "being netted"; eventually the person has to swallow the net, swallow all that binds him or her.

What binds you? All the requirements of the false personality form a net that binds you. When people first hear this teaching and want to awaken, they find they cannot because they are bound by attitudes, by all the wrong psychic functions, and so on. Then they find that they can transform these and swallow the net, and then they have more energy for awakening.

[There was a reading about the "House of the Net," from *Thrice Greatest Hermes*, by G. R. S. Mead, Vol. 1, p. 58ff.]

MRS. POGSON: This is in *The Egyptian Book of the Dead*, even older than the Hermetic teaching. This mysterious net "was supposed to exist in the Underworld and . . . the deceased regarded it with horror and detestation. Every part of it—its poles, and ropes, and weights, and small cords, and hooks—had names which he was obliged to learn if he wished to escape from it, and make use of it to catch food for himself, instead of being caught by 'those who laid snares'." He had to learn the names. Can you be freed until you see something and name it? The Work is naming first one thing and then another, so that you acquire power over it. We see these small things, one by one: the things that bind us.

When the net is turned the other way it can be used to catch food. This is why it is said that the disciples used the net to catch fish. This does not only mean swallowing the net but transforming it: using it in order to grow. The wrong manifestations which you have transformed give you power.

From the teaching of Hermes that preceded Christianity you can see that Christianity has borrowed much in the form of the idea of the Logos and the three disciples, one of whom has power, another knowledge, and another love. These are like the three disciples that Christ always had with him and to whom he gave the innermost teaching. In the Hermetic teaching, the one who represented love, the most spiritual, was left in charge. Dr. Nicoll used to say always that John was left in charge of the more spiritual teaching of Christ, whereas Peter was left in charge of the organization.

Then we come to the Greek and Chaldean teaching. Here is the teaching of the Aeon. This is in Pythagoras and Plato. We've spoken of it before—that the Aeon is not time, but eternity.

> Aeon is the power of God, whereas Cosmos is God's creation and work. The Aeon, standing between God and Cosmos, is . . . the Son of God, and the final end of man is that he should become Aeon—that is, Son of God.[2]

The Aeon could represent the Sun-Cosmos, eternity for us, the lifetime of "Real I" which has many, many lives, being so vast that for us it is eternity. This teaching of the Aeon comes from the Greek teaching. It is said that when there is this new birth in us, it can grow into this Aeon, which is eternity for us.

---

[2]*Thrice Greatest Hermes*, Vol. 1, p. 283.

The Chaldean Aeon has been described in an interesting way as "a being with lion's head, and eagle's wings, and brute's feet, and human body, enwrapped with a serpent."[3] This is comparable to the sphinx in Egypt, both having possibly the same origin.

Now, do you see what I've been talking about? I've mentioned a few ideas that come from these three main streams of religious teaching, and you can continue to make further connections for yourself. How true Dr. Nicoll thought this was, that the three kings bring their gifts.

Now, what we can think about psychologically is the idea of the net.

X: We've talked in the group about the idea of holding the net.

MRS. POGSON: Yes. If the group thinks together clearly, without any leakages, we can receive the teaching that comes from Conscious Humanity, from the invisible group. A group that thinks together can receive far more; but if there is a hole, a leakage, the whole net becomes valueless for the time being, until the hole is mended.

X: I connected this idea of the net with something Dr. Nicoll said: when we are in the Work, if we score off a person we become like a colander.

MRS. POGSON: Yes, the feeling of triumph is a negative emotion, although to some "I's" it would seem a pleasure. It is another of these subtle things.

X: The four banners of the house of Israel are represented by a lion, an eagle, a man and an ox.

MRS. POGSON: Yes, these are the four fixed signs like those represented in the sphinx. It derives from Egypt. Moses was taught in Egypt, so he would take what was purest from the teaching.

It is necessary to make these connections and see how much conscious preparation has gone into this in the schools.[4]

---

[3]*Thrice Greatest Hermes*, Vol. 1, p. 278.
[4]See sources of the Work, Beryl Pogson: *Work Talks in Brighton*, pp. 77–82, and *More Work Talks 1966*, pp. 112–120.

Discomfort
January 17, 1961

MRS. POGSON: Now to something practical. We'll go on from questions.

X: I saw quite clearly that events that are sent are very clear temptations.

MRS. POGSON: Yes, everything may test you after a certain point; once you ask to be tested, once you are on that line. When you have an aim, you are tested on that. And this can lead you on to ask what is doing the testing . . .

X: Why is it that we are always dissatisfied with ourselves? We think we never make enough effort.

MRS. POGSON: This is how you have to be—uncomfortable. Dr. Nicoll used to say, once you come to live with me here you won't be comfortable any more. I remember that even Dr. Nicoll used to look at himself as inadequate, as failing; he never felt that he was doing all he could.

X: In Graham Greene's new book there is an adaptation from Descartes', "I think, therefore I am," as "I am uncomfortable, therefore I am alive."

X: I found the "I's" talked all the more when I made an aim.

MRS. POGSON: That's how the "I's" behave when you make an aim. When you make an aim, everything comes in your way to test you, to see if you really mean it. You have to see that there is something working for you and something working against you. These small mechanical "I's" are fighting for their lives.

X: One of the ideas that makes one most uncomfortable is Mr. Ouspensky's idea that in the Work there is no forgiveness.

MRS. POGSON: What it means is that you have to see the thing is there: it can't be wiped out. Otherwise it would be too easy. In the

Work, you are shown it is there; you have to see it and live with it. It's a question of seeing not so much what you have done as what you are, what you are that's made the thing happen. You have to see it and accept it, and then ultimately it will be transformed.

X: Something in one doesn't want to be responsible.

MRS. POGSON: No, we don't want to be responsible, we don't want to make the effort. That is why Ouspensky said he wanted reliable people in the Work, people who had learned to be reliable in some sphere, no matter what, up to a point.

X: Could you say something about judgment at death?

MRS. POGSON: "Real I" judges us in the end. It is not the end for us, but we have a moment in which our consciousness is at the level of "Real I" and we see how far we've deviated from the plan that was arranged. It is only when you've touched the level of "Real I" for a moment that you can see this. People who are dying have said that what you haven't done is more painful to see than what you have done. And in such a moment you can see good and evil in terms of this—of how far you have deviated.

The most important thing for us is to do the will of "Real I"— although many of us haven't even got to the point of knowing what this will is. And then, in the moment of consciousness, we see how we've deviated from this. But we don't see for a long time where we have failed or how we fall short. Once you begin to work you are shown what to work at.

January 31, 1961

"You must realize that each man has a definite repertoire of roles which he plays in ordinary circumstances," said G. . . . "He has a role for every kind of circumstance in which he ordinarily finds himself in life; but put him into even only slightly different circumstances and he is unable to find a suitable role and *for a short time he becomes himself.* . . . To see the roles, to know one's repertoire, particularly to know its limitedness, is to know a great deal. But the point is that . . . a man feels very uncomfortable should something push him if only temporarily out of his rut, and he tries his hardest to return to any one of his usual roles. Directly he falls back into the rut everything at once goes smoothly again and the feeling of awkwardness and tension disappears. This is how it is in life; but in the work, in order to observe oneself, one must become reconciled to this awkwardness and tension and to the feeling of discomfort and helplessness. Only by experiencing this discomfort can a man really observe himself. And it is clear why this is so. When a man is not playing any of his usual roles, when he cannot find a suitable role in his repertoire, he feels that he is undressed. He is cold and ashamed and wants to run away from everybody. But the question arises: What does he want? A quiet life or to work on himself? If he wants a quiet life, he must certainly first of all never move out of his repertoire. . . . But if he wants to work on himself, he must destroy his peace. . . . A man must make a choice."[5]

MRS. POGSON: Now you see, here is something very interesting: this first feeling of real discomfort you begin to get in the Work. Everyone has to experience this personally. Shall I tell you about my first experience of what Gurdjieff describes? It was the first time I went to see Dr. Nicoll in Harley Street. At first you went to meetings, where you could be "yourself," as you usually were. Then, when he first asked you to come and see him, you could not be like this, and you found you couldn't be anything, because there was nothing to be. This is how it has to be: you have to find a place in yourself where you do not have a role.

Gurdjieff says here: Do you want a quiet life—or to work on yourself? Isn't it interesting how he defines "a quiet life"? As going on with your roles, a mechanical life. And if a person wants a quiet life, then he should never get away from his usual roles.

Do people see that you have to choose? And sitting between two stools is an uncomfortable position—which many people try, because then you can neither work nor do you have a quiet life.

---

[5]P. D. Ouspensky: *In Search of the Miraculous*, pp. 239–240.

Many people are now in this blessed state of occasionally being uncomfortable through seeing that they are speaking from a role they had not meant to go on with. So people should listen to these moments of real conscience when they come; because if they don't listen, they will stop.

We also said last time that moments of discomfort, if brought together, could lead one to chief feature.

X: The discomfort from false personality?

MRS. POGSON: Yes—if you can separate from it. The discomfort of the false personality is unnecessary suffering, but the discomfort which comes from real conscience is the other kind of suffering, real suffering. The discomfort from real conscience can be summed up in this: I do not the good which I will: but the evil that I hate, that I do (see Romans 7:15). The whole Work is in that. It is a stage—such a long stage; and everyone has to go through this stage. We can't avoid it.

Self-Observation and Self-Remembering
January 12, 1960

X: The Work speaks of self-observation as the observation of one's bad psychic functions; but it can also mean, can it not, observation of manifestations which are not bad in themselves?

MRS. POGSON: It means observation of one's whole psychology.

X: Does it then approximate to self-remembering?

MRS. POGSON: No, they are not the same. But self-observation should be done *in connection with* self-remembering, so that there is looking down and looking up at the same time. There is no reason why we should observe ourselves, unless we want self-knowledge in order to approach, and eventually unite with, something higher in ourselves.

X: So we have to remember that we observe ourselves for a purpose, and do not do it as a thing in itself?

MRS. POGSON: Yes. It cannot be done as a thing in itself. You remember at Dorton we talked about the two inscriptions at Delphi: "Know thyself," and "Thou art," in which these two things—self-observation and self-remembering—are linked.

X: It has to be done in connection with our big aim?

MRS. POGSON: Yes. Otherwise why observe yourselves at all?

X: What does it mean—looking up and looking down?

MRS. POGSON: Looking down means observing from a higher place, a more internal place in oneself, so that it is not just one "I" observing another. And looking up means looking up to the highest we know.

X: And do these go on at the same time?

MRS. POGSON: Yes, they can. I have been looking at some of the papers we read for New Year's Day with Dr. Nicoll. In one of them Dr. Nicoll said that if a person told him he was "working on himself," he took no notice. But if a person said he was working on something quite definite that he had observed clearly in himself, he took notice, he would be interested. You see, self-observation has to connect with one's big aim, but it also means observing something definite and small.

If you have been blind, it takes a very long time to learn to see. This is true for both the external and internal senses. We have to *learn* to use our inner senses, learn to see the things we try to see. And it is the same as when a person tries to see with the external senses; one has to learn to distinguish between things.

We'll discuss a task given to those who were at Dorton this Christmas. A good many people discovered at Dorton that they couldn't complete an octave. This is a good thing to have discovered: that you cannot do something without an extra shock from without.

I suggested that people assemble the Work ideas and certainties they wanted to remember and put them into a calendar for 1960. Now you all know that what is necessary first of all is to work out a plan with the mind as to what you want to do. Then you have to look forward and see what second force and what difficulties are going to be present. And then you have to visualize the thing completed. This is how I work. Now, whatever we do at Dorton by way of group work—whether it is the summer house or the mosaic—I have a vision of the work completed which I hold in my mind until it is completed. But this was not to be a group effort, using group force, but an individual effort.

What one does not take into account with people is the second force they will encounter, and which they do not see for themselves. So whoever is in charge has to see the capabilities of each person, which they don't see, and suggest how they can overcome difficulties.

X: I made excuses, but the difficulty was really in myself.

MRS. POGSON: When something has not been completed or done as it should have been done, the thing to do is to go over it and reenact it as you could have done it. We have spoken about this before in connection with going over the day, going over the events and your own part in the day and acting it differently. This is how to alter your life before death. So you can do this also with the calendar and see how you would do it differently.

We must look at this now, for this can be used as an analogy for our own lives. If we don't go through it now, it will be repeated. If we go over it now, when the event comes around again you will be awake to it. This is how your life changes, by going over it now and being able to change when the same event comes around again. The point is that when you are doing individual work, you have to visualize the whole in relation to the time allotted and just dismiss what is not possible.

There is a place at the *Mi-Fa* gap in the octave where you will stick, so you have to visualize what you will do. . . . Your calendars reveal your being. You will be able to see the state of your being if you can read it . . .

Do you see what a lot we can learn from this event by just looking at it and not being negative?

Self-Observation
January 25, 1960

[The subject was discussed with reference to a drawing by Michelangelo; see frontispiece.]

MRS. POGSON: This is an epitome of the Work. It is called "The Dream of Human Life," but it seems to me to be the awakening from a dream. It shows an angel blowing a trumpet onto a man's fore-head. Beneath where he is sitting are masks which represent his various roles in life, and around him are figures representing aspects of his personality. This is a portrayal of what it would mean to awaken and become aware of all the "I's" that surround you, and the many different masks that you can wear on separate occasions. Here are two aspects of the technique of self-observation. We are told about "I's" and we are told about the masks of the false personality, both of which we can learn to recognize. Some of the masks here are grinning; they look rather sardonic.

So you see this drawing represents man awakening to the different aspects of himself. We are awakened by a trumpet, by a shock. An angel, something from above, is doing the awakening. Until the man awoke he would not be able to see all these masks. And until we come into the Work we would not be able to see this. We would just say, "I have different moods!" With regard to self-observation, what can we see?

X: It depends on the state.

MRS. POGSON: Yes. When you are in a negative state, you distort what you see. The first thing which is necessary is to separate from what you are looking at. We have to know what to observe. Then we have to observe enough so that we can see it without coloring it with our own associations or negative emotions.

[A passage was read from *Psychological Commentaries*, "The Reason Why We Have to Observe Ourselves" on the doctrine of "I's" and how one cannot take self-observation apart from the doctrine of "I's" without doing great harm to oneself.]

> You must never say: "What I observe is 'I'," but you must know that this 'I' that you observe is in you. Now all this belongs to not identifying. Self-observation carried out with the idea of not identifying with what you observe is the keynote of this system practically, and it is a very difficult thing to carry out.[6]

---

[6]*Psychological Commentaries*, Vol. II, p. 661.

Mrs. Pogson: How far have people been able to find this idea a freeing one?

X: It's depressing if what you see you take as yourself.

Mrs. Pogson: Yes. This is why one stresses again and again the idea of separation. That is why this drawing is so good. It would be a good thing if you could see all your "I's" around you, then you could see which one had your feeling of "I." It would be good if you could remember that you have these "I's" and that they speak in your name in turn. If you could remember this when you hear your voice speaking with great emphasis, or in anger, or with melancholy, or impatience, then you could remember that one of these "I's" has taken your feeling of "I." It needn't, if you can remember in the moment. This is a further stage of self-observation: recognizing which group of "I's" has your feeling of "I"—they pass it from one to the other in the group—and, in time, withdrawing your feeling of "I" from them.

X: Even when I have separated from an event, there is still a little bit of myself attached.

Mrs. Pogson: Yes, this is a good description. This is what happens for a long time, a little bit is still identified.

X: This applies in particular to anything you might be inclined to give yourself credit for.

X: We have to be careful not to observe from critical "I's."

Mrs. Pogson: Why yes. If you are criticizing yourself, one "I"—one of these men in the picture—is criticizing another. There has to be a space between you and what you are observing. Dr. Nicoll says here that the Work teaches us that we have to take the things in our inner life objectively. We have to see what they are *up to* and what they want us to say. If you consent to them you become them; then you have no "magic circle" around yourself.

It is very good if you can remember this image. In the picture he is in a magic circle and he can see all these "I's" around him, he can see them as masks. But as soon as you step out of the circle, they fasten on to you and draw your blood.

That is why it is so important to have aim in connection with some 'I's that one knows only lead to trouble and useless suffering.[7]

MRS. POGSON: Is everyone aware of "I's" that lead to trouble and useless suffering? How do you separate from these "I's"? You make a special aim about it. First you have to see the "I's"; they have to become more important before they become less important. It is a psychological truth, however, that when you have really seen something, it recedes. Once it is in focus, you are able to take the feeling of "I" out of it. These groups of "I's" become interesting when they are connected together and when you see what is behind them.

We used to find with Dr. Nicoll that he went on and on with one thing. I remember how he used to say, we must talk about negative emotions again. And I would say, what, again? And he would say, but they don't see. . . . Now I understand that it's like this. You want to bring one thing clearly into focus so people will recognize it, and then something can change.

Now, we have this drawing of a man awakening who is in touch with something higher in himself that has awakened him. He sees himself differently. He sees himself as a series of masks that act for him . . . and of "I's" that speak for him. Who has seen his life like this? Once we have seen our lives like this, we want to change . . .

We have to see the "I's" that we are shown. We have to choose to work on the ones that come forward first, because something in us arranges the order. Everyone has to work in a different way. The order is different for everyone, although in the end it is all the same.

Self-Knowledge and Buffers
February 9, 1960

MRS. POGSON: Do you know the difference between being "out" and "in"? You can be *out* all day. This is spiritual suicide. But all you have to do is remember that these are *events*—and take them differently, not in the usual way. We all have a number of "I's" in the basement, but it isn't necessary to descend and let them speak so much.

I want to say a few words about *buffers*. They are not spoken about early in the Work. New people should learn, first of all, to rec-

---

[7]*Psychological Commentaries*, Vol. II, p. 662.

ognize the different "I's" in themselves. It is easy to observe different "I's" in other people. . . . Now I shall give you an example. Suppose you have an idealist leading a band of other idealists to redress the wrongs that exist in the world. His picture of himself is of someone leading a group to help those who are being wronged in the modern world, like a knight always working for good. Now when this man is brought into contact with an individual, a friend, who has a real need, needs money for example, he will say: This is what the world is like! What an iniquitous situation! I don't know what I can do— except get up a subscription list. And he does nothing else to help.

Now, can you see that this man has something separating what he imagines he is from what he really is? He cannot see both sides at the same time. A buffer is something that separates, so you cannot see the other side. But you cannot see the buffer. Buffers separate our contradictions. They are defined in the Work as appliances that diminish shocks.

So this idealist (who is a character in a book) cannot see the relationship between what he imagines he is and what he really is. It is long work to prick one's imagination of oneself so that one can gradually come to see what one is. This has to be gradual, so that we do not suddenly have a great shock of seeing what we are like, which we could not bear.

A person may be a lover of humanity, make speeches about it, but love no individual. And the person wouldn't believe it if you told him. This is due to a buffer. We have this imaginary idea of ourselves bolstering up the places where we are deficient. It is long work to see this. This is where chief feature is hidden.

Buffers are necessary in life. You cannot see buffers, but you can see your contradictions and work on them. You can observe contradictions and where your imagination of yourself is. The shock comes at the right time. It is no good before. When a person has nearly seen something, then he or she is shown.

Where "I's" speak with great emphasis, you can look for a buffer. Look beneath a vehement denial, there you will see a buffer. But of course you won't look! That is why the work is so slow. Buffers are dispelled when real conscience comes through, and real conscience comes through when the emotional center is purified and the middle parts of the centers are developed and we inhabit them. You have to see the difference between what you are and what you imagine you are.

What is behind this imaginary idea of ourselves? Chief feature, which works through these imaginary ideas of ourselves. We can't see this, but we can see what we decide from. You can observe what decisions you make; they are always made from the same thing. And they are always made for us. That is why we can always tell in advance how mechanical men are going to decide. When people have seen this, when they have caught a glimpse of chief feature, then there can be friction. Then the Work becomes so interesting; and people become interesting because they may decide from something else, from the Work. Here is where real conscience comes through. . . . Can any of you see your lives in this way?

X: One can see it in the way one does one's daily work. I have always tried to clear my desk of small things before tackling the bigger things.

MRS. POGSON: Yes, you've always decided or acted in the same way. Other people might act in the opposite way. But you're not doing it. Something is making decisions for you. When you see this, there are moments of choice . . .

Our enemy is the old "I's" which are deeply rooted in us and which are called "father" or "mother" in us. These are aspects of ourselves which have to be separated from. This is the cost of being a disciple of Christ, it is said in the Gospels. We have to see what these "I's" are that are so powerful that they seem right. These are attitudes in us that reach right back to childhood. Then there are the "I's" connected with the mother in us that have to be separated from. A person cannot be reborn until he or she is quite separate from these deeply-rooted influences.

X: Is there a distinction between the mother and the father, between the passive and the active in us?

MRS. POGSON: You can't divide it like that. You have to see how they are—which comes from which. Dr. Nicoll used to say to some people: "You have to overcome your mother." And to others: "You have to overcome your father."

X: This is difficult, because it is not clear to me.

MRS. POGSON: Yes, it is difficult. It is just a way of looking at some of the deeper "I's." Dr. Nicoll was, himself, overcoming his father under our very eyes. He had a very famous father and he was brought up in an atmosphere where he was always afraid of being rebuked if he talked too much. The "I's" that were brought up by his father were afraid; they had no confidence, and they produced the stammer. It was first through Dr. Jung that he learned to see this weakness and that it need not exist, but was only the result of his fear. Then, when he lost the fear, he became fluent and he no longer stammered. But it was a long process, and he was still discovering things to overcome when we knew him.

One both imitates and reacts in relation to the parents. It is very subtle. One has to see. There will be "I's" that are afraid to think and that lack confidence.

The right relationship with one's real father comes when one has overcome the father in oneself. It was transformed in Dr. Nicoll when he was able to overcome his father in him; then he could put himself in his father's place. It was wonderful to see how he re-enacted his childhood for us, how he reconstructed it. He was working on this all the time, and reconstructing the relationship because he saw how he was from the point of view of his father. This is the important thing—to reconstruct the relationship.

People can be dominated all their lives by these "I's" that go back to the nursery or childhood, and they cannot come into their own because they cannot see it. But we can become free from these "I's," when we see where they come from.

CHAPTER 4

NUTLEY TERRACE, TALKS ON COSMOLOGY

Fragments of Teaching
November 26, 1960; December 10, 1960

MRS. POGSON: I am beginning today some talks on the cosmological background of the Work. It is necessary to see the background of the whole teaching. . . . I am going to touch very briefly on the fundamental ideas. . . . This teaching was originally called "fragments of an unknown teaching," and it is presented in fragmentary form. Certain ideas are given, so that . . . we may use the ideas, as enough is given for us to go on thinking from; the clues are there. Even if you have been studying the system for thirty years, yet it is ever new, because there are such depths of meaning. These fragments are ancient truths which have been handed down orally from the beginning and have been preserved in the schools. What we speak about is very ancient teaching. It is the teaching behind all the great religions. The source is always the same, but when it becomes exoteric with rules and outward form, it falls into multiplicity and gets further from the source. It is purposely given in the form of fragments so that we have to assemble the fragments into our understanding.

Ascending and Descending Octaves
November 26, 1960

MRS. POGSON: The background of all esoteric thinking is that everything is contained in one. It is the first cause, it is the meaning of "God is One." But as the word "God" is used on so many different levels, we don't use it. The first cause is the Absolute. We are in a universe, and the universe is within the Absolute. We have to think of creation coming from within the One. Since the universe is built up on the law of analogy, we can build it up on any scale. If you are building something—writing, painting—the whole comes from out of you, and then it has to be worked out in detail. Mozart could hear a whole symphony before he began to write it.

In the ray, *Do* is the beginning of the octave of creation. At *Si* the one turns into three in order to create. There is the active force of creation, which everyone understands. . . . The passive force of resistance sets a limit to creation. The third force is the relating, preserving force—Brahma, Shiva, Vishnu.

There is a principle in every cosmos that the many circulate round the one. Our solar system circulates round one of the suns in the galaxy, perhaps around Sirius. We can see the physical sun, but all these celestial bodies are intelligences. The higher scale, the higher the intelligence. These are divine beings of which we only see the physical form. Ancient Sun worshippers originally worshipped the Sun behind the sun.

The universe looks like empty space, but what is the space filled with?

X: Energies.

MRS. POGSON: Energies and radiations. Suns that have died, and suns that are not yet born. It is a principle of an octave that there is this difficulty where there is a slowing down between *Fa* and *Mi*.

If we look at the Earth as originally a fiery body, which eventually cooled down and formed a crust, how will something that is a crust receive the vibrations? But from the sun has been created a film of organic life so that the force of the creative ray can pass downward to the Earth. It is possible that life can grow on this film in relation to what the sun gives. Life is born on every scale and life gives back something to the sun. This is all in the service of nature.

Mankind only appears in the new creation from the sun, where the film of organic life is created round the Earth. There are two reasons for this creation. One is to link the sun with the Earth. We can receive influences from the level of the sun which make it possible for us to ascend in level . . .

Our galaxy is most glorious to see. Think about it as millions of suns. We can see our sun and the planets around it. We are in the body of the sun because all the solar system is within the body of the sun.

Mr. Reyner used to explain to us very clearly how on every scale a body is mostly empty space. It is not really empty, but full of

Absolute	DO	1	
All Possible Worlds	SI	3	
Our Galaxy (Milky Way)	LA	6	
Our Sun	SOL	12	Do
Planets	FA	24	Si
	Fa Sol La		
Earth	MI	48	Mi
Moon	RE	96	Re

Diagram 4. The Ray of Creation.

energies. The sun is the heart of the solar system. Between the planets are many, many radiations.[1]

The core of the whole teaching is the possibility in us which has been written about from time to time. Here we are, created with the beasts and the plants to serve nature, but we are created with a divine spark, and because of this, it is possible for us to be recalled, to find the way back to the source.

In the great ray, the sun is the center; in the side octave, we are. We have choice whether to lead the life of the natural man, or whether we will cease to find meaning in this and receive influences that will draw us upward.

Diagram 4 explains the nature of prayer. It is impossible to pray to the Absolute; but on the level of the sun, there are beings who are connected with us. Here is the ladder that appears in legends. The descent of mankind and our return is the subject of stories in all religions and all countries. It can appear just as a fairytale. What is the fall of man? Simply the descent into a body at this level . . .

The Absolute has no influence farther down the ray except through its laws. If you create a form of government, or a game, then you have to leave the game to its laws. You can't interfere. The farther away from the source, the less influence from the source. Here

---

[1]Cf. J. H. Reyner: *God Beyond Time* (New York & London: Regency Press, 1965) and *Universe of Relationships* (London: Vincent Sheart, 1960).

we find a new idea of good and evil. Our aim is to ascend, then everything that helps us ascend is good for us. What brings us farther down into materialism is evil if we want to ascend. Evil is what makes us forget. If we are seeking new meaning, it is our real meaning which will bring us back, but anything which makes us forget is evil . . .

At the bottom of the ray is the state of meaninglessness. It is necessary to experience this at some point in life. Some of the original people in Dr. Nicoll's group had come to him because they had lost meaning.

If we think of prayer, it must be to a level with which we have some connection. "Real I" holds our destiny. There is a cord connecting that level and the level of mankind. Self-remembering is raising one's consciousness.

The Lord's Prayer has meaning against diagram 4 as well. Sun, *Sol*, heaven; *Mi*, Earth. We pray for the energy of consciousness available from this level. Ouspensky tells us that this prayer was devised to replace many of the foolish prayers that people used to say. This prayer contains everything. Sometimes devised prayers may get an unexpected response, because we may not know our own request. . .

The ascending octave begins with *Do*, evaluating the ideas; then difficulties are met at an early stage. It begins with a passive *Do*, and you don't know the end. This is the difference between an ascending and descending octave. In an octave of creation, you know the end. When you want to learn something new, you begin, but you don't know what it will be like, you just do what you can. The real thing is there, but we don't know what it is going to develop into . . .

When it is said that man is in the universe and the universe in man, it means that the laws of the universe are in us in miniature. Everything is related, and everything connected.

December 10, 1960

MRS. POGSON: The laws increase at each level. When we say laws, we mean influences, radiations, energies coming down. Influences come from our own solar system. The earth is under its own laws, and the moon is under many laws. It is a dead weight and keeps everything mechanical, going in the same way.

We spoke of the special creation of organic life around the Earth which gives the shock and makes it possible for the radiations from the sun and planets to enter upon the Earth. Then there can be an interchange between the sun and the Earth. All this is nature which has the effect of developing the ray.

The difference between an ascending and descending octave is very important. The law of the octave is the law that every process goes on in a certain order. Mr. Ouspensky said that it is very important to know in any process you happen to meet if you are in a creative octave going into multiplicity, or an ascending octave which is of a different nature. In a creative octave you have an idea, and then everything comes from what is within your mind. You go out into more and more detail. There is a point where you get stuck and you have to have a shock to get over it.

X: I have a painting that has been waiting to be finished for a week, and I realize I have met this many times before. Often I give up at this point. This pause seems most important because it enables one to stand back and see the painting objectively. By this stage one can be hypnotized by the subject so it is essential to stop and stand back.

MRS. POGSON: You step back and see what it needs.

X: There is an external gap between the conception and the result on the canvas.

MRS. POGSON: At the beginning you have eternal vision. How can you bring it into expression? Paints and canvas are parts of limitation. Everything is going out into limitation. Things are only shadows of the reality. Invisible substances are so much finer.

An ascending octave has an unknown end in view; perhaps a vision, but you don't know the way to get to it. When you are learning something, you have a vision of how it will be; you begin with valuation, but you have to be prepared to be taught. Although the distant upper *Do* echoes in the mind, the octave has to be taken tentatively, step by step. The difficulty comes much sooner and there is a slowing down at . . .

We said that good and evil can be looked at in a new way from diagram 4. There is no good or evil as such. Good for what? Evil for what? Everything that is good for multiplying and increasing on

Earth is good for nature, but it keeps us asleep; but if we remember our possible destiny, then evil becomes, from that moment, everything that makes us forget; and good, everything that keeps us awake.

The Moon is what keeps people asleep, what makes people stay as they are, not trying anything new. For emotional people the easiest thing is to go on having the same emotions . . .

If we think of the different influences that are passing through this room at the moment, one's life becomes a question of choosing the influence we want to come under. There are the influences that want to keep us as we are. But there are all the influences to help us to ascend. This is the ladder which Jacob dreamed about, and which is spoken of at the beginning of the Gospels. Angels are ascending and descending . . .

This is one of the times in the year when the cosmic influences can stir people very much. Certain energy is received which can be turned into a kind of excitement. At times of festivals, this energy can go into celebrating or rioting, or all kinds of expression. People feel the influence in some way and generally it can express itself in joy, but the influences can be received for illumination and awakening by those who understand. Influences fall on everyone, and on those trying to awaken. People can see the angels in Regent Street and enjoy them, or they can be reminded of the influence which it is possible to contact. Something new can arise in our understanding.

X: We can also think of evil as absence of what is good for awakening.

MRS. POGSON: Meaninglessness is so far away from the source that there is no meaning. . . . As thinking in a new way gives new meaning to the psychological side, so it gives new meaning in our relationship to the universe. We are not the same as animals and plants because if we seek to complete ourselves, we become solar beings. A lot of these ideas you will recognize, for they have a feeling of familiarity.

One of the laws that operate throughout the universe is the law of analogy. An atom is just like a miniature solar system. There has to be a nucleus round which certain bodies circulate; it is always the same principle. The cell is built on the same principle also. It is through the study of mankind and our physiology that many things have been discovered. The whole principle of esotericism is discovered in humans and their cells; just as a very few cells can evolve, with the right opportunities and influences, so a few men and women, if they awaken and remember, can ascend to a new state.

A great number of people live the life of Organic Life, serving the downward forces. But a few people can escape.

X: It is possible for everyone who wants to.

MRS. POGSON: Yes. It is possible for many more than those who actually attempt it.

X: I found it a very releasing idea that we are all at a different level of development and that we cannot make demands that people should behave differently.

MRS. POGSON: It is a new way of looking at people and seeing that they are at a different stage of evolution.

After a time, material meaning is exhausted. This is the parable of the Prodigal Son. In Christianity it is stated in this parable. He went into material life, enjoyed what he could and had all possible experiences and saw they were only husks; and he remembered his Father's house. This is the Christian formulation of the esoteric principle. Anything material only conducts meaning for a short time and then it is over.

A new kind of thinking is needed. People are not equal. This principle is illustrated in the example of the seeds. You sow many seeds, but you don't expect them all to grow. In the study of mankind and physiology is where the ancients found the key.

Our relationship with our cells—we aren't aware of them unless something goes wrong, but if one is going to develop, then we are aware. So it is that the level of the sun is aware of someone if he is trying to return to his source; then he is interesting. A person who is going to change becomes most interesting, and will get all the help he or she can receive.

It is said that when we are more under the influence of the moon, we respond more easily to the influences that drag us down. In order to come under higher influences, we have to be free from the influences that drag us down; there are many regenerative influences to which we can respond.

X: How can we achieve harmony within ourselves?

MRS. POGSON: One of the first things we discover is that we are scarcely ever in harmony within. If we are at peace within, it is very precious. Usually we are in chaos. Usually the conflicting "I's" are responsible for the chaos within us. As long as there are these conflicting "I's," there will never be peace, because they are always wanting something different. But when we can accept that there is another thing in us that can direct us, then we begin to be in harmony. We will have more contact with the influences that direct us all the way; the father came toward the prodigal son to meet him. The higher part of ourselves is sending messengers; it is possible to be under a higher will. In time it may be possible to develop a certain control of contradictory "I's." The psychological side shows us where we are in disharmony, gradually, one thing at a time.

January 1, 1961

MRS. POGSON: We have covered a good deal of ground in these meetings purposely so that people should have a background. Or has it gone into a maze and a daze? When anyone comes to any of these meetings, it is necessary to be present at the meeting before one gets here. If one has a journey, it is possible to reassemble what one has gathered from the last meeting, and one can think along the same lines, but if you come and expect to be reminded! We spoke of the descending octave of creation; of the side octave from the Sun; and the difference between a creative octave which is descending, and an ascending octave; this is very important. We spoke about the ascending octave which doesn't always get beyond *Mi*. People gave quite good examples of how you start something and then can't go on. If you are starting something new, you don't know what the further stages will be; soon you come to a place and need a shock to get over it. In a descending octave you sometimes get stuck and can't get any further.

You remember we said that this teaching was originally called "fragments."

X: You said that it was enough for us.

MRS. POGSON: This is very important. This is purposely given in the form of fragments so that then we have to assemble the fragments into our understanding. We have ideas to think from. Also it is very important not to think, every time you find a parallel with the teaching in some book, that it is the teaching. You find many many scattered ideas which writers use. It is important to comprehend the whole system because otherwise you can't get to the truth.

I told you that when I came into the teaching, science was very far away from these ideas. But now, diagram 4 (page 51) is almost scientific. One interesting thing that Gurdjieff says in one of his books is, that when mankind was more conscious, long ago, we were able to see the starry galaxy. Science now agrees that the universe is a continuous creation. Scien. .sts talk of all possible worlds. We live on the earth, in a place in the solar system, which is in the starry galaxy.

Then we spoke of the principle of scale. The universe is built on the principle of hierarchy. One of the reminders of this principle is monarchy, which is very valuable because it reminds us that there is one in charge of all. The ancient King-Priest used to be of a stature that he could hold all within himself. In aristocracy, the people with more understanding were in authority, and then you go out into multiplicity, to the people who knew less who formed the crowd. When this is upset, things go wrong because people don't understand that it is a cosmic principle.

X: I don't quite understand about the *La, Sol, Fa* in the middle.

MRS. POGSON: We spoke about the place of the missing semitone at which some shock is necessary. The Sun couldn't give its radiations to Earth if Earth were a lifeless crust. From the level of the Sun a film of organic life was created around Earth which makes a relationship between Sun and Earth. A further shock is that mankind is created here.

Do you see from diagram 4 how you must always think what you are within? We are on the earth, and within the solar system; we cannot think of ourselves apart from this. We are within our starry galaxy; other influences are playing on us from our galaxy and beyond. Finally we are within the Absolute, or in religious language, we are in the being of God. We cannot talk about the Absolute at all, and we cannot talk of God as Absolute. Some people come and say, "I insist on praying to the Absolute." This is ridiculous, it has to be in scale; but we can reach the level of the

Sun. From here the rope is let down. But we have to be aware that we are within the whole.

We spoke earlier about this new way of thinking about good and evil. Did this remain with you at all as a new idea, or has everybody forgotten what it was? We spoke about it in relation to this diagram. We spoke about coming under more and more laws, and of ascending Jacob's ladder, ascending to the level of the Sun. And remember, I said if you are going to think within this background, evil is what takes you out into materialism and puts you under more and more laws; and good is what helps you to ascend to the new level of yourself.

Levels in the Ray
November 15, 1960

MRS. POGSON: We need to have this system of levels clear. We are at a level where we need not stay. The more laws we are under, the fewer possibilities we have.

X: Seen from a higher level, our personal troubles seem less important.

MRS. POGSON: Yes, personal troubles become smaller, and we see that they are caused by these laws. But what are these laws that we want to become free from? I used to think mistakenly that it had to do with not having to sleep or eat so much.

X: We have to see that the different parts of ourselves are under different numbers of laws.

X: I want to put a ladder into the Ray of Creation.

MRS. POGSON: Yes, we think of Jacob's Ladder which is always double—we can ascend, angel messengers descend.

Now at the level represented by 96 orders of laws we are under imagination. It seems a terrific number. But at this level we are under so many laws through the influence of the false personality. There is a law, for instance, that you become negative if insulted if you're in false personality. And the only way to escape this law is to move away into another part of yourself. Such things are always going on. There are many small "I's" which react like this all the time.

X: Could you explain the meaning of the Sun octave?

MRS. POGSON: It's a shortcut. If people go against these laws of the personality and false personality and go into a place in themselves where they can be under certain influences, then they can ascend the ladder.

X: The sun's influences inform the spirit in mankind, the planetary influences the soul.

MRS. POGSON: Yes, the connecting force.

X: And the earth's influences inform the body.

MRS. POGSON: What happens at death? The body is received into the earth. It is said that a kind of magnetic energy—how shall I describe it?—imagination, a thing that is unreal, returns to the Moon. The personality breaks up. But Essence, what is real, goes straight to its source and can return again.

The ladder, with seven steps, represents the steps between the Sun and the Earth. You have the seven planets, sometimes represented as a pagoda, which are the planetary zones through which you have to go. Diagram 5 shows all these levels in mankind.

Sun	Do	12	Real I
All Planets	Si	24	Essence
	La		
Organic Life	Sol		Personality
	Fa		
Earth	Mi	48	Body
Moon	Re	96	False Personality

Diagram 5. The Sun Octave.

Where are you now? If you are in imagination, you are under very many laws. Or maybe you are in instinctive center, which is sleepy; or if you're in an inner part of a center you can hear with the inner ear.

X: Where are you in directed attention?

MRS. POGSON: In the inner parts of centers, in a place where you can be open to influences coming from higher centers.

X: What part is under the hypnotism of life?

MRS. POGSON: Why, here—the false personality! We are even lower than we need be. We are under all these laws, mostly caused by wrong imagination. This is the level of sleep. We have a diagram of man lying asleep and the ladder above him. He has to wake up and climb it.

Think of the Ladder as a ladder in yourself. What kind of day is it when you are in a place of depression? You don't need to stay there. You can ascend this ladder.

For practical work, register the different levels in yourself, so that they become quite real and clear. Then register the states in which you are more free. The difference is incomparable. In moments of self-remembering you can see where you've been, and you can see imagination for what it is. You have a glimpse of truth. You see many things together and your true state. It's as if you are going on a journey, and every once in a while you come to a hilltop, from which you can see where you have been. You can also see where you are going, and you might see to the next hilltop, I've noticed.

X: What is the exact process of self-remembering?

MRS. POGSON: I wish Dr. Nicoll were here! You can't talk about it like that. It is an individual process. If I tell you my experience, it isn't your experience. I can only give an analogy, which I've just done. People who have had a similar experience will recognize it. But we all have it for ourselves. The best way to have it is to want it. Even if you're disappointed, you have got it because you've wanted it. Dr. Nicoll said that the universe is response to request. But all wanting means you give up something else.

Six Cosmic Processes
January 7, 1961

MRS. POGSON: There are six processes which are taking place continually and we can study them on Earth. It is very important to see whatever is happening as one of these processes, and not to look at it in ignorance.

SIX COSMIC PROCESSES

Growth
Decay
Transformation
Corruption
Healing
Regeneration

MRS. POGSON: Growth—a process which you can observe taking place in organic life. You see the growth which takes place mechanically; this is caused by the action of the Sun on Earth. How does growth take place generally? Through multiplication. You see equally the process of decay. Growth is only for a period, then it disintegrates. This is also the action of the Sun. These are two processes which take place mechanically on Earth.

The third process is transformation. We cannot interfere with growth and decay. You have to know in observing things whether they are growing or decaying. Cultures and civilizations have their life, and then they begin to disintegrate. It is just something that happens. Growth and decay take place in the big octave of creation. Transformation is a kind of development upward. Every substance can be transformed if a higher substance can act on it. This teaching is about transformation.

You can look from this list of processes at anything you can see anywhere when you want to know what is happening.

Corruption is lack of scale when order and meaning are lost, where you find something on a lower level which becomes unduly important. You can see it in history when a person of lower being becomes too important. Lower meaning has interfered with deeper meaning. Healing. What is healing?

X: Restoration.

MRS. POGSON: Restoration to the original order. Corruption appears in the body as illness. Healing restores it to order.

X: Restores the balance.

MRS. POGSON: Corruption upsets the balance. It is interesting to remember these six processes. They are two triads. The Ray of Creation (diagram 4)—if you look at this scale, the energies that operate in the higher part of the universe are finer than the energies that appear lower down; and transformation is the change from coarser to finer. Sometimes this teaching is described as a kind of transformation. Alchemy, which was one form that this teaching took, was the science of transformation; it used the image of transforming base metal into gold. The whole principle is to let something of higher quality act on something base, to raise its level; and to show us how it works, we are given an example of transformation in the body. You realize how the octave of digestion takes substances into the body and turns them into liquid food, and then into something so fine that it can be used for thinking and feeling. This is an example of something within us that happens mechanically. The ancients said that they could study the universe by studying what was in us.

Can you see that ideas coming from the level of the Sun are of very fine quality, a very fine substance? When we receive them into our minds, they are so powerful, that they can act on our psychology and change it. This is how the whole system works. We cannot reach the level of the Sun until we have changed, because we have to be made of finer substances.

In an ascending octave, the stage that you reach is always there existing, waiting for you. The best illustration is the growth of the embryo because the next stage is always there.

The sixth process—regeneration—is the other that is not mechanical. Rebirth operates on the pattern of physical birth. Conscious effort is necessary for regeneration. It is a possibility, and here it is that the New Man exists, only we exist on a higher level of the ladder. This is a transforming idea. In fact the whole day could become a day of transformations because opportunities are endless in our psychology. Many, many stages of transformation are necessary before rebirth is possible. The Christmas festival reminds us of the idea of rebirth. Here we are reminded of the way the story is told, that something new, which we call the New Man, is born in an empty enclosed space, a very humble place where there is no noise or confusion. For this to happen, it is necessary to have withdrawn some force from the "I's" in the personality so that the place can be prepared for something new to be born. It is a long stage.

Regeneration is not natural. The natural man knows nothing. It is only the more conscious people who want this. It goes upward against the stream. Generation goes downward with the stream; it is easier. There is the example in nature, certain experiments made— the lizard and the worm are able to grow a new half a new limb, but it doesn't mean they are regenerate, only that they grow a new limb!

All the ancient religions speak of rebirth and all the instructions given are to show how to work, so that this may be possible. Can you think where we are shown the possibilities of transformation in nature?

X: A frog.

X: The cocoon.

MRS. POGSON: What is so interesting is that the grub has no idea of its possibilities. We can have no idea about our possibilities so we can't try to grow into anything through regeneration. We don't know how the baby will turn out; we don't know how the New Man will appear, but Essence brings with it the stamp of the New Man in miniature. The flower can be photographed within the seed.

One should never compare with other people, because you don't know how the person is going to develop. In the usual way, the child grows up and compares with other people, but each Essence is unique, so never try to emulate anyone else, never try to judge, because our Essence has its own development, and our destiny is arranged from a very high level.

We talk like this at these meetings so that we can have a background. We can talk of one thing at a time when you have a background.

A passage was read from *Psychological Commentaries* (Volume I, p. 30) where Dr. Nicoll speaks about not thinking one has found the system just because one finds a few ideas in the books one reads.

MRS. POGSON: Dr. Nicoll used to talk about finding things on the beach. Supposing you discovered a human hand on the beach and knew nothing about human beings, would you know what it was? When archaeologists find a bone, they fit it into the bone structure, then they know what it was, something about its meaning. The tendency today is to study one small thing without relating it to something larger of which it is a part.

Can you see the difference between two men, one of whom lives on Earth and knows nothing of his destiny, of his connection with the Sun and the planets; wouldn't his meaning be small and poor compared with the meaning of a man who understood something of the whole? In the Mystery Schools, people were taught to understand what they were doing on the earth. Real knowledge is the knowledge of the part in relation to the whole.

February 4, 1961

[The talk on January 21, 1961 concerned the process of transformation, hydrogens, and the food octave. Mrs. Pogson continued to discuss the octaves of transformation on February 4, 1961.]

MRS. POGSON: In the mechanical man (see diagram 6), the food octave works, though rather inadequately. The air octave goes up to *Mi*, and the impressions octave doesn't work at all. Diagram 7 shows a man who is more awake. This is a man after a moment of remembering himself. He has the hydrogens made in the food octave; there is this transformation in him, and he understands something. A little later he has a new idea, and the Work begins to belong to him. His breathing becomes different, and he retains something extra from the air. This may happen once or twice, but it has to happen many times before he is awake.

We will just go back to the food octave for a moment. Is it clear, that food before it is broken up or transformed is called *Do 768*? It is sometimes represented just inside, sometimes just outside the diagram. It reaches a liquid state at *Re 384*. Always in an octave, study the stage *Mi-Fa*. Here air enters the stream of the blood, and *192* really represents the food that is carried in the blood and feeds all the cells in the body. There is something very peculiar about the shock, because it causes a breaking down, *and* a building up. This blood feeds the cells all through the body. The transformations are shown in the body. This is why the alchemists and all those in esoteric schools studied mankind in every way. They knew that all the

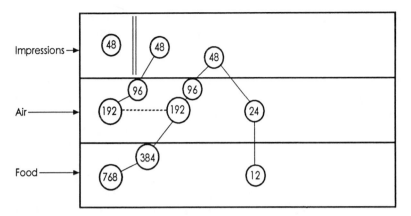

Diagram 6. Mechanical man.

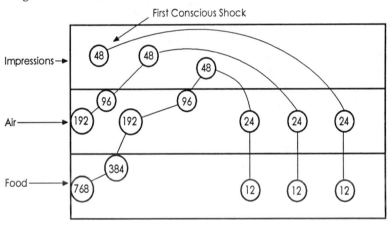

Diagram 7. Man remembering himself.

processes that happened in us also happened in the universe. We have this miracle that air comes into the blood at this stage; it has such an effect that a substance is made that can feed every cell. There is always something new at *Fa* that couldn't happen at *Do* or *Re*. How could we imagine that the shock of air could make it possible for the food to go all over the body! Something like that happens psychologically.

Here is the impressions octave. In mechanical man, there is a line drawn after *Do* 48 because impressions fall on associations. You meet a person that you see most days, but you don't really get an impression of him . . . Very small children see, and if they are still in essence, you find they see many things about people when they meet them for the first time.

The first conscious shock occurs when we remember the Work teaching about transforming impressions. A person is an impression, an event is an impression, a thought can be an impression, but you can be separated from it if you wish to take it differently; then you find that the impression comes in, and you take it in a new way, and you are related differently to the event. Everyone has things like missing trains. Can you relate newly to missing a train? It is an event I have often had to take. You can spend the interval walking up and down being angry! Instead, say: This is an event of missing a train. If it is possible, have some thoughts. You mustn't get negative with yourself. You see how the Work works every time you discover that something the Work says is true. You feel different because you feel less heavy, and you feel the current of energy flowing through you. The very fact that you have given yourself a shock enables the air octave to go on; you feel in a different state, not excited. You see the air octave has a *Mi-Fa* gap, and that is how your breathing is different.

The food octave nourishes one's physical body, the air octave does much to nourish one's psychological body, the impressions octave is what is going to nourish the finest body—the spiritual body. It is our task to work at this stage.

HUMAN ENERGIES

4) Conscious Energy;
3) Psychic Energy;
2) Vital Energy;
1) Mechanical Energy (heat, etc.).

MRS. POGSON: There are four qualities of energy used in man. The lowest in scale is mechanical energy, such as heat. We share this with tile animals and vegetables, and this goes on mechanically. It exists in all forms of life, and there are mechanical energies within the body. No amount of this energy can make the next energy—vital energy, which is the energy of life—which again we share with the animals. We have tried for thousands of years to make something come alive, we can't make anything that can live. Life is given from the Sun.

No amount of vital energy can make psychic energy. However robust a bull is, or how splendid a tiger, it can't use this energy for thinking. We are special because we have these four energies.

Psychic energy is what mechanical man uses all the time; it is not conscious energy. His thinking and feeling can go on all the time.

Can you distinguish between your psychic and vital energy? It very often happens that people who have much vital energy, which they usually use in movement, think less. G. said that they use up their vital energy quicker than other people, and get old more quickly.

This mysterious energy is conscious energy. There is a spark of this in everyone. It comes from essence, from the higher cosmos. This is the gold that the alchemists spoke of. Because we have a divine destiny, and this spark in us, it is possible to make more of this energy, so that eventually there can be rebirth. Conscious energy is a cosmic energy and on a higher scale altogether. It doesn't belong to us, but it is something we can use. All that belongs to us is that tiny spark which contains within itself the meaning of our possible destiny. Study the seed in nature, and you get the truth.

CHAPTER 5

Nutley Terrace, Lent

Regeneration
February 14, 1961

Mrs. Pogson: At this period of the year called Lent in the church, when the time is right for denying nourishment to the outer person and giving nourishment to the inner one, we have to see what is most practical to do. What is most practical is to deny some form of nourishment to the outer person, some form of mechanical talking, and so make more energy and nourishment available to the inner person.

This is connected with the cosmic process of regeneration. We've talked in the past about the six cosmic processes of growth, decay, corruption, healing, transformation, and regeneration. Regeneration is different from the others because it means going against the stream. Anything that goes against the stream can contribute to rebirth, which is the aim of this teaching and of all the great religions.

In Rodney Collin's book, *The Theory of Celestial Influence* (pp. 198ff) he speaks of this. He speaks of excreta of the mind which is an endless stream of mental waste, impossible to stem until one becomes aware of it. This is connected with the stream of daydreaming and wrong imagination and negative emotions which go on and on mechanically *until they're seen,* and it's possible then to separate. Now all this is part of the process of regeneration.

We have diagram 8 on the board (page 70) showing Undeveloped Man or Man Worked by Life: Man Machine, and Developed Man, or Man Obeying Will: Conscious Man.

Mrs. Pogson: Look first at the undeveloped man, Man Machine. The first body is the physical body which reacts to life the whole time. The point is that there is no emotional body. Mechanical man simply has changing emotions; nothing is organized, nothing can stand up against the stream of life. There is also no mental body but only thoughts, unless the person has had a training.

Now everyone has experienced this. What are the emotions of the day? Don't they depend on what happens in the day? If the emotional body were organized, it would not depend on what happened in the day. Here is the difference between someone who is more conscious and "mechanical man." Tossed about, with no stability: this is the state of chaos in most people. Life works us and our inner bodies. For example, one person may have thinking that is more developed, and is therefore more stable, but the emotional body will be undeveloped. Very seldom are both bodies developed. Some people have the system of the Work formed in them up to a point, but emotional center won't obey. You can't do what you think, you can't do what you know. This is where everyone is weak.

We have no illustration to show the state between "mechanical man" and "developed man." Here, the man is worked from the other end, but a lot of work has to go on in between. If people can make the system into a whole, without leaving the part out that they don't like, then they have a touchstone. Obeying the Work, following the instructions we are given, helps us develop a second body—develops Essence. This is what everyone needs to see.

UNDEVELOPED MAN OR MAN WORKED BY LIFE: MAN-MACHINE

Life →	Physical body Automaton working by external impressions	Desires produced by automaton	Thoughts proceeding from desires	Different and contradictory "wills" created by desires

DEVELOPED MAN OR MAN OBEYING WILL: CONSCIOUS MAN

Life ←	Body obeying desires and emotions which are subject to intelligence (1st Body)	Emotional powers and desires obeying thought and intelligence (2nd Body)	Thinking functions obeying consciousness and will (3rd Body)	Master " I " Ego Consciousness Will (4th Body)

Diagram 8. The "man machine," and the conscious man.

Can you be sure you'll be in the right "I's" even if you go out to an evening of pleasure?

X: You can't even be sure you'll be in the right "I's" at a meeting.

X: I had an example of this. I was in a mechanical state at my work and I found that I didn't want to get out of it.

MRS. POGSON: No, an undeveloped emotional center doesn't want to obey. That's why it's sometimes called the rogue elephant. This is why I talk about obeying the instructions of the Work, so as to have a developed emotional center. As they are, people haven't got anything to work through that will obey the Work.

The fourth body can occupy the place within and control the whole. Then we are linked and can fulfill our real destiny. Here we do the will of "Real I," which is not our own will.

The undeveloped second body is not will at all. What do you desire? A cup of coffee, sleep, first one thing and then another. There has to be a vehicle formed here in order to connect, so that you can live your real life. The bodies have to be clearly formed. That is why we spend such a long time studying the instructions of the Work, and you can see to what purpose.

X: How does this relate to work on Deputy Steward?

MRS. POGSON: Work on Deputy Steward connects with work on both bodies. When Deputy Steward is formed, a person then has a center of gravity. But you cannot have a center of gravity until there are "I's" formed that want to do the Work.

Sacrifice

MRS. POGSON: Have we spoken in this group about creating energy through dying to something in yourself? We have talked in some of the groups lately about the state of entropy—a state of disorder, of meaninglessness—where you are far removed from your source, which is unity. When you feel scattered and chaotic, you can experience a loss of meaning. You may remain in this state until you receive a certain kind of shock: the shock which can break it is a sort of death, for whenever you die to something, you release energy, and as energy flows, entropy decreases. So also, on a larger scale, when the world reaches a state of entropy, a new savior is born, and through death, the savior releases great energy, and a new civilization is created. Here is a way to create energy, through some kind of death. What happens is this: the finer and the coarser are separated. Something goes down and something goes up. This is the meaning of sacrifice as it is taught in esoteric teachings. You must die to something in order that something new may live.

[A passage was read from an unpublished paper of Dr. Nicoll's.]

> Death is a great cosmic event in which all beings participate. We are accustomed to think of death in a very narrow way, particularly of the death of the bodies of animals and the death of our own body. But really there are many kinds of death. *All death is separation.* Whenever there is separation of energies there is dying. For example, as I speak to you, my words, as I speak them, die. Separated from me they die and in their death a certain energy is liberated. My thoughts as I think them die. And as they die something comes from that moment of separation. Everything that dies sets free a definite quality of energy . . . Dying is a perpetual and ever present event. Everything that comes into existence has to die and everything has a life-cycle corresponding to its own essence . . . We live in the midst of a perpetual dying of all our automatic functions.

MRS. POGSON: We have recently had a new birth in the royal family (Prince Edward). How much sacrifice was necessary before this new prince could be born? His mother gives up certain energies which she denies to herself so that they can be used for the baby's gestation. In every human process there is an analogy with a cosmic process and with a psychological process as well. And so, when we deny something to ourselves, energy can be freed. The Work operates on this principle: when we observe certain things in ourselves clearly, we see what we have to deny ourselves in order that the New Man can be born. And then we have to start by denying ourselves some of the manifestations of the thing which we have observed. This is the meaning of separating the coarse from the fine as the process is described in alchemy, in the Emerald Tablet, and all through esotericism. If you can separate from some aspect of the outer man, a finer energy is born which can go to the New Man.

I want to speak now about increasing effort with particular reference to temptation. Temptation is associated with this period of the year, so that the greatest force may be called forth to make what happens at Easter possible. There is something in us, a certain aspect of the divine sometimes called Satan or Saturn, that will test us at certain points. . . . At certain stages we are tested. This can happen on different levels. (Dr. Nicoll says that once we are in the Work, we are only tested about things relating to the Work, not about other things.)

[The story from Genesis Chapter XXII concerning the testing of Abraham was read to the group.]

MRS. POGSON: Abraham is instructed to sacrifice his first son, Isaac. He makes his choice; he is ready to do what is commanded as he interprets it. But to slay Isaac is not what was really meant. Perhaps when Abraham received his first instruction, it did not come from the deepest place in him; there are different levels from which our promptings come, and it is possible to misinterpret them. But then comes a second vision in the form of an angel. Abraham is shown what he really has to do, and he sacrifices the ram. From this test a new phase of his life begins. This story of the sacrifice of Isaac foreshadows the crucifixion drama.

Do you see what energy could be released through being willing no longer to keep something for yourself but to give it?

Temptation
February 23, 1960

Let us come to what is most practical. If you have a clear aim, you are tested on it by something inner. It is a great mystery, what this second force, this tester in us is, which brings into focus whatever we need to work on. The main thing is to stop using certain energies for ourselves. Isn't it true that we spend most of our energies keeping up false personality? If we deny ourselves something, then these energies can go to the new thing in us. We must see what is taking our energy which needn't have it. And then we have to die to this thing in ourselves. What manifestation of false personality takes your energy? If you are to become part of this organism of the Work, gradually something will work on you. So it is necessary to let some manifestations be weakened in order that something else can have more room.

X: Does work against pictures of ourselves come into this?

MRS. POGSON: Certainly. You have to give your picture less time. If you see that you are in its power four hours during the day, be in it only three hours! Then you have more energy for something else. We have to create energy which can be used by the powers in us that are working for our transformation.

X: It takes great energy even to observe oneself.

MRS. POGSON: Yes, we don't yet have enough energy to work. But from any conscious act you gain energy. Then you have more for working. Once you have an aim, amazing things can happen. If you make an aim seriously, then testing comes. It is to see if you are serious. These events by which you are tested come down the perpendicular line of eternity. They are *extra* things, not the ordinary things we meet in life. But you have to be awake to meaning all the time; you can't be in a state of chaos.

We get energy from aims. Each week we have new aims in the group, and then you have your personal aims. Your aim has eventually to be directed against chief feature, but before that it is against certain mechanical manifestations connected with chief feature. You have to work in the present moment on the mechanicalness that you can observe in yourselves. If you are interested in the Work and want to let the Work change you, then make an aim about something which you have observed, and wish to weaken. Then see if you are tested.

[A passage was read from the record of a meeting at Great Amwell, July 19, 1952.]

> DR. NICOLL: You must remember that when you are in this Work you begin to come under its influence and certain things are bound to happen to you. It is bound to increase your difficulties. This Work, which is real work, does not make it easier for you. When you come within

the influence of the Work, you will be tempted in various ways in which you have never been tempted before.

The whole of the house which life has built in us is founded on self-love. The whole thing has to be taken down since the mortar and bricks are of self-love. It has to be done gradually.

MRS. POGSON: This is rather refreshing. The Work is not just added onto us as we are. We have to be rebuilt. You can see from this why the work has to be gradual; you can't pull down the house all at once. It is so consciously devised that each idea dawns gradually in the mind. "No," you say, "This brick is not very good!" So you just let one brick go after another. Some bricks in the personality can be used. Then the Work builds up its own structure. You have to give up only what you see is useless, then the whole structure doesn't tumble down.

Something else in us builds the house. Except the Lord build the house, they that build it labor in vain. This is the meaning of building Jerusalem, a city that is at unity with itself, built on a clear structure.

Inertia and Effort
April 5, 1960

No effort—do work: no work—no awakening: no awakening—death.

What creates stimulus for work?

MRS. POGSON: On the board you'll find a very telling quotation of Dr. Nicoll's. I wonder how people would answer the question on the board, which is a question someone asked Mr. Ouspensky.

X: Seeing one's mechanicalness.

X: Dissatisfaction with one's state.

MRS. POGSON: That is the answer given by Mr. Ouspensky—the realization of one's state. This is what we're going to talk about. Everyone has to answer this question for himself or herself.

I asked you to observe inertia. Eventually we have to get behind it, see what it is, and work against this delaying force. In the meantime, however, we just have to observe it. It is the main thing we have to work on, this thing that always holds us up. It's our share of the cosmic delaying force. Now what observations do people have on inertia?

X: We don't see it, but think of it as our normal state.

Mrs. Pogson: Yes. . .

X: I have felt the importance of urgency.

MRS. POGSON: Yes, of course you have. You have observed that, for you, inertia lies in intellectual center. The "I's" that want to learn are not strong enough. We see that there is so much to learn—but what stops us?

X: Inertia with regard to making effort.

MRS. POGSON: Yes. You often see that if people avoid making effort in intellectual center, they make moving center effort instead. It is a way of justifying.

One person observed inertia in the form of impatience, which arose if she couldn't understand or connect with something in a flash. Another gives an example of the inertia which came when reading something in attracted attention, at the point where some passage required the effort of directed attention. We need to think about diagram 9, the intellectual center, here, with its three divisions showing "I's" in zero, attracted, and directed attention. Take, for example, reading a Work book in attracted attention. The tendency will be to go on reading in attracted attention and not give the directed attention to places which require it. But you can go on only so far with attracted attention.

When we are reading, the "I's" in zero attention will be thinking of something else or going off into associations. The "I's" in attracted attention are looking for new ideas; they have a feeling for what is higher, and they can passively appreciate what is given. But every now and then we have the choice of using directed attention. If we

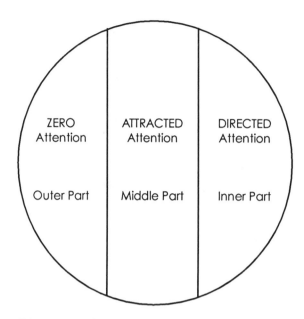

Diagram 9. Three qualities of attention.

have our minds well stored with connections, we can take some idea and go on thinking about it and make it our own. Here we are using the active mind.

But if it becomes too difficult, and you don't want to make the effort to think on these lines, then you may fall back into zero attention.

Are there any more observations on inertia and seeing that it is our enemy?

X: You make connections which should be written down, but inertia keeps you from doing it.

MRS. POGSON: Yes, this is a useful thing to see and remember. The same thing can happen with a dream that one doesn't write down because one thinks one will remember. One thinks things will stay in one's memory, but they won't. We have to experience the fact that they won't, but even then we don't act on our experience. It is important to make the effort to get a pencil and paper and write things down; otherwise they are lost. What you do more consciously, with directed attention, you have in your memory. When you have worked out something for yourself with constructive thought, you have it and do not need to bother about it.

X: Does work in attracted attention leave any memory?

MRS. POGSON: Yes, there is memory but it is not a specific memory. For example, people tell me about books they've read in attracted attention. When I ask a question, they can't say anything specific about the book. One sees only the impression it has made on that person.

We will read some passages from Mr. Ouspensky's novel, *The Strange Life of Ivan Osokin*, which are applicable to inertia. Here is the young schoolboy who has visited the magician and has been given another chance to live his life differently, having memory of his life. But he doesn't live it differently, because of inertia. It could be the same with us. This curious, heavy influence keeps us doing the same thing.

"I won't go to school to-morrow," he says.

"Why not?" says his mother, astonished and frightened.

"Oh, I don't know; I've a headache," he answers, using the schoolboy's stock phrase. "I just want to stay at home and think. I can't be among those idiots for so long. If it were not for these stupid punishments I should not be staying at home now. I can't go on like this. They'll shut me up again for two or three weeks."

"Do as you please," says his mother, "but I warn you it will only make things worse for you at school. If you don't go tomorrow they will take it as a challenge on your part—but you must decide for yourself. You know I never interfere in your affairs."

Osokin knows that his mother is right, and this makes him feel still more angry. All this dull reality of life, and the necessity of thinking about it, distracts him from his sad thoughts, from the strange sensation of two lives, from the troubling memories of the past and the future. He does not want to think about the present, he wants to escape from it.

"I won't go tomorrow," he says out of sheer obstinacy, although in his heart he feels how unpleasant this is for his mother, and he realizes that he is going against all his own resolutions to arrange his life in a new way.

"Well, this will be the last time," he says to himself. "I'll think things over tomorrow. I must have a day at home. The school won't run away. Afterwards, I'll set to work."[1]

MRS. POGSON: You see the idea that you can just "think things over" is only playing for time. He's got this memory of his life, but he can't act from it. At every node of his life, he feels this repetition, this inertia, that makes him act in the same way.

X: Although we don't have this memory we know this even in our own lives.

MRS. POGSON: Yes. There are nodes where something might be changed if only we made the effort and remembered to act differently. Now, why doesn't he live his life differently? Because he keeps putting things off. He has to realize the difference between tomorrow and now. A shock or something has to make him realize that *you can only work now.* He has memory of his life, but not understanding. That is why we emphasize understanding in the Work, for without it nothing is possible.

X: We might feel the truth of that at a meeting, but not tomorrow morning.

MRS. POGSON: Yes, that is a very good remark. We might realize this at a meeting and see that we have to live in the now and not put things off. But tomorrow we say: "That was an interesting chapter we heard!"

---

[1] P. D. Ouspensky, *The Strange Life of Ivan Osokin* (New York & London: Holme Press, 1947), pp. 66, 67.

What is the stimulus for effort? A very strong aim, so strong that we can walk in the protection of our aim. Then we can do something on ourselves. There is a quotation somewhere that goes something like this: "You must throw your heart in front of you and then follow it." We might throw our aim ahead today, as a group aim, but tomorrow we have to begin to follow it, slowly, gradually.

If a person doesn't know that there is a cosmic force, doesn't know that this inertia is real, but thinks of it rather as an accident, then he or she is more a victim of it. We are taught there are these forces, so that we can be aware of them and know their power. But there are also the forces of the spirit which are stronger.

X: When we realize that inertia is a cosmic force, it makes it less personal and takes the feeling of guilt out of it.

MRS. POGSON: Coming back to the question asked Mr. Ouspensky: "What creates stimulus for work?" Mr. Ouspensky himself answered:

> Realization of one's present state. When one realizes that one deceives oneself, that one is asleep and one's house is on fire, always, permanently on fire, and that it is only by accident that the fire has not reached one's room at this very moment, when one realizes this, one will want to make efforts to awake and one will not expect any special reward. Since we do not realize that our house is on fire we always expect a special reward. What can one do in sleep? One can only have different dreams—bad dreams, good dreams, but in the same bed. The dreams may be different, but the bed is the same (*The Fourth Way*, p. 266).

MRS. POGSON: Bunyan saw this when he left the City of Destruction. He saw the urgency of it and that one need not be destroyed oneself. We'll read what Mr. Ouspensky had to say on the importance of aim:

> We are never the same for two days in succession. On some days we shall be more successful, on others less. All we can do is to control what we can. We can never control more difficult things if we do not control the easy things. Every day and hour there are things that we could con-

trol and do not; so we cannot have new things to control. We are surrounded by neglected things. Chiefly, we do not control our thinking. We think in a vague way about what we want, but if we do not formulate what we want, nothing will happen. This is the first condition but there are many obstacles (*The Fourth Way*, p. 260).

MRS. POGSON: It's interesting how he says it is important to control what one can. You won't believe this. I didn't. One thinks one can learn to control more difficult things. But one has to practice on smaller things.

X: You have to practice the technique.

MRS. POGSON: Yes. Then, when you've practiced a technique, it— and you—can be relied on.

What we need *in the group* is to create a nucleus that can be relied on.

What small things can be worked on? *Mechanical talking* can always be worked on; *imagination; impatience* is a good one to work on; and not putting things off—smaller things.

This is very much connected with entropy. There is no effort at all in a state of entropy. Then only a shock, coming from outside, will get you out.

X: What about physical tiredness?

MRS. POGSON: You have to see it for yourself. Maybe you have to rest at certain times. You can see if it's physical or not. Effort can help even there. For example, there may be energy in another center. We might over-exhaust one center and not realize there is energy in another center.

X: I have difficulty in getting up in the morning.

MRS. POGSON: Meaning will get you up. Dr. Nicoll used to go over things in his mind in the morning and find that nothing had meaning. There was nothing to write, breakfast had no meaning for him, and perhaps it was raining outside. Then he would remember the Work and that there was so much to do for the Work, and he would leap out of bed. You get out of bed to meaning. As you go on in the Work, there are more and more sources of meaning. You get up by combining with meaning.

[A passage was read from *Living Time* by Maurice Nicoll (p. 112) about one's life as a unity, and about feeling one's life together, as one.]

MRS. POGSON: You see, from any moment it should be possible to feel the life as a whole. Here's the important point: it's a question of re-living it as one. The whole life can be experienced as one, and it is in this way that we can see our life at death. And then, when we see its whole, we see its meaning.

X: It's like seeing the whole growth of the Bower.

MRS. POGSON: Yes. We see purpose, we see what we're here for, and, seeing this meaning, we are able to enter into a new life. The purpose of the Work is to enable us to see meaning before we die. It would surely be the most bitter pain one could have, to see one's life at death and say: "This is my meaning, and I got off on the wrong track."

X: You have to see where things recur.

MRS. POGSON: Yes. I often see people in the groups getting into diffi-culty, and I see it is the same difficulty that always happens to them. I wonder if they will take it differently this time. But the person can't see it like that. She thinks it shouldn't happen that way. And so the difficulty will have to occur again.

X: Don't you think some people do know their pattern?

MRS. POGSON: Yes, thank God, some people do! If we could really become conscious and aware of our meaning, nothing could remain the same. Such thoughts can attract us; but you can go on thinking about them and make them your own, which means applying them to your lives.

X: Dr. Nicoll expresses it as: We labor in the permanent field of our lives.

MRS. POGSON: If I speak about this with feeling, it is because I have seen it happen—that it is possible to be in your own life. There is a reason for urgency.

[A passage was read which says to those who are indifferent or think they have many births before them, that they must not put off working from day to day, thinking they could do so in another life; for when the circle of perfect souls is completed, the light will be shut off.]

MRS. POGSON: This is a solemn warning, that one can't put off work forever.

Easter
March 24, 1959

X: What is meant by a new birth of Essence?

MRS. POGSON: It is a new birth *from* Essence. It is possible to have many small births before the real birth takes place—before "Christ is born within us"—just as it is possible to have many small deaths. In fact, this is how the Work proceeds.

This is very much connected with Easter. The vernal equinox is a time of new beginnings and is recognized in all religions. March 25th, Lady Day, is equivalent to a special feast in ancient Egyptian teaching when there is a conjunction between the Sun and the Moon. This time is also recognized in Mexican, Babylonian, and Roman teachings. A period of fasting and small sacrifices precedes this time in preparation for it.

X: It is a period of intensification of forces.

MRS. POGSON: Yes, because of the strength of the sun more things are possible—something may be born, but there must be sacrifices first. Have you thought how infectious negative emotions are and how people affect each other just by their presence?

X: If you are too long with a person whom you like he often irritates you. What can you do?

MRS. POGSON: You are irritated by the other person's mechanical-ness; see that it is this which irritates you and then wait for it to pass.

X: One can realize that one may be irritating the other person.

X: With a new friendship, you can see the friendship building up and then comes a time when you get bored or annoyed with the other person. What can you do about this?

MRS. POGSON: When you live in close contact with a person you see him or her in small "I's" and you have to see whether you have contact with them in other "I's." If you value your friend and find what is real in him you can bear his mechanicalness because you have a real connection with him. On the other hand, he may be a person with whom you have no real connection.

X: At first we meet the façade of the other person and then comes a time when "the honeymoon is over."

MRS. POGSON: Yes, we are attracted by glamor at first, but when we are in close contact with the person, his or her mechanical habits irritate us. It is interesting to see what mechanical habits irritate us; this tells us something about ourselves, and if we can look at the matter from this point of view, then the person can help us a great deal, and after much self-observation we become grateful to the other person.

X: What is meant by wasting our feeling of "I," which you spoke about at another meeting?

MRS. POGSON: This is a very important question. Dr. Nicoll describes this feeling of "I" as spirit. It is the most precious thing we have, and yet we allow any small "I" to take this feeling. Try to discover where your feeling of "I" is during the day. It is necessary to give this feeling to professional "I's" for a time during the day, but how often is it in false personality? How often are you feeling offended, for example? This feeling of "I" must be taken out of small "I's" and placed farther inwards in "I's" which are responsible, which can give some directed attention.

X: Can you say exactly what this feeling of "I" is like?

MRS. POGSON: Who can give a good example?

X: When small "I's" take this feeling of "I," they do not want to relinquish it.

X: It is one's soul.

MRS. POGSON: Yes, it is where you love. It is in the wrong places. Look at your day and see what takes your feeling of "I." When you see what takes your feeling of "I," you have choice. Your feeling of "I" is owed to "Real I."

X: Sometimes I see I am identified, but I have not the strength to separate.

MRS. POGSON: Life is very strong, but eventually you can separate if you really want to. It is necessary to make an aim about what you have seen and the next time you are about to become identified you will be given some help. Aim must be made before the event.

X: The meaning of religious festivals is to help you to put your feeling of "I" into bigger things.

MRS. POGSON: It is merciful that these times of Easter and Christmas exist, because we may for a time become more conscious of levels. Our feeling of "I" may be drawn into inner things.

X: Is there more force at such times?

MRS. POGSON: Certainly. If many people are together they receive a certain force which can be set against the negative forces in the world.

I want to show you Dr. Nicoll's method of studying Easter. It is to take a particular aspect of Easter and study it from a psychological point of view. We will consider the descriptions of the robing and mocking of Christ, and the choice of the people in releasing Barabbas and having Christ crucified. Gurdjieff, Ouspensky, and Dr. Nicoll taught that the drama of Easter is a consciously planned drama having an inner as well as an outer meaning. There was nothing fortuitous about it. In the Old Testament there are many prophesies of this drama because in esoteric schools the inner meaning was known, and this is the same meaning contained in all the Mysteries. The manifestation of the drama might vary, but the purpose of it is always the same. It illustrates what happens psychologically in life every day. Barabbas, the pseudo king, is chosen and the real king, Christ, is put to death. Barabbas is described in the Gospels as a robber, murderer, traitor, and rebel. What is the robber in us? It is the false personality. Barabbas is in us. The crowd in the drama represents the multitude of "I's" in outer parts of centers, who, turned outward to life, seek to destroy the inner. Christ here represents "Real I" and this is what is crucified in our daily lives when we give our feeling of "I" to violent emotions.

[Accounts of Barabbas from the four gospels were then read: Matthew 27: 15-21 describes how he was chosen instead of Christ; in Mark 15: 6-15 Barabbas was not alone, but with a group of rebels who had committed murder; Luke 23: 18, 19; and John 18: 39, 40, where he is described as a robber.]

MRS. POGSON: Do you know Barabbas in yourselves? One meaning of the word Barabbas is "son of the father." He is contrasted with Christ, placed side by side with him, and in a way he is the other side of Christ, the false personality, chief feature.

X: One of the gospels says that the crowd was influenced by the chief priest.

MRS. POGSON: Small "I's" have not much will, just a collection of little wills, and are influenced by another force. They always choose for their master the pseudo king, the false personality. Notice that these small "I's" dislike a person one minute and the next minute like him; they are for the Work one minute and against it the next.

X: It is interesting that the same crowd that welcomed Christ a few days before now demanded his crucifixion.

MRS. POGSON: Let us study the mocking of Christ by the soldiers.

[Accounts of this were read from Matthew 27: 27-31; Mark 15: 16-20; Luke 23: 8-12 (this describes Herod and Pilate becoming friends together: for before they were at enmity between themselves); and John 19: 1–3.]

MRS. POGSON: Christ was dressed in a purple robe, a crown of thorns was placed on his head, and he was hailed as "king" in a mocking fashion. The false personality will mock and scorn what is real. It is worth thinking about the part played by Pilate. His wife (the intuitive side of him) knew that Christ was from a higher level, but his self-love was too strong to allow him to act from his understanding. Have you observed that you know better than you behave? How many people see that the drama of choosing Barabbas and destroying Christ is enacted in their lives every day on a small scale?

Have people thought why the physical suffering of the crucifixion is stressed? It may be because physical suffering is the kind of suffering which everyone understands something of, and if we are greatly moved we may get a glimpse of the psychological suffering of Christ. We have to try to think what the suffering of God—in our language, "Real I"—might be. When we give our feeling of "I" to false personality, this is robbing "Real I" of what belongs to it alone.

X: No real satisfaction seems to have followed the crucifixion of Christ.

MRS. POGSON: The satisfaction was at a higher level. After the death and resurrection of Christ, his chosen apostles were able to teach and to heal; they were able to *Do*.

X: Christ talked to the multitude.

X: It is difficult to understand his love for the multitude.

MRS. POGSON: To understand how Christ loved the multitude is far beyond us, but we have to look at this. You have to accept all "I's" and when you have lived with them for a long time, perhaps there is a certain tenderness for all "I's." You are responsible for your "I's." After a long time the level of the whole being can be raised if enough effort has been made.

X: Where is the choice between the pseudo king and the real king?

MRS. POGSON: When you really want the pseudo king to die, there is a choice. The Work will eventually lead you to where a final choice must be made, and if at that point you choose the real king, then a reversal takes place. But there are small choices in each day when you make effort. What you give up on one level is given back to you on another level but, in a way, changed.

The Reed-Bearer is a common figure in the Mysteries. In the Easter drama, he offers Christ a cup of bitter wine or vinegar symbolizing that he must accept all experiences, however bitter. Christ drinks it and then says, "It is finished," thereby showing that he has accepted all the experiences which have come to him and his incarnation is finished. The acceptance has included all sides of himself and his incarnation is complete—finished.

It is interesting to study symbolism, but we must relate all this to ourselves, to our everyday life. We must see Barabbas in ourselves and not just as a figure in a distant drama.

X: We can only see one small aspect of Barabbas every Easter.

MRS. POGSON: Yes, but this is something. If we could die to that it would leave space for something new to be born in its place. Easter is a time for a *new beginning*.

[This is also discussed in chapter 9 of Commentary on the Fourth Gospel.]

CHAPTER 6

EASTER AT DORTON

The Theme of Reversal
April 3, 1959

MRS. POGSON: When it comes to your daily life, you don't apply the instructions given in the Work. In the ancient Mysteries, candidates received instructions for a long time in the lesser mysteries, for a long time they had not only to acquire this knowledge but also *apply it* to themselves. They were not allowed to go on until they had applied it. In the groups now people don't apply what they learn, yet they go on asking for new ideas. Being lags behind because they don't *live* according to what they know. I will think of examples: you don't really see what to work against mechanicalness means. We gain new knowledge here, at Dorton, but whenever we aren't actually doing constructive work (not actually in a meeting, discussing the Work, or engaged in activities connected with it), people lapse back into everyday "I's." The aim of Dorton is to awaken something that can be still aware in periods between Dortons. To make it worth the effort here, we must be able to carry through, to retain some kind of consciousness, some continuity of awareness. Otherwise we shall have to discontinue Dorton. To lapse back into one's ordinary "I's" between activities does not represent any change of being; change of being is shown by some continuity of awareness.

There are people here from different parts of the country. How do you relate to one another? Mostly you relate by enquiring about personality things and comparing notes about personality things. And yet here is a chance to try to connect in a different way, to see the person essentially, without reference to personality and his or her usual background. At Amwell, we worked with people and related to them differently without ever asking them about themselves, or even, in many cases, knowing about them until much later.

X: It's not necessary to talk, but it's difficult for both people to be in the right place so as to make a real connection.

MRS. POGSON: Through the neutralizing force of the Work, it is possible to see a person differently—without his house on his back. We want to connect with the real part of a person. Just being with a person makes this possible, for through that we get a feeling of the other person and so connect more essentially. Getting to know someone socially comes later.

X: Can't ordinary conversation touch off something deeper?

MRS. POGSON: It can. But you like to limit everything to polite conversation. It would be an exercise for you not to. This would then be a reversal in yourself. You should all try to remember and minimize conversation, limit it to what is necessary, avoid personality conversation. Light conversation is, however, different and has its place. Dr. Nicoll valued it.

X: We all come from such different parts of the country and have such different personalities, it seems to me that the ability to talk to different people might also require effort—at least for some people. Is all such talking mechanical?

MRS. POGSON: You can make a new relationship through the Work, through what we talk about. The thing is to be related apart from your environment.

About the habit of unnecessary talking, you remember what Mr. Ouspensky wrote in *In Search of the Miraculous:* that this is the great difficulty; that people wouldn't struggle with it because it always seemed to them right or positive. They call it "wanting to be sincere, to help someone, to ask questions" and so on.

X: If we could stop automatic talking, it would make us very much more conscious.

X: I tried to stop unnecessary conversation in the office, but found it resulted in there being a strain in my relations with the other people.

MRS. POGSON: Something was wrong. It has to be done from the third force of the Work. Mr. Ouspensky said that the habit of talking touches everything. It could become the center of gravity for work on oneself. He said how much easier complete silence is. It is much more difficult to be nearly silent.

X: Isn't it nervousness—always wanting to talk?

MRS. POGSON: Yes, but all these are habits to become separated from. They only belong to self-love; they are bothering about oneself.

There are curious gaps—as when we hear the Work at meetings and say we are in the Work, but do not do it. Everyone has a high aim and wants to hear about how to attain this aim, and to hear about the wonderful possibilities. But the near and the tangible, that is the last thing anyone wants to hear about or do.

X: It is as though you can't resist these habits.

MRS. POGSON: You don't want to. We want to be as we have always been. But the Work sets up a friction; something in you doesn't want to be as you have always been: one group of "I's" wants the Work.

X: If you make the personality approach while observing or self-remembering, it's different, isn't it?

MRS. POGSON: Yes, if you do it consciously, or if you have a certain reason for doing it. That's the difference. There should be more and more people who begin to know what they're doing.

X: You have to begin by seeing what kind of approach you have.

MRS. POGSON: Then you can have a little choice. The following from an early meeting of Dr. Nicoll's was read:

> You cannot see [your chief feature] until you have suf-
> fered a lot. The Work becomes harder and harder until
> you are driven to find a place in yourself from which you
> can see. You may occasionally see your chief feature
> objectively before that and for a very short moment—but

you cannot see it properly because it is you. When you get into a bigger self (which is all around this smaller self but you do not know it) then you can really see it, but everything by which you live, enjoy life, or which has any color, will have gone, and you cannot bear it unless there is something to take its place.

In this bigger self whatever is real in the smaller self will find a place; it will be the same but magnified and it will have lost its color. Even if there is something real in the smaller self it is mixed with what is false, and this colors it; when the color is lost, we lose what gave us interest before. We feel strange now and do not know what we are. But from here we can begin to do. From one place in us doing is always possible and is not so difficult as we think it is.[1]

Reversal in the Emotional Center
April 4, 1959

[Mrs Pogson returned to the theme—the need for a complete reversal in oneself. She quoted again from the Acts of Philip: All the world is turned the wrong way and every soul in it. . . . Unless you make that which is beneath to be above, and the left to the right and the right to the left, you shall not enter the Kingdom of Heaven. . . . *A complete reversal* is necessary.]

MRS. POGSON: We have to think during the next few days about the conditions of complete reversal. What does that mean? It means giving control to the side that has not got it and taking away from that which has. It means a turning, a reversal in everything, in our thinking, our emotions, in our whole life.

Our theme for the next meeting will be how this reversal has to take place in the emotional center. Reversal is chiefly connected with the soul. It is a turning round, as with Mary Magdalene, who first loved man, and then turned round to love Christ. We turn round to

---

[1]At the next meeting Mrs. Pogson commented: This "coloring" comes from self-love, self-interest, through which we feel ourselves. With loss of color, meaning and interest remain, but in purer form: white light includes all the colors.

love what is within. It is a long process of friction, during which we love ourselves through this or that person without realizing that it is self-love. The mind knows that there are other things, but the choice continues to be directed to self-love for a while. When we begin to work, the Work starts a friction in us which can begin this process of reversal.

Try to see what it is you put before the Work. At the simplest level someone might say that they couldn't go to a meeting on a certain day because he or she always did something else, had always done so. These objections exist, of course, on every level. Try to see what it is you prefer to the Work.

X: We tend to become identified over the Work. When something interrupts my reading of a commentary or a quiet period I become upset or irritated.

MRS. POGSON: That often happens, but the Work is about transforming events, not about carrying out selected Work activities. Dr. Nicoll always interpreted "Blessed are the meek," as "Blessed are those who do not resent." When you feel resentful, remember that it is the outer man. You have to live the Work and win it through friction. Remember the pearl. The inner man is always there, even when the outer man is resentful, and he has to bear both outside difficulties and inner resentments. He may be weak due to lack of nourishment.

X: You say that the group gives opportunities to provide friction. Do you mean that the group creates events that make for friction?

MRS. POGSON: Directed group work gives better opportunities for friction than you can get working by yourself.

[Mrs. Pogson continued the discussion of group work and friction as the means of work on oneself, quoting from *The Fourth Way* (p. 274ff). Opportunities depend on the amount of effort you put into the Work. If you give little, only a little will be required of you. The more you do, the more you will have to do; the more your responsibilities toward the Work will increase.]

MRS. POGSON: In a group you are surrounded by mirrors, you can study your "I's" in other people. We should be grateful toward those who give us an opportunity to work on ourselves! Where friction is greatest in working with someone else, there you are being shown something very important. . . . In a group, we cannot expect other people to think about us. If you stick in your own work, I mean in the first line of the Work, you are able to give yourself a shock by turning to the other two lines.

X: Is it never possible to work on the first and third lines of the Work without work in a group?

MRS. POGSON: You cannot work by yourselves. It goes into imagination if you are not in a group. When the Work is taught orally, you are able to get into touch with Influences.

Groups are accumulators. How many of us contribute, and how many only draw from the accumulated force of the group? New people are able to contribute by their interest, their questions, and their willingness to absorb.

X: Does all friction of the outer man help to feed the inner man?

MRS. POGSON: The outer man is continually complaining. He has to become quiescent. When many people are together, it is necessary to learn to accept things.

X: Wanting things to be different can be a complete block. I remember an occasion when I had brought my husband to meet Dr. Nicoll and was wanting him to be impressed with the Work. Dr. Nicoll spoke only of hunting tigers, not the words of wisdom I expected to hear. Suddenly he turned to me and said: "Why are you so negative?" I found out afterward that my husband had been very much impressed, and remembered all he had said about tigers, while I could not remember a thing. It seems that anticipation of a certain event or situation is at the root here and makes one deaf to anything else, except what one is expecting to hear.

X: Is friction arranged in a group?

MRS. POGSON: Yes. Practical work at Dorton and with Dr. Nicoll is designed to teach us not to be identified with what we do. But you can be negatively indifferent. In schools we are also taught how not to be caught by vanity.

[Mrs. Pogson continued reading extracts from *The Fourth Way*. She mentioned in particular the question of how one can "give back to the Work." To do this it is necessary to know what is useful to the Work without reference to oneself. The group was asked to work on choice by trying to observe instances where choice is possible, as between, for example, resenting and accepting. In conclusion, there was a reading from "The Antagonism between the Self-Love and the Work" (*Psychological Commentaries*, Vol. V, p. 1618ff).]

April 6, 1959

MRS. POGSON: We've been talking since we've been at Dorton about the need for a complete reversal in the mind and emotions. The biggest reversal has to take place in the emotional center. We can keep on talking about this, but nothing happens. To do the Work, you must take force from the self-love, so that the feeling of "I" can be taken inward. This feeling of "I" can then be used to give attention in other directions. It is best if we think of love as giving attention. This is the nearest and first approach to another kind of affection. It's all we've got to give inwardly. In self-love we have no attention for the other person, because we are glued to ourselves and hypnotized.

X: Does all sense of gratification come from self-love?

MRS. POGSON: Yes, all meaning is through self-love until you're able to find meaning elsewhere. We can begin to find new meaning outside ourselves, especially in other people. The supreme example of giving attention to the needs of others is that of the Good Samaritan. We must widen the field of those to whom we can give attention. The power of attention increases as you use it. In the intellectual center the ability to give attention to studies can be acquired. In the emotional center, we must clear away the illusion of how well we mean toward others.

All the time in meetings, when this subject is mentioned, people retire into themselves saying, "Yes, of course, but this doesn't apply to me!" Or, "I know it already." We don't bother to make efforts, because we think we give enough attention to others already. We have to accept the fact that we can't really be bothered with others.

X: We can make room for them.

MRS. POGSON: Just by remembering to give room, you are already giving attention. But you can only give attention if there is a space between you and the thing or person. When you don't give people a space, you are wanting to change them, asking questions, making requirements, and so on. You must leave space for the person to be as he is. You put a spell on him if you make no space for him.

It's much harder to transform in ourselves the things we think are right than the things we think are wrong.

X: I have just realized that, in spite of our utterly different facades, all of us at Dorton are wanting essentially the same thing.

MRS. POGSON: That was a very real experience.

April 8, 1959

X: I found that my mind was unadaptable and that I was only able with difficulty to move from one center to another.

MRS. POGSON: One of the principal things about this training is that it teaches us to move about in ourselves and to be adaptable, also to move from one center to another. Everything in oneself should be accessible.

When you find yourself between centers you have the least energy, because you are not in touch with any accumulator. In a center you have energy, enough energy to switch over to another center. When you find yourself between centers, go as quickly as you can into one center—it doesn't matter which. Go for a walk, eat something, or whatever, but give your attention to something.

When the second body is organized, a person is able to create emotions he or she would like to feel, and is not at the mercy of emotional reactions. The chief instruction for the formation of the second body is to obey the Work. Instead of a kaleidoscope of emotions you will have an emotional center that can function.

X: I am sometimes nervous about working for fear I shall be confronted with something I don't want to see, or with a test.

MRS. POGSON: It *seems* to come when it is a little beyond us or when we are not ready for it, but in fact it doesn't. The test is always given to us when we are able to bear it, and we can bear it by reaching a little beyond our being.

If you want the whole system to be clear, do not object to anything difficult, but leave it and wait until light is thrown on what you have objected to. See your objections; this is the emotional center not cooperating. Objections are for the most part to the practice of the Work. Where do your objections come from? Often from pictures, or places where you think you are right. If you are sure you are right, that is often the very time when you meet with a test.

X: I found difficulty in following the many instructions of the Work simultaneously. Should it not be possible to follow them one at a time, working through each one separately and more or less finishing with it before going on the next? Does one not after a certain period of time reach the point where one no longer has consciously to remember all the instructions separately, but that they function more or less automatically within one?

MRS. POGSON: You are taking it much too heavily.

[The following five basic instructions were put on the board (plus one that was connected with all of them).]

> Do not express negative emotions;
> Do not identify;
> Do not justify;
> Observe yourself;
> Remember yourself;
> Work against imagination (this is put separately because it comes into everything).

MRS. POGSON: This last one is essential, because it is possible to imagine you are working. You should have all these instructions in an accessible place so that they can be called upon as required. There is then always some idea which can help you to relate to events differently. There is always an instruction available and hence a choice is possible, a choice in relation to your aim.

Reversal in the Intellectual
Center: Psychological Thinking

[Referring to an answer of Christ to Pilate which is not in the Gospels (see the Acts of Pilate), Mrs. Pogson quoted the following: "Pilate asks: What is truth? and Jesus answers: Truth is of Heaven."[2] Truth is shown here as belonging to the level above. This belongs to reversal. There is no truth on earth. The senses lie to us.]

MRS. POGSON: The processes of our life on Earth are simply reflections of the processes in the invisible world, and if we want to know about processes in the invisible world, all we have to do is study this world. What a source of knowledge that is! We have talked before in this way, for instance, about modern inventions. They represent what can happen in the inner world. The escalator—up and down; it is like the angels ascending and descending. There is the upward movement and the downward movement. The telephone represents communicating with people from a distance. The inner process is telepathy. Television is clairvoyance—seeing people from a distance.

X: The electronic brain is interesting. It shows us processes of calculation and computation that go on without our knowing about it.

MRS. POGSON: Buying and selling is a definite process that can happen on any plane. You have always to have something to give in order to obtain anything. You have to give something in exchange, and this is buying. We generally say in the Work that effort is our money. Effort is asking, and you are bound to have a return. Dr. Nicoll, in a very interesting chapter, says that we always get what we ask for although we do not know that it is what we have asked for.

X: I wanted time to read, and then I had a very long period in bed. I knew that I had asked for it, and so I did not resent being ill but was able to enjoy reading.

---

[2]*The Lost Books of the Bible and the Forgotten Books of Eden*, Nicodemus 3: 11, 12 (New York, Meridian, 1963).

X: Things never turn out quite as you had expected.

MRS. POGSON: Yes, you buy and the thing is disguised. It is in a parcel. Perhaps something else is there as well. When we come to the question of prayer, we must use this creative faculty that we have. If you want something from the spiritual world, and it is a spiritual request—for instance, if you want something to be changed in yourself—you must visualize yourself in this new state; you must be very sure how you want to be—have it clear.

X: How can one visualize what one has not yet experienced if it is on a higher level?

MRS. POGSON: I mean in small things—for instance, not to judge. You have to prepare, rehearse, going through the day and looking on people differently. Take one person and rehearse the day differently. You don't know how much the Work depends on this preparing.

[The following statement was written on the blackboard.]

No one who is not free from suffering can work.

MRS. POGSON: This means mechanical suffering. This is the price we have to pay. You set aside mechanical suffering, and then you can begin to work. This is another form of reversal, to give up mechanical suffering and suffer consciously. You see, you haven't got the energy to work if you are always letting it drain away by mechanical suffering.

For this reversal it is necessary to see all the different forms of useless suffering so that one can be free from them. It is the small "I's" that have mechanical suffering, but real suffering is in an inner part of the center and has a quite different quality. Christ said, "If you had known how to suffer you would not have suffered." This is how it should be in the Work. People should learn to suffer in the right place.

The moments of real suffering are very short, but we do sometimes have a sudden vision of what we are really like and that is great suffering; but there is a curious thing about it; it can turn to a kind of bliss—after the suffering you have bliss. There are not many such moments, but they are very precious and they stand out.

Reversal on Cosmic Scale
April 9, 1959

[There was a reading on evolution and involution from *In Search of the Miraculous*, p. 308.]

MRS. POGSON: This is the principle of evolution in every cosmos and on every scale. The one hope for humanity is that a conscious nucleus shall be held together and be able to stand up against the force of the mechanical downward pull. And so it is in a group. The hope is that some people will be able to form a nucleus and will be strong enough to stand up against all the manifestations of mechanicalness that pull the other way. And in ourselves this is the formation of Deputy Steward. Deputy Steward is formed of all the "I's" that can work, so that there is something built up which, in the end, can become stronger than the multitude of "I's" that are liable to be hypnotized by life. This is the principle of evolution. The involutionary process begins consciously in the Absolute. At the next step it already becomes mechanical. But the evolutionary process becomes more and more conscious as it develops.

You can think of ways in which two hundred beings from the level of conscious humanity could work to transform humanity, supposing they were to inhabit the bodies of certain people, such as the heads of important organizations and institutions, religious bodies for instance.

X: Probably such intervention would not be considered as right unless things had got to such a state that it could not go on any longer.

MRS. POGSON: Yes, that is what I think. But we have to think of ourselves and how we stand between these two opposing forces of involution and evolution, and how our hope of strengthening our aim is to put ourselves under the influence of the forces that will lift us up.

X: I am having some difficulty with the idea of involution.

MRS. POGSON: It is a downward force. It is used simply in connection with going downward into manifestation, becoming more and more material.

[Diagram 4 of the Ray of Creation with the side octave was now put on the blackboard (p. 51).]

MRS. POGSON: Can we look at this diagram and conceive of all possible worlds? We cannot do it, we can't think on that level. But then we come to our galaxy—the Milky Way—that we can conceive. We can begin to know something of its size, something of its scale, and we have our own wonder about it through seeing the sky at night, and there we can see how the Will of the Absolute goes out into creation. Within the galaxy we can see our solar system. It is a good thing to go to the planetarium where we can see the Sun with its planets, and our Earth among them within the galaxy.

This outward movement is not a question of good or evil. Is it evil for the Divine Mind to make all possible worlds, or the galaxies, or the planets? It is not evil, it is simply what is brought into manifestation; it is a way of manifesting in more and more material density. But for us, if we are going in the other direction, it is evil. This is the escalator which is going at a great rate downward, and there is terrific momentum.

X: It is not evil going down, but our business is to go up.

MRS. POGSON: Yes, it is not evil for people who do not know there is a ladder. We must remember this because there is a tendency in the Work to criticize people who are not in it. If they are interested in life on Earth, it simply means that they are under this influence (Earth) and want to fulfill all possibilities of material life. That is where they are.

It is only when they get a tweak of the cord, as it were, that they begin to want to go in another direction. Something on this higher level with which we are connected begins to think, "Well, perhaps he might want to turn in the other direction."

X: It is as though we have a Work responsibility, having been shown the ladder.

MRS. POGSON: Yes, it does give us responsibility. Call this to mind when you think of your aim and of the difficulties of working—that there is this ladder, and that as soon as one has got separated at all from the level of life, it is possible to come under these influences (on the side octave) which can enable us to go upward.

Logical and Psychological Thinking
April 10, 1959

[Mrs. Pogson referred to Diagram 10 on the board.]

MRS. POGSON: This makes clear what *metanoia* is—thinking beyond our usual mind, beyond the senses. This connects with reversal. . . . People are not aware of how much they still think from the senses. And yet you are becoming used to interpreting parables and myths; this is an exercise to teach you to think psychologically . . . One should be able to think on every level. Where is logical thinking useful? In practical work, observation in life, etc. Where is it used wrongly? When taking a person as a single "I" . . . it is necessary to leap to the level of relative thinking. There is no truth without relative thinking. For example, to study one organ of the body by itself, without considering the whole, is ridiculous. We have to know to what everything belongs. Historical thinking is interesting because it shows relationship. We must study humans in relation to everything else.

On each level of mind there is a different kind of memory. The logical mind remembers details and facts; it is sequential. It has to do with the pendulum of opposites, with yes-or-no. It is related to ordinary time, to one dimension of time. The psychological mind remembers through connections. It has another kind of relationship to time. . . . The logical mind remembers things which are of no use to us; it remembers from habit. See what you remember unnecessarily, because we have only so much force for remembering. When you make new connections you have a new memory. . . . Our attitudes lie in the logical mind. They are blank spaces in the mind. The logical mind is the place from which our justifications come.

```
Greater Mind
Psychological Mind
— — — — — — — — — (discontinuous levels)
Logical Mind
A-logical Mind
```

Diagram 10. Levels of Mind.

[A commentary was read on psychological thinking (*Psychological Commentaries*, Vol. III, p. 1019ff).]

MRS. POGSON: Whenever you recognize *argument*, see that it is in small "I's." When the Work is being argued about, this is in small "I's." The level of the Work falls; you must try to stop it immediately. Psychological thinking must prevail and logical thinking must become subordinated to it.

X: Logical thinking is useful in its place. And the negative part of the intellectual center is a useful counterbalance.

MRS. POGSON: Greater Mind plays down through the psychological mind. When the mind of a person becomes receptive, new ideas may fall down at any moment from Greater Mind.

X: Psychological thinking is a balanced way of thinking. It doesn't create argument or raise second force in another. The person goes with it.

MRS. POGSON: Logical thinking only engenders a memory that has to do with time and space. Recollection is one of the most important tasks. Every moment of self-remembering strengthens our memory. Memory below the line is a travesty of real memory. Things below must be there, but not for themselves. What is above must govern. . . . *Every connection we make in the Work is recollection.*

  X referred yesterday to choosing what we must forget. Choosing what to remember is easier. Writing it down is one way. In order to forget an emotional experience you want to forget, you must make a new connection with it. There are some experiences which we live through for years and years afterwards—like having been made a fool of. If another instance comes, the new emotion can replace the old experience. But it must be stronger than the old one. But two centers have to do it together. The previous emotion is then dissolved in the new emotion. There are only so many experiences and these repeat themselves. When one of them comes around again, you work on it, and on all the others which are of a similar nature, and so connected with it. With regard to memory: you *recall* what is already there. The awakening of true redeeming memory is a theme of the Work.

In the next paper Dr. Nicoll says our logical man cannot under-stand the Work. He must jump and catch the rope suspended above his head. He speaks of understanding the inner meaning of the Lord's Prayer: "Give us this day our daily bread"—praying so that we can awaken. Only through psychological thinking can this be understood—ideas must be seen in the light of the Ray of Creation. Relative thinking is with the whole Ray of Creation in the back-ground. An example of relative thinking: whatever keeps you awake is right, whatever puts you to sleep is wrong. A man awakening can-not be understood by logical man.

April 11, 1959

[Mrs. Pogson referred to *Psychological Commentaries*, "Positive Ideas in the Work" (Vol. III, pp. 984–990) and to the diagram on p. 986, which is reproduced here as Diagram 11.]

X: Is psychological thinking related to both the emotional and intel-lectual centers?

MRS. POGSON: Yes—it is emotional thinking. . . . Humanity cannot change without a shock to connect it with positive ideas. Mechanical humanity does not have positive ideas. One must get to the place where life reasons become irrelevant, before one can contact positive ideas. The Work is a forcing house to produce in people positive ideas to make the transition possible. "A certain inner positive pres-

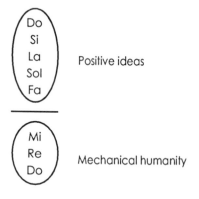

Diagram 11. *Mechanical humanity and* do, re, mi.

sure of attention is necessary to make ideas grow". . . . Plants, seeds—things on all levels—can grow better with attention. The Work is like a plant that has to be given attention and nourished, in order that it may nourish us. A special energy—an invisible substance—comes from the human care of things. This is what we have to give. It can often best be seen in the care people give to plants and animals, but it is often forgotten about in relation to grown-ups. Dr. Nicoll speaks about the increase of consciousness: "To have more consciousness requires a not going to sleep inside, for that is to invite and encourage darkness. Going to sleep means not doing anything in any of the three lines of Work" (*Psychological Commentaries*, Vol. III, p. 985).

In difficult periods, ". . . you *will* the Work, as a small guarded plant, between your two hands, and keep your eyes on it enough. That means your attention and the two hands mean inner and outer consciousness—consciousness of yourself and consciousness of others. This plant begins to die if you do not look at it enough" (Vol. III, p. 985). In the periods between Dortons many people neglect the Work and don't give attention to it, forgetting it has to be kept alive all the time. It's as if they didn't even water the plant. It can nourish us—but it has to be nourished in return.

X: I've had some help lately just through taking care of a plant someone neglected and I had taken over to tend. It kept me in mind of the Work the whole time I was tending it.

Mrs. Pogson: This is a good idea—but don't identify with the plant and forget what it means. You might come back to Dorton simply having fine cyclamens.

It does help Essence to grow, having something like that. These things are given to us for the purpose of making analogies. . . . Our relationship with other people is also a delicate plant. We should have a greenhouse of these young green plants. They have to be cared for. Yet sometimes you say to one of them: You can't have any water for a couple of weeks. . . . Love and attention is called "heat" in alchemy.

This discussion has arisen from what Dr. Nicoll said about the necessity for a *certain inner positive pressure of attention* to change being or grow. And one has first of all to understand from the Work "that one's life on earth means that one has something quite definite to do or else one would not be here" (*Psychological Commentaries*, Vol. III, p. 986). This is a positive idea. But people have not enough force because they have no *distinct positive* ideas about the Work. These ideas have to do with reversal.

[A further commentary on positive ideas (Vol. III, p. 990) was read.]

MRS. POGSON: A positive idea makes Essence grow. Negative ideas seem to make personality grow. The idea that we cannot do may sound negative from the life point of view, but it is positive from the point of view of the Work—a reversal. . . . We may define a positive idea as *that which lessens personality and increases Essence.*

Laws Concerning Leaven
April 15, 1960

MRS. POGSON: This Easter I tried a new way of including the people who weren't able to come to Dorton by sending out a question relating to what we would be talking about. I have received many replies already. Many people have connected with us. The question was about meaning: the reason why, on the eve of the Passover in the Jewish the master of the house searches the house for all the leaven—even to the crumbs—which then has to be destroyed; and for seven days only unleavened bread is eaten.

["The Search for Leaven" from the Passover Seder Hagadah were read as follows.]

> The search for leaven is usually conducted the night before Passover eve; that is on the eve of the 14th of Nisan. It is preceded by the benediction:

> "Praised are Thou, Eternal, our God, King of the Universe, Who in sanctifying us with Thy commandments, hast enjoined upon us the removal of all leaven."

> The search having been concluded the following is recited:

"All leaven on my premisis, which has escaped my notice
and has not been removed, is herewith declared of no
consequence and equivalent to mere dust."[3]

MRS. POGSON: I have an interesting observation from one person
who writes that she read recently in a newspaper about the Jews
who sell what is unlawful for them to keep, on the understanding
that they can buy it back after the feast of the Passover. But instead
of commenting on the iniquity of the custom she has made a connection with herself, drawing a parallel with the Work and seeing how
she also sells the Work for a time in the hopes that she can buy it
back later. Well, how is this done psychologically? . . . People let the
Work go at a time when they feel they don't want it, and then hope
to get it back later. But people don't realize they're doing it. They do
it mechanically.

This theme of "becoming free from Egypt" is expressed in different ways in different religions. We have been discussing how it is that
we can only learn *intellectually* from any other teaching. Only the
teaching we are *practicing* can change our being. Although we may
study other systems, they make no impression on our being. But now
that we are practicing the Work, it is possible to study other systems
and see how the same ideas are expressed in other teachings.[4]

X: Would you clear up the literal meaning of leaven?

MRS. POGSON: Leaven is used very often as an image in the Bible. A
very small amount of this substance can have a great effect; it has a
fermenting quality; it increases—for good or evil; it has infinite possibilities; it gives life. The point is that it can do this in whatever it
touches, but it can't be kept.

[An observation was read to the group: one must search out the old
leaven, the wrong thinking, the wrong meanings in oneself, before
one could come out of Egypt; one could not add the new onto the
old or mix the new with the old; and that then a period of seven
days—a space—must be left.]

---

[3]*Home-Service for Passover Eve*, translated and edited by William Rosenau (New York:
Bloch Publishing, 1943), p. 1.
[4]It should be clear that Mrs. Pogson is not saying that the Work is the only teaching
through which there can be change of being.

MRS. POGSON: This space is so important. It is the idea expressed in all teachings. One has to be aware of what is old in one. It must be destroyed, and then there has to be a space in which you become free from the influence of the old attitudes. Then you can become open to the new, and there is a chance that the higher centers may let something through.

X: Can we think of it in connection with meaning?

MRS. POGSON: Yes, one has to lose one's old meaning. It is no longer valid. You cannot keep even a bit of it—not a crumb. But it takes a very long time to see what one's old meaning was and then to realize that it no longer conducts meaning.

X: It is difficult to carry about an empty space!

MRS. POGSON: In there is an empty space, it is there in one's being; and there it is possible to be present and hear what is said. In the place of old attitudes we cannot hear without mixing things up. The new ideas have to fall on this empty space, not on the old attitudes. Here you can make the ideas your own. This searching out of the old leaven in the house and the seven days of "space" is not taken over into the Christian teaching, but the washing by Christ of the disciples" feet corresponds to it in some degree. The passage from slavery to freedom is expressed most graphically in the Old Testament; but we don't always see that for us it is the same thing.

X: Why is it called Good Friday?

MRS. POGSON: It is the most Sacred day in the Christian church. The most holy day. I think the explanation is as simple as that.

The Crucifixion

[Mrs. Pogson then spoke about the crucifixion drama.]

MRS. POGSON: "The time is at hand." Dr. Nicoll points to the arrival of certain Greeks from Greek schools to show that the time was right. Then we have the words of Christ which connect his teaching with the Greek and Egyptian mysteries: "Except a grain of wheat fall into the ground and die, it abideth alone. . . ." He is telling us that the same thing which he is going to enact, was enacted in the Mysteries. Mr. Gurdjieff, Mr. Ouspensky and Dr. Nicoll all believed that the Crucifixion was a drama which had been enacted in the schools.

The Crucifixion has to be connected with the time of the vernal equinox and the Jewish Passover; at this time there is the force to connect with. Then those who were saved by the blood of the lamb are now saved by the blood of Christ. There has to be this correspondence. And why the full moon? This is a time for fulfillment. The time of secret initiations, for beginning something new, was the time of the new moon. But festivals were celebrated at full moon, when everything could come to its full development.

X: There was an *Egyptian* sacrifice of the ram at the same time.

MRS. POGSON: Yes. It is said that our cosmos has to be in correspondence with the greater cosmos.

We have spoken before about the choice of Barabbas by the multitude. Dr. Nicoll always asked us to see the characters taking part in the Crucifixion drama as in ourselves. This is how one can be redeemed: by seeing how it could take place in oneself. Everyone knows the multitude by now. Most of your "I's" prefer to have the robber released, not Christ. Who is this robber?

X: He robs the inner man.

MRS. POGSON: Yes. He robs us of nourishment that should be given to the inner man. This is the choice. Then there is Pilate in us—someone with knowledge, superior to the other "I's." He *knows* better than he *does*. The disciples in us are trained in the Work; they can understand something. But even they cannot be relied on. They deny Christ; they can't stay awake until they have failed, until the great shock comes; then they can change. It's the shock that failure gives that makes it possible to become different. Only the women in the Crucifixion story remain loyal. Women represent the emotions.

And then you have to see Judas in yourself. This is psychological. When you think about it as a drama, you see Judas in a different way. Mr. Gurdjieff and Dr. Nicoll say that Judas was the chief disciple because he had the most difficult part to play.

X: Why did he destroy himself afterwards?

MRS. POGSON: Because he had to play the part of an evil "I," and an evil "I" destroys itself in the end. It is simply in the part.

X: Do you mean the other disciples acted consciously running away?

MRS. POGSON: No, I do not think so. But Judas had to act consciously. The very name "Judas" means "he who is praised." This part is well-known in the Mysteries, although very little is known to us of their practices. We do know that there were two kinds of teacher. One was the *hydrophant*, who baptized with water and gave the early training to the candidates. They were handed over at a later stage to the hierophant who was responsible for committing the candidates to their final test, which was a crucifixion, lying on the ground. It was a symbolic crucifixion, meaning dying to himself. It is possible that Judas was playing this rôle.

You have heard of the term "vicarious atonement" which is often misleading. Christ cannot die for us, but his death shows us the way. Dr. Nicoll couldn't die *for* us, but he showed us the way. It has to happen in us. You can see that it cannot be otherwise.

In Robert Grant's *The Secret Sayings of Jesus*, he refers to the Apocryphal Gospel of Peter. This Gospel was rejected for several reasons. One reason was that it said of Christ: "He kept silence, as one feeling no pain." But it wouldn't be necessary to feel pain in his physical body. The suffering is elsewhere, higher than that. It hasn't to do with physical suffering at all but with psychological development. We speak in the Work of right suffering, conscious suffering, which means Suffering because of what we are. We see Barabbas in us, we see the disciples the better "I's," and we know that not even they can be relied on. This is the kind of suffering meant—psychological suffering.

Stages of Practical Work
April 16, 1940

MRS. POGSON: I want to talk about crossing this *Mi-Fa* gap (diagram 12 on p. 112). This is how Dr. Nicoll represented the Work octave for us on a smaller scale in his own private diagram. The Work octave begins with valuation at *Do*, then *Re* is applying the ideas, and *Mi* is working on personal difficulties (cf. p. 77). The gap at *Mi* cannot finally be crossed for a long time, but it can be represented many times on small scale. You have to cross the gap many times before you finally cross it.

Let us take the idea about minding. What happens? First an idea is repeated in the group. There will always be some people who don't hear it at all, for people are at different stages and in different states at the meeting. Some will dismiss the idea, thinking they've heard it before. Some resist it. And some hear it only vaguely. But after many repetitions someone may hear it. And then at the next meeting someone else may hear another idea, and so on. Then they know the idea. That is the second stage. Then there is a further stage of acknowledging it by applying it to oneself.

Then comes the next stage, understanding. There is a bigger gap here, between acknowledging and understanding. Understanding comes from acting according to what you have acknowledged in yourself, and then it becomes part of your being. A person is measured by his or her understanding. You act according to your being. Your being is your understanding. If I were to say how I thought of all of you, it would be according to your understanding. Then the octave continues and goes much faster—deciding, willing, doing.

X: On the right side, *Do-Re-Mi*, we remember after we act; and on the left side, *Fa-Sol-La-Si*, we remember before we act.

MRS. POGSON: Yes, that is a good description. Every small increase in understanding makes you realize how much more there is to understand. . . . There can be many octaves like this. Can anyone give an example?

X: Not to be impatient when something goes wrong.

MRS. POGSON: Yes, if you have really seen this and can act from it, then something has changed in your being. This is how a person learns to do, very gradually. In order to do, you have first to love the idea. Does anyone have an example of an idea you love?

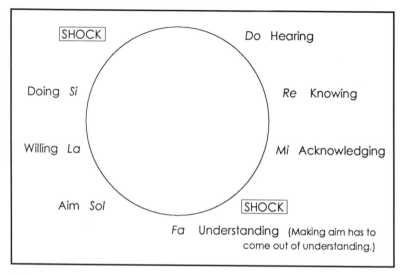

Diagram 12. An octave of learning.

X: Mr. Ouspensky's bird.

MRS. POGSON: Yes, many people have found that image valuable. Dr. Nicoll had a dream when he first met Mr. Ouspensky that he was able to be quite still when his feathers were ruffled. This is a good example X has given, because you can visualize Mr. Ouspensky with his hair being ruffled and yet unaffected by it. This is an image to retain.

[Mrs. Pogson turned to the subject of the main Work Octave.]

MRS. POGSON: In the *Mi-Fa* gap a lot of work is covered. You have to see the pendulum in yourself and not identify with the opposites. As long as a person identifies with the opposites there is no question of his crossing the gap. And a person has also to be able to inhabit the inner parts of centers, so that one can stand in oneself and is not knocked about by outer events. When a person has been in the Work for some time, one works on personal difficulties; one works toward the stage of "balanced man." Many times one has to cross the gap. This is a time of choices. The person will make an aim for the day, and then there are choices: will one follow the line of least resistance or act from the Work? The choice is whether to go against one's mechanicalness or not. For a long time one has to suffer the fact that one can't make the right choice.

Then there is work against chief feature. Work on personal difficulties leads us in this direction. At this important stage energy is needed. Where does it come from? It can only come from doing the Work. Then we see that we have to stop losing energy through wrong psychic functions or negative emotions. A person may want to go on but not have the energy; he or she is too weak. One has to remember that it is necessary to save energy and not lose it by wasting it. And then one has not only to save energy but to gain it by giving attention, by observation, by self-remembering.

April 20, 1960

> And lest I should be exalted above measure through the abundance of the revelations, there was given to me a thorn in the flesh, the messenger of Satan to buffet me, lest I should be exalted above measure. For this thing I besought the Lord thrice, that it might depart from me. And he said unto me, My grace is sufficient for thee: for my strength is made perfect in weakness. Most gladly therefore will I rather glory in my infirmities, that the power of Christ may rest upon me (II Corinthians 12: 7–9).

MRS. POGSON: People have been asking how to be freed from something that appears too difficult to work on. After long work on yourself you come to a point where you are helpless. Here in Paul we have a key to what is possible. Here is the "thorn in the flesh," which may be physical or psychological. It is too much, he cannot be freed from it, and he gives for all time the only answer: "My grace is sufficient for thee: for my strength is made perfect in weakness." If one asks from a place of humility, in this place of weakness and knowing one's weakness, it is "possible that one might be freed by Grace." This is the only way, we find, to be freed from the deep negative emotions.

Now real conscience, which is said to be buried, comes through very gradually and shows you the truth. Its action is always very gentle. It says, "there you are," it's like that. So you don't have to hear the "I's" saying: How awful! Here is real shame. It brings you to the state of St. Paul—a knowledge of your own weakness, humility. And real suffering is connected with real conscience. We suffer every time we have a real awareness of some manifestation of the false personality.

[A passage was read from *The Fourth Way*, p. 151. Mr. Ouspensky speaks of the "aim of the system being to bring man to conscience."]

X: The experience of real conscience could almost be described as pleasant.

MRS. POGSON: Yes, I know what you mean—but that's not quite the right word. There is a kind of pain with the experience of real conscience, but also a blessed relief.

> At first when conscience manifests itself in us, it turns against us, and we begin to see all our inner contradictions (*The Fourth Way*, p. 152).

MRS. POGSON: Do you agree with this? Do you agree that "all our life, all our habitual ways of thinking, have only one aim—to avoid shocks, unpleasant feelings, unpleasant realizations about ourselves?" (p. 153). Yes, that is the way it is.

April 20, 1960

MRS. POGSON [Reading observations people had written on the task, which was to observe and record the different feelings we had about the Work]: These are very interesting. So many of you have been through the same stages. Many have described the initial interest, the excitement, or joy they had on discovering the Work. This was from the Magnetic Center. It may have been remembering in Essence. It was an essential feeling, wasn't it?

One of you has observed feelings of annoyance on being told that one's truth before meeting the Work is without foundation. It isn't quite like that. The Work doesn't say this, so you may have understood wrongly. The point is that when one meets the Work one is then given a clear foundation which is linked with the source of all esoteric teaching, and the truth one had before can be linked with this. . . . Yes, I think one must at some point feel how great the Work is and how great the distance is between one's own level and the mark at which one is trying to shoot.

What is important here is to be aware that different "I's" speak in different ways about the Work; there are different emotions that both love and hate it. And they are in everybody. When I see people having doubts, I don't think: "Well, that's the end!" I just realize that people are at this stage. You have to see how the Work is received by the "I's" that get to know about it. That is why it is so necessary to have this group of "I's" called Deputy Steward which are like the disciples. They fail probably in an emergency, but they can hear the Work and they can be trained. . . . When Deputy Steward is formed, there is a certain kind of stability, discrimination, reliability. Deputy Steward has a sense of scale, inner taste; he doesn't go with all the "I's," he knows about states and something about his own weakness.

Socrates
April 17, 1960

MRS. POGSON: Did you make the connection between what Socrates was dying for and what Christ died for? We read yesterday at lunchtime about Socrates in Zenophon's account. What was he accused of? He was accused of despising the old gods and corrupting the youth of his generation with new ideas. And what was he really doing? He was doing for the Greeks—for the youth of Athens—what Christ later did for the world. He was trying to show them the inner meaning of the gods that they worshipped—showing that they represented forces in the universe, showing that they could only connect with the gods, with these forces, through something in themselves, and showing them how one had to connect with what he called the "dæmon" in oneself. It is a kind of foreshadowing of what Christ was to do for the world. The literal level always tries to destroy the higher level which it doesn't understand. We see the parallels between Christ and Socrates. Socrates tried always to obey and never go against his own demon, his inner instructions. And then his death came about, being based on false accusations; his prompting said he was not to defend himself, so he didn't try to justify.

The Sabbath

MRS. POGSON: We have often spoken of how Christ was all the time trying to explain the inner meaning of Judaic Law. One of these was the law regarding the Sabbath. He consciously healed on the Sabbath day in order to demonstrate an inner process; how it is possible when you are within yourself to make another person whole. The original meaning of the Sabbath in Genesis is "returning," returning to your source. It is described not as a day at all but as a fact. From this we understand what it means when it is said that we cannot know the Father unless we keep the Sabbath. In Exodus it is generally implied that Sabbath means "rest," a rest from oneself. If we think of it in connection with the return to our source, we see there is this inner movement and then rest. For the inner movement, the return, includes rest and peace, if peace is in the center and one returns to one's center.

X: Would you say that the Jews understood the inner meaning?

MRS. POGSON: I don't know how much they understood. The multitude saw the literal meaning, but there were many who had more understanding. The Commandments are full of inner octaves, but only the literal meaning, on stone, has been handed down to us. I remember reading of a vision in which the stone of the Commandments, when looked at more closely, was seen to be covered with hieroglyphs all over, smaller and smaller ones. The inner octaves are there.

It is known how the Essenes and others kept the Sabbath. The seventh day was spent differently, not in work-a-day "I's." So there were different activities—music, study of the scriptures, sacred dances, communal activities. And in order to make it more possible to be in a different place, certain things were forbidden, for example, to wash the vessels, because these things were usually done in small "I's." This is how the prohibitions arose. And it is strange that we tend to remember more easily what we mustn't do. The point is that the Sabbath was originally the day of Saturn, the day when the Mysteries were celebrated that gave self-knowledge. So it should have this meaning, as the day when one comes through to self-knowledge.

It was a day which those who retained the inner meaning of the Commandments were able to keep. This is the point of esotericism, to retain the inner meaning. For when the forms have become crystallized, fewer and fewer people are able to understand the inner meaning, although it has always been preserved in schools. So Christ taught the inner meaning and showed it, for example, in the story of the man ploughing on Sunday, to whom Christ said it was all right if he knew what he was doing, otherwise he was simply breaking the law. If you have a good reason, you can take the responsibility for what you are doing. Christ tried to show that in this a man was free; that a man who could be within himself could do what he liked. So David could eat the bread and the priests sweep the temple on the Sabbath.

[A passage was read from the 12th chapter of Matthew concerning the Sabbath, in which Christ says: "The Son of man is Lord even of the sabbath day" (12:8).]

MRS. POGSON: Do you understand about the priests? That they could sweep out the temple on the Sabbath because it was accepted that priests could be within themselves and sweep, whereas others couldn't. It was accepted that priests knew how to remember themselves, so they have charge of sweeping out the temple.

I think this inner keeping of the Sabbath is stressed more than anything in the Gospels. You see, healing has to be done on the Sabbath; it is impossible to heal a person when you are in small "I's." In order to make another person whole, you have to be whole yourself.

And then ritually you have to arrange a day, the seventh day. For the Jews it was the seventh day, deriving from the Chaldeans. For us it is the first day of the week, the day dedicated to song and music. This is stressed almost more than self-knowledge. Whichever day it is, there has to be this rhythm, that after six days" preparation there is an in-drawing. It is the natural rhythm for self-development.

[A paragraph was read from *Psychological Commentaries*, "The Psychological Meaning of Foot," Vol. III (pp. 859–860) in which Dr. Nicoll comments on the passage from Isaiah (58:13) which begins: "If thou turn away thy foot from the sabbath" (58:13).]

MRS. POGSON: All this must originally have been included in the meaning of the Sabbath when it was devised, and this was the meaning of the fourth commandment; it is referring to all the "I's" that shouldn't work or be allowed to speak.

Herman Wouk in *This is my God*[5] speaks of small actions which have to be excluded on the Sabbath. He says that avoiding a small action is a ceremony. It becomes this through the effort required to remember not to do these small things. One day has to be different: a day of going against oneself. The first Sunday I ever spent at Tyeponds was not like Sunday at all. The point of it was to go against oneself. What Dr. Nicoll stressed was that it was to be a day of rest from the self-will. Do you see how the self-will is always draining you, and how there is frustration all the time? Sunday is a time to rest from this.

---

[5]Herman Wouk, *This is My God* (London: Fontana, 1976).

The Work Group Scrapbook

G. I. Gurdjieff.

P. D. Ouspensky in Ceylon, 1914.

Beryl Pogson and Maurice Nicoll, 1949.

Above: Mrs. Pogson, who made this study group possible.
Right top: Dorton house where the group met. Right bottom:
One of the study groups poses on the steps in 1956.

Mrs. Pogson is painting Dorton Church.

*Christmas at Dorton House, 1958. Top: Beryl Pogson sur-
rounded by her group at the Christmas feast. Seated on the
couch from left to right are Jane Malcomson, Lewis Creed,
Margaret Jeans, Joan Cooper, and Beryl Pogson. Bottom: An
informal talk after supper.*

Building the sundial, and the sundial finished.

Building the zodiac, and the glass mosaic finished.

Building a water garden at Dorton House.

This is the beginning of the group project scheduled for Easter Week, 1957. The group painted the Twelve Labors of Hercules. Each labor is related to a sign of the zodiac, and during this week of work, Mrs. Pogson discussed the esoteric meaning of each labor. The group interpretation of this work reads: "As is the case with most allegories, not every detail can be fitted into its place, but the meaning of the whole theme seems clear— that of the hero perfecting all sides of his being through overcoming the psychological difficulties connected with each of the twelve astrological signs." The work was difficult. The people in the group were not painters, and the surface they worked on was painted brick. One of the participants said, "No one who sees the results of our efforts will ever be more surprised than we were ourselves when the Twelve Labors emerged." Details of the "work" are on the opposite page.

The group's rendition of Alice and Wonderland *painted in the summer of 1958 at Dorton House.*

"The Great Feast" from St. Luke (Chapter 14:15-24) is brought alive by this group wall painting done at Easter in Dorton, 1958.

We couldn't resist showing the group's interpretation of Sir Gawain and the Green Knight.

CHAPTER 7

NUTLEY TERRACE, WHITSUN AND TRINITY

Work on Associative Thinking
April 21, 1959

[Mrs. Pogson talked about the power of associative thinking and how one can free the mind from it. She read from a book by Rear Admiral E. H. Shattock, *An Experiment in Mindfulness* (Rider, 1958), which describes how the author is instructed for three weeks at a meditation center and how he acquires a technique which leads to heightened powers of concentration, to awareness and to peace of mind. Each day the author has intensive training. He discovers at first it is impossible to direct the mind without it going off into associations.]

MRS. POGSON: This is the Work teaching which shows us that most of our inner talking goes on when we're unoccupied. Always the same associations go on. Admiral Shattock is shown one of the secrets: to *direct* your attention when you have associations which waste force. Go back to see where the associations came from. This is the thing to do to create the energy to compensate for what you have lost.

X: This is a kind of Judo.

MRS. POGSON: Yes. Go with the enemy, observe the enemy, make him give back the force he was taking from you. Observe where the associations begin. What word leads you off? This is done in connection with an aim. . . . One of the exercises given the admiral was to walk up and down and visualize each movement before it took place: lift leg, swing leg, put foot down. The exercise was to last for twenty-five minutes and alternate with an exercise in observing the rising and falling of the diaphragm. Different parts of the brain are involved. The admiral soon discovered that he could not direct his attention but went off with his trains of thought association. Once barking dogs took his attention: "Why are dogs allowed in? And why can't they be looked after?" This is a thoroughly English observation! It was five minutes later when he realized that he'd been taken away from his exercise by associations. And five minutes seemed a terrible waste, for he had only three weeks in this school. When he told his master about his observations of his mind wandering, he was told to observe what made it wander and he'd get back the energy lost.

X: You can do this exercise of observing your associations anywhere.

MRS. POGSON: Yes, but you have to have a very strong aim. The author of the book had to have a very strong aim. But until he found the method of observing associations he could not get on.

X: Do you observe them, go with them, or stop them?

MRS. POGSON: You observe them. Each time the mind strays, record it. There must be "tireless persistence in noting, checking and pressing on." This is the Work. In the book the author says he was told to categorize the word that began the train of associations: is it imagining, remembering, planning, or just wandering? Later he was able to have nonassociative thinking. Admiral Shattock had a clear motive: to be master of his mind. Our aim is for the mind to become free and still and no longer the slave of associations, so that the inner teacher can speak. This comes near self-remembering. On p. 151 the author describes beautifully a moment of self-remembering. He recognizes a place in his mind where Buddhism and Christianity are one. In this special moment he puts a glass of wine down. The light is reflected through the wine—the color is part of the moment. He sees the unity of everything. He sees two powers are the same. But he fears he may lose this moment. The sensation is part of the living moment in eternity. In a moment of self-remembering everything contributes. "Breathless ecstasy."

X: I tried giving my attention in different ways, such as listening, looking, writing, eating. I found that it was always taken away by imagination, and that I was afraid of having a *blank* in my mind and rushed back to myself to fill it.

MRS. POGSON: These blanks are going to be important.

X: I found that while reading, my interest in words led me away into analogies and associations. I wasn't sure of the borderline between making connections and associative thinking. But I observed that, in the case of associations, the moving center went on reading, whereas when I seemed to be making a connection there was a dead stop in the mechanics of reading.

MRS. POGSON: Making a connection is always done purposely. [She then drew attention to the diagram 13, which Dr. Nicoll had drawn after reading what Lord Adrian had discovered about brain rhythms.]

These tracks are laid down in us, so that we are bound in associative thinking to go along them. They lead often to very disagreeable places. Something new happens when you make a new connection; you stop and take a different path. You want to make light, to make new comparisons. The Work is *to redeem the mind.* What is wrong?

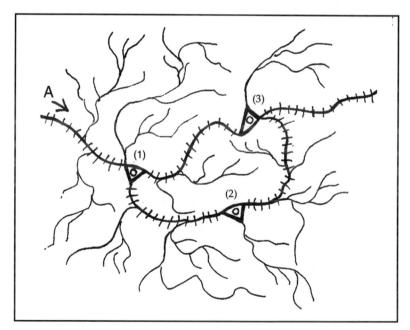

Diagram 13. The three brain-cells.

Our mind is full of associations. When one stops for a moment, various things are possible. New connections begin to furnish the middle parts of centers. The *spaces* which are created when you stop are very important; it is only when there is a space that something can come through from higher centers. Usually the doors to these centers are closed. This is the point of the exercise. Work in directed attention helps to furnish the inner parts of centers.

If you've read the book, you remember that at a certain point something happened to Admiral Shattock. He began to scratch and fidget. When he had his interview with his teacher, he didn't want to report it, it seemed too trivial. When at last he did, the teacher said that he had reached a certain stage of becoming aware of body-irritations that were going on all the time, but he only became aware of them after he had made a certain space in his mind. (Mrs. Pogson read the relevant passages from the book, pp. 52–54.)

Thoughts are a stream of fragments of mind. We must make blanks so that we are free to observe. When there are spaces, strange new thoughts can come in. Only after having directed one's attention for a time is one rewarded. There is a time lag; then something new is given. This is a religious technique. It is the associations which prevent us from experiencing something new.

We have very old associations. If you can find associations that lead to negative emotions, here is a place to work. These can be pointers to one's negative emotions. One of the tracks may be an account, which is one of the most dangerous habitual associations.

X: Each time it is traveled over it becomes stronger.

X: I found myself unable, upon awakening, to get back and make connection with a dream I wanted to recall.

MRS. POGSON: The mind is "bludgeoned" by mechanical associations as soon as it awakens. It is important to remain absolutely still, both physically still and still in the mind.

X: What is it? Like inner talking that goes round and round, and maybe you notice it the third time round?

MRS. POGSON: Yes, it is inner talking. Repetitive associations are the most mechanical. (She referred to the circular track on the diagram.)

X: Do all tracks—or associations—lead to the same place? And all smaller negative emotions lead to one chief negative emotion?

MRS. POGSON: This is a true observation. You should all know where these end. If they are allowed to go on, a habit of negative associations is formed.

X: The word *Elysium* in the Greek Mysteries meant to find one's way in a maze.

MRS. POGSON: If you have become aware of your powerlessness, you do feel as if you are lost in a maze. The author saw how associations interfered with the impressions he took in. Do you see how this is connected with our teaching about the first conscious shock: that we have to learn to be conscious at the point of incoming impressions and not take them mechanically.

[Mrs. Pogson refers to the intellectual center (see diagram 9 on p. 77).] Mechanical associations are in the outer part of the center which works with zero attention; the middle part of the center works with attracted attention, the inner part with directed attention. Mr. Ouspensky said that it was necessary, as an exercise, to stop thinking. Then one could see how difficult it was to do it. "Association" is a procession of "I's" holding hands. Consciousness is passed from one to the other. If something in us is aware, we can bring our consciousness back. In the inner part, energy is created through being in attention. It is through this that new understanding can come. Speeds are interesting to note here, because in zero attention you have no time; in directed attention there is more time because the work is done at greater speed with a higher hydrogen. If you have been concentrating here, something may open and come in from higher centers. Mr. Ouspensky said that intuition cannot reach the conscious mind as long as there is all this associative thinking.

On Becoming More Receptive
May 5, 1959

MRS. POGSON [Reads excerpts from Dr. Nicoll's paper (unpublished) of July 17, 1935]: Higher centers are working all the time but the doors are shut. Dr. Nicoll, in this paper, speaks of influences that play on us in times that are difficult on Earth. At such times these influences are more easily available to us. If we are in a negative state, these influences would possibly make us go mad.

> Some influences play on the earth directly. It we could be sensitive to these influences, we would not have to talk about man's not evolving . . .

> This Work is the study of how to prepare ourselves for the action of higher centers. If we are always negative and if higher centers played on us, we would be only more negative. If man could awaken a little, these Higher Minds could cause man to evolve. . . . Man is said to be governed by the moon because he is in that state of receptivity that he can receive influences only from the moon.

> The Work makes one more receptive. For this to happen *daring* is necessary—not the daring that is based on fear, but *on a sense of beauty*.

> Each set of influences dies out and others come in. This age may be called the age of scientific materialism. Matter became important, but again nothing has come of these influences because matter has been taken wrongly . . .

> If we think of man as a receiving apparatus and the influences coming in as different colored lights, these different lights as they change would help him to evolve if only he could awaken; but he interprets them wrongly and they produce bad results. This is one reason why it is good to remember that man is not isolated or living in a dying universe. There is help, and the universe is growing. The help comes from the kind of radiations playing at our own period. It's no good thinking what wonderful things he could do in another period with the inventions we have now. We can only grow with those influences which

belong to our period. The teaching is adapted to the period—the Work accepts science.

To be more receptive man must work. We have a certain kind of will and power of choice on our own scale, for example, whether we will go with these "I's" which stand near us at the moment or not.

About striving. First consider nature. The plant grows through the brick floor; the bird crosses the ocean, it does not think of results, it does not pity itself, it just goes on doing what it does. The enemy to striving is all fear, all self-pity, and insipid feeble manifestations of oneself, all sickness of spirit, all making small things big, all magnifying of handicaps, all giving up trying to learn anything or see anything.

Personal relationships. People think that personal relationships are necessary only for emotional life. They are necessary, not only for this, but for the collecting of influences that reach this planet. "Where two or three are gathered together," i.e., you cannot work alone.

Growth of Being. The most important thing is to collect wise observations. All moments of self-realization go to a special place and are stored there. What does "Give us this day our daily bread" mean? If you lift yourself a little then you get the force of the day. If we try to conduct this force, this directed daily bread, it means finer energies, means growing intentional sensitiveness towards everything.

Do not use negative phrases. Don't say "I can't understand," "I can't remember." This is starting from negative part of the thinking center. Say instead: "I did not observe myself enough." This is making personality a little more passive. If you speak differently, you will think differently, which is just the opposite of what we are taught in life.

About our chief trouble. What is our chief trouble in the Work? A kind of indolence. We cannot rouse ourselves. All daydreaming is lack of spirit. You want to give up.

This must not be gone with. This is just heaviness. This means moon for you, this thing that sucks you down. You cannot bother to move or act. Quite a different thing from needing rest. We must be able to distinguish, not try to go on when the octave may be finished. Indolence is really deeply negative, a denial of everything. Depression is absolutely forbidden, it is quite useless. Animals are not depressed. Look at a rose when you are depressed—it will give you nothing. We should at least be equal to organic life. Being conscious in organic life, i.e., $H\ 24$, is a much bigger thing than we think.

Organic life is like a big accumulator around the earth. Certain of these influences are used for the growth of plants and fishes. But if a quantity of people together try to collect these influences, they can pass through them. Humanity is always transmitting influences to the moon, which is all good for the moon.

MRS. POGSON: This is recalling to us all the possibilities that there are. The outer people could meet together week after week and nothing would happen. They are collecting no influences. Dr. Nicoll was always telling us how brave the birds are. They go on and on. These are the people necessary to the group—the ones that go on and on. No one was ever killed by overwork, though sometimes it may look like it.

Basic Instructions
April 26, 1960

MRS. POGSON: I thought we would go back to the year 1931, when Dr. Nicoll was first taking his group, and see what instructions he gave, instructions that came on the board meeting after meeting.

DR. NICOLL'S FIRST INSTRUCTIONS

Remember Yourself;
Observe Yourself;
Do not Internally Consider;
Do not Identify;

Do not Express Negative Emotions;
Struggle with Imagination.

MRS. POGSON: These are five simple instructions which could be carried out. Sometimes there were only four: remember yourself, observe yourself, non-considering, and nonidentifying, which people could begin with. At the bottom of the list we have "struggle with imagination" because imagination can interfere with and take over all work done in carrying out these instructions.

You would not think it easy to remember yourself straight away, but do you remember what is said at the beginning of the teaching? That a number of people, when they first hear the idea of self-remembering, can have an experience of it right away? It is the newness of the shock when the idea is first received that makes this experience of self-remembering possible. Self-observation takes a long time. One observes only a few things to begin with.

Now can you see how imagination takes over? People can imagine they observe themselves, or that they are remembering themselves, when they are really only talking about it. Can you see how these simple instructions could change a person quite soon, *if he or she followed them?*

Now in considering the whole teaching as given by Dr. Nicoll, what stands out the most? What did he emphasize the most?

X: The quality of will that knows no resentment.

MRS. POGSON: Yes, in the last years of his life, but what did he emphasize in the early teaching?

X: To have control.

X: To purify the emotional center.

MRS. POGSON: Dr. Nicoll said that what Mr. Ouspensky emphasized most was the importance of work on negative emotions. You must be able to discriminate between the different people who have taught this Work. Mr. Ouspensky classified the different negative emotions so that we could come to see the different kinds and the different techniques for working on them. Now what did Mr.

Gurdjieff emphasize? He emphasized the importance of weakening personality and especially false personality. Now what about Dr. Nicoll?

X: He stressed the self-love.

MRS. POGSON: Yes, in the last years of his life he stressed self-love. But in the earlier days he stressed the idea of giving ourselves the first conscious shock. This is the secret of the sly man's way of life. The Fourth Way is the way of sly man. And the sly man has this special technique so as to be able to walk safely through life without being touched by it.

The first instruction—remember yourself—means give yourself the first conscious shock. When enough energy is made over a period of time through self-remembering, there may one day be enough energy to give the second conscious shock, which is work on purifying the emotional center of negative emotions.

Suppose people say when it has been possible to give themselves the first conscious shock. Most of the time we are suffering uselessly through inner considering, imagination, negative emotions, etc. The only way to become master of the technique of sly man is to practice it. Can you give a simple example of a situation which makes you habitually negative and where, if you can remember that the Work says it is possible to take things differently, something can be changed?

X: I was able to receive differently the event of a letter. I took it simply, instead of studying it and becoming identified with it.

MRS. POGSON: Yes, this is a very simple thing. A letter can upset you for the whole day if taken mechanically. The Work gives a background of ideas, which together form a canopy. These ideas can be applied. You applied here the idea of *scale*. Sly man knows what is important and what is not important; although to the small "I's" letters might seem important.

X: My example is of getting up to shut a door which someone had left open and feeling resentment as I shut it. I then remembered my aim and was able to transform it.

MRS. POGSON: This is one of the simplest forms of self-remembering—remembering your aim. Do you see that this is the way to go through life differently?

X: I had to entertain people to dinner. I made an aim to enjoy myself and to be aware of restaurant events. In this way I was able to remember my aim and not let restaurant events take me away.

MRS. POGSON: How important it is to make an aim beforehand on the basis of what one has observed as the events most likely to occur!

We have to gather together the things that are important. In assembling the ideas of Dr. Nicoll, we find that he emphasized first of all the idea of scale and, with this, the scale of energies. Then connected with this was the idea of the four bodies, expressed so wonderfully in the parable of the horse, carriage, and driver. Reading through the notes of the early meetings I find that this was what he emphasized again and again—and, of course, also the Ray of Creation.

X: Could you talk about the connections between the first conscious shock and energy?

MRS. POGSON: The first conscious shock transforms energy so that it becomes *Mi 12*. It is necessary for this energy to be continually transformed so that we eventually have enough of this fine energy in the body to transform negative emotions. We work on the first and second conscious shocks together in a way. Only Dr. Nicoll said not to ask about the second conscious shock until we had given ourselves the first conscious shock over a period of time and had enough energy to transform negative emotions.[1]

X: Is no *H 12* produced naturally?

MRS. POGSON: Yes. From the food and air octaves there are forms of *Mi 12*: *Si 12* and *Sol 12*; but in the impressions octave the energy is younger and has more possibilities. Do you all see the difference between these?

---

[1]See diagram 7 of "Man remembering himself" on p. 65.

X: Cannot *Mi 12* be used wrongly when one has made it?

MRS. POGSON: Yes. The negative emotions can use *Mi 12* also.

X: Does one give oneself the first conscious shock at the point of choice?

MRS. POGSON: Yes. The first thing is to be aware of choice. That is why it is good to prepare the day and see what is coming, then it will be possible to have this choice. For a long time however you choose in the old way. You notice the choice, but nothing seems to happen.

X: What energy is the second body created from?

MRS. POGSON: Fine emotional energy contributes *H 12* and *H 24*. When the emotional center works rightly it works with these energies.

Dr. Nicoll said that the chief thing to remember was that people were our events, and our ways of taking people are what we have to transform. Our danger lies in our reactions to other people during the day. What Work ideas can we use here to transform our reactions, our ways of taking people?

X: Our being attracts our life.

X: That we have to give people room to exist.

X: That we don't see all of the person.

MRS. POGSON: Yes. You have to remember that you see only one aspect of the person, one "I" or group of "I's." You are receiving the person as one "I." The person also has Essence. It is advisable to take one person at a time, when you are thinking of working on taking people differently. Think about the person when he or she isn't there. Then you get to know more about him or her. Gather together your impressions of the person in his or her absence. This is how I do it. Then you begin no longer to be irritated by people, because your impression of them includes more of their being.

When you are identified with a person you are stuck to him or her. As long as you are identified, you can't see more than a small part. You not free, you are a prisoner, you can't let go. It may happen through love or hate. It is like this in our inner life. "Identified" means being *the same as*. Now when you let go you can see far more because there is a space between. As long as we are identified we want to force the other person to go *our* way, whether we love or hate him.

Now I want you to think about the idea that imagination can interfere in all work, and eventually it is possible for the self-love to take over all the work one does. At a certain stage, it is important for people to see what part of their work has been taken over by the self-love. This is what can happen when, for example, one's knowledge outstrips one's being. For example, someone may understand something of the system and be able to give oneself the first conscious shock or be able to observe oneself. But then one thinks that *one* can do it. *One* can work! I'd like everybody to accept this idea first and then see what the self-love has taken over in your own work. The self-love can take over knowledge and you then feel that *you know*. It can compare you with other people, and you feel you know more. This is the robber that will steal from the Work. Then there is *showing off* in the Work, appearing as if you were working. At Amwell, Dr. Nicoll said that people should not appear as if they were working. For example, they shouldn't look solemn. There is also giving people advice from the Work.

X: One can feel superior to people in life who aren't in the Work.

MRS. POGSON: Yes, all this is stealing from the Work. Then it comes in like this, too. In the early days the Work was stark and bare. You went to a meeting. There were no books. You could only get hold of one or two ideas at each meeting. No one spoke to you. It was all very slow. You tried to connect ideas together with difficulty. You just had the bare Work. It was clearer. Now people read so much. The groups have more activities. Knowledge is given more quickly; things are speeded up. Once it could be said: "In five years you'll understand that!" Now it isn't like that. I think time is different and anyone may understand anything at any time—don't you agree? The change is necessary because there doesn't seem to be so much time.

So we don't go slowly now and say: "Ask that again in five years!" But the self-love can just as quickly take this knowledge away again.

You have to think what you would have to fall back on in the Work if everything were taken away. It is this which is important. You have to see what is accessory, and what you really value.

X: Everything is mixed up together.

MRS. POGSON: Yes. The wheat and tares grow together. But one sees where a person is working from the self-love, and where there is also some valuation and one has to get the person to fall back on that. Eventually a separation will be made for you. In the meantime things are mixed.

The Law of Three
May 19, 1959

MRS. POGSON: This law is seen at its most exalted level in the Christian Trinity. But the three forces are present in every manifestation. We must study them, and think carefully about the method of working we must adopt in order to make the Work our third force instead of life.

You should notice that there are three forces present in a question. If rightly asked, the question is the passive force. We ask it from our need to know, and in a passive, awaiting state. The answer we get is active, and the result, the neutralizing force, is the explanation we receive. Something is made clear to us, making it possible for us to ask another question. These questions passively asked in the desire to find the truth are always answered for us, and this is how understanding is brought about, in a series of triads.

But this only applies to the right kind of question. If your question comes from a wrong motive you will not gain understanding. It is possible to ask a question in order to serve the false personality. One can ask a question in order to air one's knowledge, for instance. In this case the *question* is active. The person asking is not seeking truth but is wishing to put himself forward or perhaps to belittle someone else. In this case the answer would be passive force and the neutralizing force would be self-glorification.

The Three Forces
June 2, 1959

X: I couldn't see the third force in life, I could only see the third force of the Work.

MRS. POGSON: The third force is why you do something in life—your motive. It takes some looking for. The whole thing is to act from the third force of the Work, not from the third force of life.

Dr. Nicoll said that we can see second force by struggling with certain things such as habits, the expression of negative emotions, suffering, imagination, etc. We have been talking about trying to see the three forces, but the first thing is to see what it is that obstructs the Work in us.

X: Struggling with *habits*, I found that they seemed to be focused in the moving center. First force was in the intellectual center in the form of an aim, second force in the moving center, and then a Work "I" came in as third force and helped.

MRS. POGSON: The neutralizing force is why you do it at all. You have to do it from the Work. There is no special harm in habits as such, but they are so very strong and we always tend to follow the line of least resistance and do what we have always done.

X: Mechanicalness is always second force.

MRS. POGSON: Yes. The more we work, though, the stronger the Work influences will become.

X: Second force altered as soon as I saw the reason why I was doing something. For example, when I saw I was doing something in order to impress.

MRS. POGSON: All this is preparatory to seeing that it is necessary to work from the third force of the Work.

X: I was struggling with suffering. When it could be named it was no longer second force.

X: I found that requirements made me negative and made me suffer. I then saw I was being negative and worked on it, but it wouldn't give up.

MRS. POGSON: This is a very subtle thing to struggle with. All these things can become second force in us when we are trying to work. Everything we try to do, observing ourselves, remembering ourselves, trying not to identify, etc., comes up against second force. First there is habit, as it is always easier to do what we've done before; then negative emotions, suffering (which we don't see for a long time), and imagination. We must try to become aware of these things as always existing in us, trying to keep us from achieving our aim. By studying second force you must learn to see what it is you want—what is first force.

X: It seems to me that what varies is third force; it can be either the Work or life.

MRS. POGSON: Yes, it is important to see this.

X: Yet even in a life triad we might see something, as when we find that no one listens when we self-justify.

X: Is forgetting a form of second force?

MRS. POGSON: One of the strongest forms of second force. One can forget the whole idea of taking things differently. Ignorance is another form. It is first of all necessary to discover the form of second force which exists in oneself, one's special form of mechanicalness. One has to know one's adversary. It is necessary to count the cost and prepare in advance.

[Reference was then made to the diagram on categories of thinking from *The Fourth Way*, p. 195. It was based on what Mr. Ouspensky says: that everything can be divided into seven categories.]

	No. 4	Opposites reconciled, understanding.
Ordinary thinking	No. 3	Theoretical, logical thinking, thinking in opposites.
	No. 2	More emotional, based on likes and dislikes.
	No. 1	Chiefly imitative.

MRS. POGSON: The first three categories refer to ordinary thinking, the fourth to the beginning of thinking in a new way. Number 1 person takes ideas chiefly from others. Number 2 imitates the thinking of someone he or she likes. Number 3 thinks in a theoretical and logical way, which is useful in its place, but there will always be someone to contradict on the level of logical thinking, always an opposite theory. In the thinking of Number 4 opposites begin to be reconciled. When one is standing in the middle, back from the opposites, one can see something of truth.

What was the nature of the second force with which Admiral Shattock struggled?[2] It was his habits of thought. These constituted his second force when he tried to fix his attention on walking or work on his associations. He felt that if he could learn to still his mind, something new could come through. And so it is with us. We must see what we are up against and what prevents our aim. People aren't really systematic enough! When you see something preventing your aim, you have to look at what you really want. It may be another person who seems to be keeping you from working. This person represents something in yourself that you have to work on. You need the reconciling force of the Work in order to relate to the person in a different way. Then you no longer think he or she is a nuisance.

[There was a reading from *Psychological Commentaries*, "Commentary on Second Force in Oneself" (Vol. II, pp. 543–544).]

> What is the 2nd Force in us in regard to the wish to self-remember, to awaken? You see at once that the Work tells us what are the forces that resist awakening in us. The whole Work can be understood in this light. If I am very identified with some life-ambition this will be 2nd Force in me in regard to the Work. It will put me to sleep. Now suppose we could do everything from the Work. Nothing would change in what we were doing perhaps, but the inner relationship would change . . .
>
> You can often see by self-observation that one 'I' in yourself opposes another 'I,' or one group of 'I's opposes

---

[2]See *An Experiment in Mindfulness*, pp. 57–59, and 99.

another group of 'I's. When the opposing force gets the upper hand it becomes 1st Force. Some 'I's may, for instance, be talking wrongly and other 'I's may see that this wrong talking would stop if you could remember yourself. Which group of 'I's is going to become 1st Force? I said some time ago to you all that you should be very careful on getting up in the morning to work carefully on yourselves and, in fact, before getting up. All sorts of unpleasant 'I's may start talking about their troubles and taking a certain view of the day and if you listen to them you will be absorbing negative impressions and so starting the day well-poisoned. . . . So it is the 1st Force that one has to look at and observe, and gradually become conscious of. What do you want?

MRS. POGSON: There are two chief things we have to do in the Work: to observe ourselves and to remember ourselves. What prevents us? What do we want? We very often do not know what we want, we don't know first force until we see second force. For example, we can recognize very great ambition by the terrific second force it raises. What we want in the Work is to awaken. This is our aim. Then other "I's" come in and seek to prevent us.

If certain people live under the canopy of the Work, it is possible in this age of ours for the forces of regeneration to have a focus. So the groups are important as focuses for receiving these influences. Dr. Nicoll says in one of his papers that the regenerative influences are coming down all the time and can be received if there is something to receive them; otherwise they go straight through and produce only violence. If one cannot receive this force, what does one do with it? Ride a motorbike fast? That's why speed satisfies some young people.

X: What would one need in the inner parts of centers in order to receive this force?

MRS. POGSON: Understanding.

X: And something more that can use it? A training, as a scientist, for instance?

Mrs. Pogson: Yes.

[Diagram 14 was put on the board.]

X: One doesn't always realize that a rich personality is needed to feed Essence.

MRS. POGSON: There must be material. The Work is for the strong. There was nothing Dr. Nicoll objected to more than wishy-washy people. We need good strong people in the Work. And once inner man is in control, a person can be used for very good things. People have to have finished octaves in life. Then the group can become an organism, and the people's talents can be used. The main purpose for the group is to become a focus.

X: It is said that we have to enrich personality as well as make it passive. Is this a contradiction?

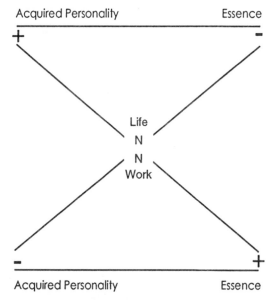

Diagram 14. The two triads.

MRS. POGSON: The real work to begin with is on false personality; at the same time everyone can enrich personality. A "wishy-washy person," Dr. Nicoll might have said, is someone who has never finished octaves. If you can finish one thing, you can finish another, or if you know one thing really well, then it can be used.

X: These two triads would be alternating constantly.

MRS. POGSON: Yes. Remember these triads during the day; you will see that they alternate.

How important it is how we start the day! Usually we start by wanting things to go pleasantly, to be happy, to have a good lunch, etc. But we can also start from wanting to remain awake during the day.

X: By trying to learn something new in the day, we are deliberately making personality passive.

MRS. POGSON: Essence seems to flourish on new things, and on new impressions, impressions from nature, for instance.

X: I find it very difficult to know what to do when it comes to making decisions involving what I owe other people. It takes a lot of energy thinking over the pros and cons of a decision, and it seems necessary to do so. I suppose later on real conscience decides for us in a flash.

MRS. POGSON: Real conscience can decide now, if you give your attention to the question and then leave it and ask to be shown what to do. But real conscience can only show you if you ask your question after having given real attention to it. And you must be prepared to accept what it says.

X: It takes time, and it is difficult to avoid thinking about what you want, and doing that.

MRS. POGSON: Yes, it takes time. You have to be prepared to listen. Actually we nearly always make ordinary life decisions from chief feature or false personality. But in the Work you can present your question to something more internal that can decide for you. Are we going to act from the third force of life or of the Work? We can deceive ourselves.

Our task for the last fortnight was to see how far it was possible to use the ideas of the Work, how far they were accessible to us.

X: If you can be just a little more aware, the ideas come to meet you.

MRS. POGSON: In a state of greater awareness you are nearer to your Work memory where the ideas are stored.

X: On one or two occasions when I found myself about to do battle with a situation or negative emotion, I remembered something you once said: "Just accept it." And this made me stop.

MRS. POGSON: When you use violence against violent things, they become more and more violent. But if you accept, what can they do?

X: I had a situation the other day in which I had to be with a very boring person who went on talking about his hobby for two hours. I realized beforehand that I was going to be bored, so I tried to think what Work idea could transform the situation. I went mentally through many ideas, and one would connect, then I forgot and had to look for another. So I spent two hours passing between the Work triad and the life triad, trying to connect with the right idea.

MRS. POGSON: Eventually the ideas will present themselves and you won't have to seek for them in this way. But what is the answer to this kind of situation? The mechanical reaction is to separate from the person and wait until he is finished. This makes him more mechanical. But put yourself into him. Look at him, think about him and what his hobby means to him. Listen to him; people become more responsive if you listen to them.

X: It seems to be the self-will that cuts one off from people.

MRS. POGSON: Yes. It says: "I shall not have much chance to shine in this conversation, so I'll just wait until he finishes. Then I'll get my innings."

X: You said that if we cannot love people, we can at least give them our attention. But I have a situation with an elderly person where I find myself alternating between giving attention and just being patient.

MRS. POGSON: Many people have this situation. The thing to do is to give as much attention as possible. . . . Now to return to X's battling with negative emotions. I found an answer to this in something I was reading last night.

[Mrs. Pogson read a passage from *The Wheel of Life* by John Blofeld, (p. 78).]

> Of all the elements, the Sage should take water as his preceptor. Water is yielding but all-conquering. Water extinguishes Fire or, finding itself likely to be defeated, escapes as steam and re-forms. Water washes away soft Earth or, when confronted by rocks, seeks a way round. Water corrodes Iron till it crumbles to dust; it saturates the atmosphere so that Wind dies. Water gives way to obstacles with deceptive humility, for no power can prevent it following its destined course to the sea. Water conquers by yielding; it never attacks but always wins the last battle. The Sage who makes himself as water is distinguished for his humility; he embraces passivity, acts from non-action and conquers the world (quoted from the 11th century Taoist scholar, Tao Chêng of Nan Yeo).

MRS. POGSON: For those who haven't been here recently, we have been talking about the three forces necessary for every manifestation. People have been observing second force. Third force always answers the question of why we do a thing. We have seen it is possible to do something either from life or from the Work. You said last time, X, that you found it difficult to see when third force was from life. But surely it is normally from life? Take Mrs. X again. She quite rightly sees the negative emotion as second force in herself. First force is her aim not to be negative. But why does she have this aim? If she is remembering the Work idea that she has a right not to be negative, and wishes not to be negative, she is using the third force of the Work. If she is doing it because professionally she doesn't want to show negative emotions in public, then she is using the third force of life.

[Then followed a reading from *Psychological Commentaries*, Vol. III, pp. 972, "A Note on Effort."]

> The secret lies in taking your life as an exercise. To do this interesting thing, a certain vision of life is required. All the background of the Work, all the teaching about the Cosmic Ray, the Sun-Octave, and the significance of Man, can give this vision, if you know it well mentally and then imagine it so that it better connects with the Emotional Centre. . . . Then you see your life as a miraculous adventure—that ceases to be so once you identify with it. . . . With this attitude we gain the sense of being *in* life, not *of* life or caused by life, and this is a preliminary to that form of Self-Remembering where the three factors, (1) the seen object in outer life, (2) my observed reaction to it, and (3) I myself, constitute a triple simultaneous consciousness—a full triad—that is, a being conscious in 3 forces at the same time. . . . One must get this vision—in which the centre of gravity of the whole Work lies—a vision of the Work that lifts us above life—in short, this Rope which we have to catch hold of. *Hold this Rope,* when you catch it.

MRS. POGSON [Referring to Mrs. X's example, which was drawn on the board as three forces: Mrs. X, first force, her enemy the negative emotion, second force, and a Work idea as third force]: The battle can go on between first and second forces until one remembers an idea of the Work, then one can become conscious in three forces. The situation may be resolved for the time being, but it will come again. After a time the ideas become more accessible.

> You have to see that a person is not outside you but is your *idea* of him, your imagination of him, your reaction to him (or her), and not the object you see *via* your senses. Here begins the real effort as regards the second line of Work—work, that is, about relationship, work about enduring without negativeness one another's unpleasant manifestations. Only in this way can an accumulator be made among ourselves that eventually gives force to all of us (p. 973).

MRS. POGSON: A group can become an accumulator. Some people take from and some people give to the group. Here is one way to increase the force of the group, by working against one's negative emotions.

> . . . Under the 3rd force of life, things always divide, disunite, and are at war—as life shews us. . . . Now the 3rd force of the Work unites. . . . The supreme effort that has to be made in the Work is to *feel the Work*. Seek the Work first, fight for it, keep it alive—and then all the rest follows. Remember that all temptations in the Work-meaning are about feeling, valuing, cherishing the meaning and reality of the Work, of esotericism. This is faith—a thing requiring much and constant effort of mind—an inner daily action in both mind and heart (p. 973).

MRS. POGSON: Here is the very profound truth which Dr. Nicoll talks of: the necessity of keeping the Work alive in oneself and nourishing the Work as a whole. He mentions faith in this connection. The only way something alive in you can grow is through continually acknowledging its presence and acting as though it were there. Remember that there is this something in you that always knows how to act in any situation. *But you have to be aware that it is there.* Let us talk about the different ways in which you can act from the Work.

X: I find I can sometimes work for my own sake, but not for the Work's sake. If I am becoming negative I may recognize what is happening, in which case a Work idea is presented to me, and I am faced with the choice of following it or not. I find it very difficult to be aware of the reality of esotericism as a whole in the world and of the necessity for working for it.

X: But we all come to the Work first of all from our own needs, and then gradually we realize its "greater life."

X: There seem to be three stages in the Work: (1) doing it for life reasons, (2) doing it because you are in the Work, and (3) doing it to make yourself a receiving instrument for higher influences.

MRS. POGSON: That is well described. It is necessary to become aware of the whole body of esotericism on a larger scale: to think of the people everywhere who are trying to evolve and of all the groups which together form a being that can regenerate the world. It is also important to think of the pool of force belonging to each group. Once the pool of force is built up, anyone who is in need can draw on it. Those who are not in need should remember this and not draw on force. You can contribute to the pool by working: by transforming life and remembering yourself, by forgetting your own personal troubles in order to work for something bigger.

Three Lines of Work
June 16, 1959

MRS. POGSON: We start with the first line of the Work, *work on oneself*, in which we become familiar with the ideas and begin to apply them to ourselves. We have to be able to work and see the possibility of living differently, before we can work with other people.

The second line of the Work is *work with other people*. Mr. Ouspensky makes it clear that this does not mean *helping* other people. This is a thing to be avoided in the beginning. It means working with other people under direction. What is the key to this? It is seeing that a person is not outside you but is your *idea* of him. It is seeing the other person in yourself. If you live in the front of yourself you see everything outside you, not realizing that, for example, when you are alone it is your idea of the person which you call up.

X: I find this awfully difficult, because so many people share the same idea of a person.

MRS. POGSON: I am glad you are finding it difficult; it shows you appreciate it. This is a very transforming idea.

In order to extend one's consciousness it is necessary to inhabit "I's" which can feel more deeply about other people. When they develop, deeper relationships become possible and it is possible to call up and consider the things you like and the things you dislike about a person to get a balanced view.

X: It is mechanically easy to see people in absolutes—as good or bad.

Mrs. Pogson: The people who irritate you most are those who point out something you won't accept in yourself.

The third line of the Work is *work for the Work itself.* This means keeping in mind first of all the whole idea of esotericism, its purpose and its destiny—once it is in mind, it flourishes—then the work that is going on, our teaching, anything practical to help what we are doing. One also works for the third line of the Work by never harming the Work. This is also important. What harms it?

X: Setting a poor example.

X: By arguing about it.

X: Talking about it in small "I's."

X: Being negatively connected in any way with Work people.

X: Taking force from the accumulator.

Mrs. Pogson: Yes. People have said: "I'm negative. The Work will help me." Help is available in all circumstances, but only if we give something first. This is a law. What do we give? If we give affection, belief, and effort we are repaid in full measure. Very important also is our accuracy in talking about the ideas of the Work. Be careful. Everyone is responsible for not distorting the Work.

Nourishing Essence
May 10, 1960

X: We speak of feeding Essence, but I can form no picture in my mind of what happens when Essence is fed.

Mrs. Pogson: Shall we think about this? Ideas are given out in the Work, and at first the ideas are taken in by personality. It has to happen in this way. Then suddenly an idea strikes, and you recognize it. It falls on Essence, on the child in you, and you join with the idea. It then becomes part of your understanding. When you act from an idea, then it is in your understanding. Don't you all remember back to the first time you conjoined with the idea of the first conscious shock, or the idea of how our being attracts our life? Essence has the power of recognition because it has known these ideas before; or if it hasn't known them, it knows anyway that they are true.

Dr. and Mrs. Nicoll used to tell us how one night they came back from one of Mr. Ouspensky's meetings with the same thing to tell each other. The same idea had struck both of them at the same time: that negative emotions are no good! Of course, even after you had seen the truth of this, the negative "I's" would still go on reacting, but now there would be something else that knew differently.

In some cases the chief feature can take over the Work. This happens in rather clever people; simple people aren't in this danger. Then it will tend to sweep them out of the Work. But if the chief feature doesn't take over, these people can be very valuable.

When we were with Dr. Nicoll we might sometimes be surprised that someone was in the Work, someone who was difficult to get on with. But Dr. Nicoll would say: "Don't you see? Don't you see?" For *he* could see into what the person could become. He had a kind of radionic camera in himself that was able to see these stages and the Essence in a person. And so he would be infinitely patient with him.

X: Was it the development of Dr. Nicoll's Essence which enabled him to see the Essence in other people?

Mrs. Pogson: Yes.

X: Does this intelligence about what it is to become exist in the embryo?

MRS. POGSON: Yes, I think so.

X: How can we see Essence in us? It all seems rather vague.

MRS. POGSON: At first we are not asked so much to see Essence in ourselves as to see Essence in other people. We have to see that if people are here, accepted as part of the group, then the Essence in them is capable of growth. You have to see what is *real* in people. . . . Essence is invisible, and what is invisible is the cause of the manifest. Essence causes personality: it attracts to it a personality to do its work in the world and a false personality which has to be overcome.

It's interesting to think in relation to other people: What is that person going to grow into? That is how I think of all of you. A person in the Work is in the right condition for this development; but life doesn't develop these seeds in us. . . . The chief way of nourishing Essence is by self-remembering, and also through love of truth and beauty. When something you know about becomes real, then it passes into understanding and becomes part of you. This happens when you apply a Work idea to yourself. When you say, "This is how I really want to live," then Essence is nourished. Inertia is the enemy of all growth of Essence.

X: How could you find the essential qualities in another person?

MRS. POGSON: It is where the truth is. It is what you like about a person. I recall a conversation with Dr. Nicoll in which we were talking about someone in the group whom we both liked. He had an admirable personality. I said to Dr. Nicoll that it wasn't for this that I liked him. And Dr. Nicoll answered: "What do you think I like him for?" We both liked him for something simple in him.

Are there any questions?

X: I want to ask more about Essence. When Essence grows does it grow by extending its range or by becoming more intense?

MRS. POGSON: I think almost entirely through increasing its understanding.

X: What happens to personality when Essence is developed?

MRS. POGSON: You have to *use* your personality. That is why it is important to have a rich personality which can be useful when it no longer serves the self-will. A child shall lead them: this means that Essence shall lead because it knows the way; personality doesn't know the way. Essence is the mediator between personality and

"Real I." In a series of choices who is going to decide, the self-will, which is chief feature, or the child in us?

X: Do people have different sizes of Essence?

MRS. POGSON: Essence is something which returns again and again, every time taking with it added treasure which is the understanding it has gained. So some people are young in Essence and some are older; people vary very much in Essence. . . . What really becomes your own cannot be taken from you; it is part of Essence.

Dr. Nicoll brought back so much understanding with him, which we can see from reading his early books; and then when he found the Work teaching it was all joined together.

Choice
May 24, 1960

> Thought during the night very much of eternal life. What is there in ourselves that we would wish to make eternal? (Dr. Nicoll's diary for July 19th, 1941).

MRS. POGSON: This is an extract from Dr. Nicoll's diary on one of his birthdays. One would think very much about this on one's birthday. It is indeed something to think about.

As Essence grows, it approaches nearer and nearer to the source. And if we choose rightly, this will bring us into a new state of ourselves. Of course we all choose wrongly at first. You will find, if you go on with the Work, that your life is presented as a series of choices, through events which always recur. The choice is between what can lead up to a new state and what will delay us.

X: We never have to think it's too late, because we'll always be presented with the choice again.

MRS. POGSON: Yes. This is how a man can begin to fulfill himself. And if we think of a man as having more than one life, then he fulfills more in each life, approaching ever closer to the source.

X: Is there any connection between one's own possibilities, and what other people have to do?

MRS. POGSON: No, it has nothing to do with other people. Although on the invisible level people are linked together in a group, we do not all have to have the same experiences. But psychologically we go through the same stages. However, we don't all have to become lawyers, for example.

X: What we have to do first is create the body of ideas called Deputy Steward, and then it is up to us whether we act from them or not.

MRS. POGSON: Yes, we have to train Deputy Steward which knows which ideas to apply in each case. Then the choice is whether or not one acts from Deputy Steward. That is why it is so important to connect the different ideas of the Work together. There can be no real choice until after the formation of Deputy Steward.

X: The choice is important even if we choose wrongly.

MRS. POGSON: Yes, we learn very much from choosing wrongly. This is where the idea of "sinner" comes in. The sinner is at least someone who is aiming at a mark. Those who are not aiming are of no interest at the moment; their time will come. The sinner aims at the mark and misses. Every time, after a certain stage, when you aim at a mark and miss, there is a kind of conscious suffering which will enable you to choose differently another time.

X: What is the difference between conscious suffering and mechanical suffering?

MRS. POGSON: It is a matter of inner taste. When you have made an aim and see yourself unable to keep it, you suffer in a sense because you are still like that.

X: It feels to me like self-criticism.

MRS. POGSON: There is all the difference in the world. There can be self-criticism in the beginning, but this is from pride and feeling that you should be different. The other is a kind of helplessness if one is sincere. Then help can come and next time you can possibly choose differently.

X: Don't you think that we ought to . . .

MRS. POGSON: "Ought"? You cannot work from saying "ought." Do you see why not?

X: It belongs to personality.

MRS. POGSON: Yes. Acquired conscience says "ought." We are brought up on "ought." In the Work you have to work from love, from affection for the Work, and because you want to be different. But it is possible to make an aim from personality, because you get a new idea of yourselves.

X: Is there a test?

MRS. POGSON: Inner taste, which belongs to the middle divisions of centers. You know then.

X: Even inner "I's" sometimes seem to say "ought."

MRS. POGSON: Then they are still using the language of the outer "I's." There can be no "ought," no compulsion in working.

Look at what is written on the board. This was always Dr. Nicoll's aim. It was more real to him than his ordinary life during the day. He was always thinking of the real life that was waiting for him after death if he could connect with it.

"What is there in ourselves that we would wish to make eternal?" It isn't possible to live on that plane of reality unless there is something. Love of truth, love of any kind can draw us up. Only very simple qualities can be used. Humility. It was interesting to see when we were talking recently about the emotions belonging to the middle parts of centers that humility also exists there.

X: Then the answer to this question of Dr. Nicoll's is *nothing*.

MRS. POGSON: Yes, in a certain state he might have answered it like this. There is nothing in us that could exist at that level. But we have to create something.

June 7, 1960

MRS. POGSON: Dr. Nicoll taught us always to name our events and talk about others as having certain kinds of events: So-and-so is having a certain kind of event. And we were able to do this in the group, and so the event wasn't added to by useless suffering.

If we think from Aeon, we can know that the events we attract, if we accept the direction of what is real, will be the events that belong to us. You have to visualize a kind of pattern. If you go off the track altogether through vanity or negative emotions, then you do not fill in the pattern. If you are in a state of self-remembering, the event can have meaning. But if you have brought on something that doesn't belong to you, then you have to get out of it! . . . Dr. Nicoll sometimes advised people to squeeze something out of their lives that didn't really belong to them. For example, people would say they were going to follow up a relationship with someone they had met on board ship, and Dr. Nicoll would ask them if they wanted to give time to it. Yes, you have to contract some events and expand others, because the life cannot contain everything.

Two things stand out in the early life of Mr. Gurdjieff: how he seized every opportunity which was given to him and how every event had meaning and was part of a pattern. . . . Dr. Nicoll told us to value especially the people who had been at our crossroads.

The Science of External Impressions
July 5, 1960

MRS. POGSON: Although at this stage you cannot choose the impression you want to make on other people, Dr. Nicoll said you should know the impression that you do make on others.

X: I have noticed that certain people are always on the defensive with me.

MRS. POGSON: This is a good example. There can be many reasons for this. It may be in the voice; you don't often hear your own voice. It could be rather fierce.

X: I observed how my voice changed when I was talking to someone else, after I'd seen how people were on the defensive with me.

X: We are responsible for the impressions we make on other people.

MRS. POGSON: Yes. But we weren't told this at first in the Work. It was only after some time that Dr. Nicoll told us this. It was a shock when we first heard it. We have to see what impressions we are making on others and be responsible for them. Then there will be an intermediate stage of not knowing what to say to a person, as some of you have already experienced. Another important thing comes in here. When we are more aware of the impressions we make on others, we can remember what we have said; otherwise, where we are not awake, we remember our part in the conversation wrongly. . . .

X: I have been reading a book on the presentation of the self.

MRS. POGSON: It might be about the impressions of the personality; there are many such books. You study in life how to make impressions from personality, and from the Self-love how to make impressions in false personality. But this is different.

X: At first one can only be silent with a person.

MRS. POGSON: Even that changes something.
    We have also to look at the subject the other way round. Have you seen what puts *you* in prison? It is worrying about the impressions you are making on others, inner considering.

X: Inner considering becomes very apparent when you are with several people to whom you relate through different "I's."

MRS. POGSON: Yes. You find yourself in a muddle, and you can't link the people together.

For next time take someone in the Work or someone you see daily and see if you can step back a little. Be aware of the impression you make on this person, and try to act with more consciousness.

If we were writing a paper on the science of external impressions, what more would you say? Dr. Nicoll talked a lot about this in the house. It was important there, particularly the impression we made on new people. The impression you give to new people in the Work is very important. You are all responsible for the impressions you give.

X: This reminds me of the instructions which Dr. Nicoll gave to the group on going to Gloucestershire, about behaving in a normal way and not giving an impression to the villagers of being different. . . . The danger lies in giving an impression of being superior to those who haven't got the Work.

X: I have been trying not to sound superior but would nonetheless use certain ideas of the Work on occasion. For example, when someone was critical of another person, I would say: "Everyone has his faults!" Later I realized how irritating this must have been to others.

MRS. POGSON: This is a good example. We must be aware of the effect of what we say on other people. This belongs to the science of impressions. We have to protect the Work. This belongs to the third line of the Work. There are two things we have to do—not harm the Work, and protect the Work. The two belong together. We have to protect it from the small "I's" of other people.

X: And from our own small I's.

MRS. POGSON: Yes, and not let our own small "I's" harm it.

X: It helps to realize that we are in the Work because we need it, and other people may not be ready for it.

MRS. POGSON: Yes, not force it on them.

MRS. POGSON: One of you has made an important observation, that when you are negative you make quite a different impression on people from the one you think you are making. You might think that you're hiding your negativeness, for example. This person also made an observation about the kind of impression which is made if someone is talking from a sense of duty. Now, what impression does it make on you if someone is speaking to you from a sense of duty?

X: You are bored.

MRS. POGSON: Yes. You see, here you have to be careful, because you don't know what impression you are making, if you are acting from a sense of duty.

X: I was having people stay with me, and inner talking about their not offering to help with the breakfast. When they did help, one of them suddenly said to me as I was looking over her shoulder: "Are you being critical of me?" This provided a shock which enabled me to see how critical "I's" in me kept people from helping me.

MRS. POGSON: Yes. We aren't aware of these critical "I's." They make people feel inadequate.

X: I've been thinking about the impressions made by physical manifestations, such as the way one screws one's face up or frowns, and how these make impressions on other people.

MRS. POGSON: Yes. Here is something important which X says: "We can't help making impressions; and if we think we aren't making an impression, we may be making one of aloofness or superiority." Yes, haven't some of you seen this? But when we're really giving attention to someone, they receive an impression of our good will.

X: Could it make people worse if one is passive to them?

MRS. POGSON: It could, but not if you are really passive.

X: You spoke about self-righteousness the other night.

MRS. POGSON: Yes, whenever we feel we know better than the other person or whenever we act from self-righteousness, we create a barrier and put others on the defensive.

When the false personality is making an impression it gives quite a different impression from what one imagines one is giving. Others see it, but one doesn't see it oneself.

Now, we need more actual examples. One of the best was sent by someone who couldn't be here tonight. She discovered that when she felt tired or ill she made a wrong impression on others. Haven't many of you seen this? We don't make the impression we want to make, or maybe we don't care what impression we make. So when we are tired we have to be very careful.

X: Is it true that in some relationships other people take their color from you and in some relationships you follow other people?

MRS. POGSON: You have to think about why that is for yourself.

X: Is St. Paul's "being all things to all men" connected with this?

[There was a reading of Paul's First Epistle to the Corinthians.]

> For though I be free from all men, yet have I made myself servant unto all, that I might gain the more. And unto the Jews I became as a Jew, that I might gain the Jews; to them that are under the law, as under the law, that I might gain them that are under the law. . . . I am made all things to all men, that I might by all means save some. And this I do for the gospel's sake, that I might be partaker thereof with you (I, 9:19–23).

MRS. POGSON: You see, St. Paul has different approaches to different people. Do you see what he is meaning here? He is acting consciously, choosing the best way of approach when he is meeting new people on his travels. He speaks to the Jews as a Jew, from the background of Jewish thought. St. Paul was specially equipped to do this because of his knowledge of many systems of thought and religions. His sermon in Athens is an example of his wonderful knowledge of the Greek background of thinking.

It is adapting to people, finding the best way of talking to them, finding the best in them. I watched Dr. Nicoll do this time and time again. He was extremely flexible. Some people would have a shock straight away, and others he would treat with special kindness.

The Next Thing
July 19, 1960

MRS. POGSON: I thought tonight we would speak of Dr. Jung, and Dr. Nicoll's connection with him. Here is something Dr. Nicoll wrote:

> Jung once told me that he had had a dream about me. He said: "You were working on the same tree as me, but you were one higher branch. I can't understand it." He said it without venom. A few years later I met the Work. It is much completer than Jung.

MRS. POGSON: Dr. Nicoll took this dream to mean that the Work represented what he was doing, working on a higher branch, because the Work went further. Dr. Nicoll met Dr. Jung in 1912, at a time when Jung had separated from Freud. Dr. Nicoll chose definitely to go to Jung instead of Freud, which was very important for him.

[Several excerpts from the article on Jung in the *Sunday Times*, July 17, 1960, were read about Jung's stone tower in Bollingen to which he often retires and how he finds "human satisfaction in a host of purely material activities."]

> Dr. Jung, indeed, has a special phrase for this part of his life. He calls it "Following the claim of the object." To mystified visitors he explains, "There's some wood which wants to be cut, a piece of meat which wants to be cooked, or a swan which wants to be fed. So I follow the claim of the object. I cut the wood, cook the meat and feed the swan."
>
> Just recently he has been following the claim of a large block of stone in the wall of the house at Bollingen which was, apparently, calling out to be carved. So he obliged it, and has laboriously chipped from it an attractive relief of a bear holding a ball in its paws.

MRS. POGSON: This is clear. This is what Dr. Nicoll taught us, to do the next thing, whatever it was. To go to it and conjoin with it. That is, go toward it, whatever it might be.

X: If we could approach it like this, would it separate us a little from identification?

MRS. POGSON: Why, yes. Dr. Nicoll told us about a time when he was staying with Jung and had to give a lecture across the lake. They didn't want to go. Then Jung transformed the situation by getting up and saying: "Come on, Nicoll, let's go to it!" That's *willing* it. A change of attitude had to be made at that moment, otherwise they'd have gone on losing force. It was natural not to want to leave the garden and cross the lake to give a lecture. Haven't many of you seen how difficult it is to make the change, and how interruptions always seem an extra that shouldn't be there? This is something to remember.

[Interested students should see Beryl Pogson's *Unforgotten Fragments*.]

Work Memory
April 25, 1961

> What you love you remember and love never sleeps.
> Many other sides of us may sleep (Dr. Nicoll).

MRS. POGSON: The chief thing to remember is the necessity of canceling new accounts. This is possible because they haven't got very strong.

X: A most effective way of dealing with accounts is to remember the parable of the servant who owed and was forgiven millions but wouldn't cancel his own small accounts.

MRS. POGSON: Yes, this is our parable. We are forgiven so much the whole time, yet we do not forgive other people. We talk about this now, and we've spoken about this before; now you see the truth of this, but then you forget. It doesn't stay with you, but it should always be in the background of your work. *Everything which has to do with our relationship to the higher level should be in our Work memory and accessible all the time.*

X: The higher level can't be active, it can't compel us.

MRS. POGSON: No, it can't compel us. We have to make the effort first. . . . Shall we think now about the Work memory? How can you increase your Work memory?

X: Doesn't it depend on types? Can some people increase it through attention?

MRS. POGSON: Yes, through directed attention you are closer to Work memory. We can build up our Work memory through connecting things together in our understanding so that the ideas of the system are connected together in a place where they are accessible to us. But until that happens you cannot call up an idea when you need it.

X: You have to make an extra effort.

MRS. POGSON: Yes, and then act from it.

X: One way to increase Work memory is to connect what you've heard at a meeting with your own observations.

MRS. POGSON: Yes. Once an idea has become emotional and you want to live with it, then it is yours. You have to fall in love with the ideas one by one. Some ideas you don't hear for a long time, then they come round again and maybe you connect.

We've been speaking in the past ten days at the new house about *being present,* which is the beginning of self-remembering.[3] The beginning of this is to see that you are not present, there is no one at home. You can see in a person when there's no one at home. Even at a meeting people are not all present. You have to select continually, and then what is not necessary can go. You have to choose special things you want to remember.

If people could just remember to come back when they see they're not present! The thing is to see you've gone away and then come back.

X: It is good to have something specific to come back to, such as one's aim.

---

[3] The group had moved to its new center at the Dicker on April 14th, 1961.

MRS. POGSON: The more times you can come back to being present, the more it becomes the way you live. The real point is that when you're present it's possible for something to come down the pendicular; you're on the line of self-remembering and could be there if anything came down. Otherwise you don't hear, you're not there. Do people realize how much they miss by not being present? Some days you are identified all day, and no message from another level can reach you because you aren't there. Our connection with this level depends on our being present. As Dr. Jung said: "If we could simply do the next thing, instead of objecting. If you look at the next thing, you don't have to think whether you like it or not, *you just do it.*"

X: There's a certain art in recognizing the next thing.

MRS. POGSON: Yes. You relate yourself to it by going straight towards it without daydreaming and without objecting.

X: There is a danger in the other direction of becoming identified with whatever is the next thing to do.

MRS. POGSON: If you give *attention* to the next thing, then there is a space between you and it.

X: If one is present there is a kind of effortless opening up which reveals connections as if they were already there.

MRS. POGSON: Yes, you put yourself into that place and the connections are there. Once you are raised up along this perpendicular line at all, you are open to connections.

X: When I am able to be present what has previously been a problem seems to be lifted from me.

MRS. POGSON: You have gone away from what you call the "problem." You were in anxious "I's," whose job it is to be anxious, and you moved away into "I's" that have to be in attention, into a better room in the house of yourself, and that is why the problem seemed to be lifted from you. "Cast your burdens on the Lord," it says. *You* don't have to carry these anxious "I's." Can you all think about moving about in the house of yourself? Do you remember this idea? Do you think of this house? Until you see it in this way, you're stuck.

All these ideas should be in your memory; they help us to live. Once they're present with you, they make the Work more possible.

X: It is possible to be in a better place and connect with the Work ideas when alone, but more difficult in life.

MRS. POGSON: The Work is *in life*. We mustn't think of life as something separate. In the Fourth Way we are in life. When we are alone there is much that is possible, but when we go into life the Work goes with us.

At one place, Dr. Nicoll says that the Work is sometimes called Good News. It is Good News to know we have a right not to be negative. It is Good News "to think that there is another meaning to life that will explain everything," and so on. The thing is to remember all this Good News that is given us. If it becomes real to you that there is this possibility of something reaching you from a higher level which begins by small contacts, then external events can't touch you, because they are received more consciously. Remember that the canopy is the beginning. Another state of consciousness is near you, up above. The Good News of the Work can transform our past.

[The concluding passage from *Psychological Commentaries*, "Commentary on Memory" was read.]

> I remember G. saying one night: "Remember, remember, remember, remember why you are in the Work." Why are you in the Work? Why are you here? I have often thought about this and I thought very much at the time when he said it. I realized that one could get nothing of the Work save by wanting it quite genuinely. Certainly many mixed motives may exist but nothing is recorded in the memory save through affection, and so no real Work-memory can arise in a person unless there is affection for it. What you love you remember and love never sleeps. Many other sides of us may sleep (p. 594).

MRS. POGSON: That is the most important thing to remember: "What you love you remember and love never sleeps." These are the ideas you love and make your own. But how do you love an idea? By recognizing that it belonged to you in the past; by practicing it and seeing the Good of the Truth. Then you cherish it and love it.

The Four Bodies
May 9, 1961

MRS. POGSON: I want to speak on the idea of the universe as vibrations, to remind us of the quality of vibrations which varies according to the level in the universe, and about the diagram on the board showing the seven orders of materiality, seven levels of vibrations.

[There was a reading from *In Search of the Miraculous*.]

> From this point of view, then, the world consists of vibrations and matter, or of matter in a state of vibration, of vibrating matter. The rate of vibration is in inverse ratio to the density of matter.
>
> In the Absolute vibrations are the most rapid and matter is the least dense. In the next world vibrations are slower and matter denser; and further on matter is still more dense and vibrations correspondingly slower (p. 87).

MRS. POGSON: This is to show how, on a higher level, atoms are finer and vibrate faster.

Look at Diagram 15. This represents the bodies of man in corresponding levels and qualities. At the level of the physical body we can see physical matter with our physical eyes. But we cannot see the astral and mental bodies, and the fourth body is of a different quality altogether. So we have this teaching of interpenetrating bodies. It is necessary to develop the finer energy to create second body so that we don't drift about at death. A person whose emotional body isn't organized, who in life is at the mercy of all his likes and dislikes, would drift about on the wind at death. Hence there is the need to see the state of the emotional center now. Don't you drift about at the mercy of wrong psychic functions, with no choice of state or where you want to be in yourself? *That is how we are without the Work.* And this is why we have to have a picture of the state of ourselves, so that there can be choice.

People have always wondered at the saints, that they are able to walk around serene, whatever happens. But that is because they can choose where they'll be. They don't have to be angry. . . . You see the difference between having scattered emotions and having a fully vibrating, controlled emotional body. This body is made from energy created from choice, from the effort involved in making choices. But it is necessary to practice; then something is possible.

I will speak a little about the mystery of the fourth body in relation to Ascension Day. I'll read some verses from Mark's Gospel from the new translation of the Bible:

> Afterward he appeared unto the eleven as they sat at meat, and upbraided them with their unbelief and hardness of heart, because they believed not them which had seen him after he was risen. And he said to them, "Go ye into all the world, and preach the gospel to every creature" (Mark 16:14–15).

This is the core of the Christian teaching.

> He that believeth and is baptized shall be saved; but he that believeth not shall be damned (Mark 16:16).

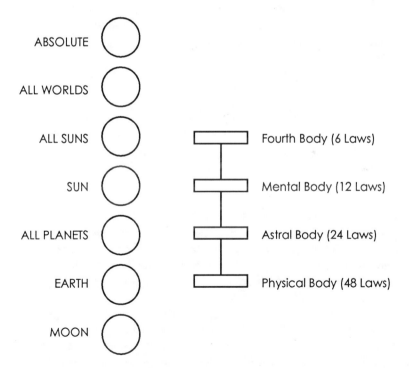

Diagram 15. The bodies and corresponding levels and qualities (from In Search of the Miraculous, *p. 94).*

What does it mean, "will be damned"? They are their own punishments. They remain in outer darkness: there you are in the darkness of your ignorance. But the others are those who can see the possibility of the new way that has been opened. Christ is called the Door and the Way. The door has been opened; this is the gospel.

The Work teaching about the fourth body is that it exists, but we are not connected with it. This is shown very clearly in the Hymn of the Robe of Glory. The prince receives the beautiful cloak when he returns, the radiant body, the body of light. It is also called the body of resurrection because it means the body in which one can live having risen to this level. In this body one is immortal. But until the other bodies are formed and organized and can obey the instructions coming through from the fourth body, nothing can be changed. This is the body of will. At that level it is known what we have to do in this life, and from this level instructions are given. In another diagram we have Steward, who comes from "Real I," as a messenger.

The whole thing is dramatized for us in the teaching of the Gospels. The mystery of the body in which Christ appeared after death is revealed in various passages.

> And as they thus spake, Jesus himself stood in the midst of them, and saith unto them, Peace be unto you. But they were terrified and affrighted, and supposed that they had seen a spirit. And he said unto them, Why are ye troubled? and why do thoughts arise in your hearts? Behold my hands and feet, that it is I myself: handle me and see; for a spirit hath not flesh and bones, as ye see me have (Luke 24: 36–39).

MRS. POGSON: The point is that from the level of the fourth body you have power over matter. What is below you you have power over, and it is possible to assemble the atoms and form a physical body. And he did this in order to demonstrate to the disciples that he was in the fourth body. And so also with the example of eating and drinking, so that they had proof.

There is another faculty of the fourth body, which is appearing in many places simultaneously. Christ appeared to many disciples in many places at the moment of death. There is an interesting example from the death of St. Columba, where he appeared to a monk in Ireland. Milarepa appeared in many different places. I think you might put it like this: that at the moment of death, they are with anyone who wants them to be with them.

X: It seems to happen only at the moment of death—except with Christ.

MRS. POGSON: Yes. These faculties are well-known and this is in all great teachings, the possibility of inhabiting the fourth body. But we have to rise to be conscious at that level in order to inhabit that level. This is theoretical teaching, but what is described can become real to anyone, otherwise the teaching wouldn't be given.

The Work teaches that you are at death as you are before you die. Dying doesn't change you. When you die, you shed the physical body; then you are present in the invisible bodies. This is why it is long work to prepare the psychological bodies so they can be absorbed into the fourth body. It doesn't happen naturally. It all works up to this, but it is long work.

To be immortal in the solar system means you can choose what you will do. There is the example in Christ who had the power of choice, his choice being to inspire the Christian church and to be with anyone who seeks his presence. The whole mystery can be enacted in us, on our own scale. There is a Christ for us.

Otherwise, what would be the good of working on negative emotions, of purifying emotions, if there weren't some end in view? But it takes many lives.

X: It is difficult not to mix up working for results, and purpose.

MRS. POGSON: One can work toward an aim. At death everything real is there and can't be taken away. What you've understood can't be taken away.

Whitsun
May 30, 1961

MRS. POGSON: I want to talk tonight about what is meant by "doing," and not being able to "do."

We could say that before the crucifixion the disciples were not able to do, despite contact with Christ. They went to sleep when they were supposed to keep awake, until they had this shock, which was a shock away from themselves in personality.

X: Even when they were awake, they wanted to take the experience for themselves, for example, Peter.

MRS. POGSON: Yes. But we are shown they were quite different afterward.

X: Why is the question of the higher aim connected with Whitsun and not with the Resurrection?

MRS. POGSON: The Resurrection happens first, but it affected each disciple separately. It wasn't until they were connected as a group that they became connected with the higher aim, and for this they had to be prepared further so that they could have this further shock, which we could call the second conscious shock. *Through being together as a group,* as they were at Pentecost, they could know their aim and be able to connect with the force to carry out their task.

We have had several meetings about real will and how to attain to real will, and how centers have to be prepared; for it can be dangerous if higher centers come through to an unprepared person. In the Work the chief task is in the preparation of the emotional center. Before Pentecost the disciples couldn't "do." Now, how do you understand this?

X: They still thought they could "do."

MRS. POGSON: We are shown how we can begin to learn to do, and it is important to notice what is said in the teaching about how we can begin to do. We speak of the three-fold man as thinking, willing, doing; as the three centers, intellectual, emotional and instinctive-moving centers. In Mr. Nott's book,[4] he refers to the triad of centers, where the intellectual center is the active force, the instinctive-moving center is the passive force, and the emotional center should be the reconciling force. But because the emotional center is not developed and is filled with negative emotions, it doesn't func-

---

[4]*Teachings of Gurdjieff* by C. S. Nott, Routledge & Kegan Paul, 1961; New York: Samuel Weiser, 1962.

tion as reconciling force. So the emotional center has to be changed. But how?

X: Getting rid of the self-emotions.

MRS. POGSON: Yes. The feeling of "I" has to be taken from the self-emotions, and the "I's" developed in the inner parts of the center which are facing inward. And negative emotions have to be worked on, first of all by not expressing them.

Mankind cannot "do" until we are balanced. What does this mean to you, cannot "do"?

X: You cannot do with yourself as you wish.

MRS. POGSON: Yes. You can't help yourself or other people. Why is the emotional center spoken of as the reconciling force?

X: It supplies the motive.

MRS. POGSON: Yes, the wish is there. Did you see the importance of wishing, willing, which was stressed in Mr. Nott's book, wishing from the right place? But if we inhabit the self-emotions, the aim which was made in a deeper place is not fulfilled. The other "I's" go the way they want and don't care about the aim.

Now, what is it we are told we can begin to do? We can observe ourselves. A person can begin to remember himself or herself and just begin to externally consider. It is only through self-observation that we begin to learn something about ourselves. Through self-remembering we can begin to pray a little.

X: When the disciples were able to withdraw their feeling of "I" from their self-emotions, they became humble.

MRS. POGSON: Yes. It's only when you're in a place of humility that something can come through. When the disciples were together, they were in a place of humility, of nothing; then something could come through so strongly.

Again and again hints are given in the Work of how a person can begin to do. G stressed beginning with small things. Mr. Nott records that someone asked the question: "What can I do?" And Gurdjieff answered:

> There are two kinds of doing—mechanical, automatic doing, and doing according to your real wish. Take some small thing which you are not able to do, but which you wish to do. Make this your God. Let nothing interfere. Only strive to fulfil your wish. If you succeed in this small thing, I shall give you a bigger task (*Teachings of Gurdjieff*, p. 66).

MRS. POGSON: No one can do anything big who hasn't practiced on something small.

> At present many of you have an abnormal appetite for doing things which are too big for you. This appetite keeps you from doing the small things which you could do. Destroy this appetite. Forget these big things. Make your aim the breaking of some small habit (*Teachings of Gurdjieff*, p. 66).

X: It could be a mechanical phrase.

MRS. POGSON: Yes, or a habit in the moving center. When we were first at Dorton, we worked on mechanical phrases. People began to see them.

X: If you stop one, you acquire new ones and have to keep on working.

MRS. POGSON: Then G goes on to say: "If you *wish*, you *can*. Without wishing you never can."[5] People can work for years, but unless there's a real wish nothing happens. It has to be a conscious wish, in the innermost part of yourself. Everything depends on how much one wishes to change and what one wishes. It's only in a very deep place you can wish to change. Small "I's" always want something else.

X: You've talked about inhabiting deeper "I's." This is one way, by carrying about a wish with you.

Mrs. Pogson: Yes.

---

[5]*Teachings of Gurdjieff*, p. 66.

X: Can we say that what we really wish we do?

MRS. POGSON: Yes, I think we could say that. . . .

In this center which should be the reconciling force, there are so many denying "I's" working in the opposite direction, against the Work. So our work for the time is on the purification of the emotional center.

It is interesting to observe everything that happens to St. Peter. The contrast is greatest in him. When there is a terrific change, the person is very strong.

X: One of the most marked things is that he is fearless afterward.

MRS. POGSON: Yes. This is one of the great changes. Fearlessness was characteristic of all the disciples, St. Thomas in India, Philip in Greece, and so on. We are shown that they were able to go on to the next thing, whatever it was. If a person didn't carry out instructions, he couldn't be used.

What are the disciples able to teach, after Pentecost? X wrote in his observation that they were shown that there was no such thing as unknown or unmanifest and that because the higher level had become manifest there was a kind of vista of a whole series of higher levels. What were the disciples really being shown?

X: How to inhabit the fourth body?

MRS. POGSON: It's all here if you really study the Gospels, the Acts and the Epistles. The way is shown: that if it is possible to lay down the psychological life, the self-will, and live as a whole person and do the will of something higher, then it is possible to inhabit the fourth body at death. Then you're free to live on any plane; you have choice. It is sometimes called the body of will because you can choose. Conscious Humanity, this body of minds, is able to help the world because they have this freedom and are able to influence through the mind. But ordinary people cannot do this. We have no will. Death will only mean seeing what we haven't done so that we can make an aim of what to do in the next life. And so there is return; return, with no choice. But for Conscious Humanity it is different. This is the only force that can redeem humanity. They have the power to do. The disciples had reached this level, they had put aside what *they* wanted to do so that something else could do through them.

Shall we talk about what is necessary before we can do? First of all, to work with three centers together in harmony. This is within everyone's power eventually. People can do it from time to time. You recall that special feeling of harmony that comes from willing what you are doing. People should remember examples of this. When could this happen in daily life? The centers have to be trained, and the only way is for something in the emotional center to turn round and will the event. Everyone should see the events that come in the day.

[The following passage from the Persian mystic, Nasafi, was read.]

> Some travelers of the path (the theologians) spoke: Let us learn the craft of the scribe and inscribe all existing things on our hearts with the ink of study and the reed of repetition in order that a copy of everything sensory and supersensory that exists in the world may be written in our hearts. Whatever is inscribed and recorded in our hearts is well preserved. Thus our heart will become the Well-preserved Tablet. But other travelers of the path (the mystics) spoke: Let us learn the polisher's trade and make the mirror of our heart clean and shining with the stone of spiritual struggle and the oil of contemplation of God, in order that our hearts may become transparent mirrors, reflecting everything sensory and supersensory that exists in the world. A reflection in the mirror is more accurate and free from doubt than writing, for in writing errors and fallacies are possible, while in the reflection, they do not occur. Moreover, there are many branches of science, and even many categories of science, and life is short. Hence life is not long enough to make the heart the Well-preserved Tablet by means of study and repetition. But by means of spiritual struggle and contemplation of God, life can make the heart a mirror, disclosing the whole world.[6]

MRS. POGSON: We have to think of the cleansing of the emotional center so that it becomes a mirror.

---

[6] All efforts have been made to credit the source for the passage from the Persian mystic, Nasafi. If any reader knows this material and can supply us with information, please contact the publisher.

Conscious Love
July 14, 1959

MRS. POGSON: We have spoken sometimes of the Essenes. Our Work is closely connected with the tradition of the Essenes, of whom Mr. Gurdjieff said they were the one group which had kept the teaching pure. It was said of them at the time of Christ that they loved one another more than any other group. What a wonderful thing to have said! It shows that they had an understanding of conscious love. One of our studies, to which Dr. Nicoll was continually returning, was to act from conscious love, to develop "I's" where it was possible to consider externally.

[There was a reading from the *Psychological Commentaries*, "The Work and the Wrong Love," Vol. V, pp. 1554ff.]

MRS. POGSON: Dr. Nicoll is talking about this new kind of love which is capable of relating you to something new and higher. This is only possible in the inner "I's." When consciousness grows in these inner "I's," your relationship to other people will change as well. You will find that your relationship to other people depends on your relationship to yourself. If someone has a relationship to something higher in himself, the "I's" at that level of consciousness look on other people differently. These "I's" have the power of giving attention. They can see in other people what they know in themselves. Dr. Nicoll spoke of connecting with what is good in other people— not being blind to their mechanicalness, but making a connection with what is not mechanical. The only possible way to have a deeper relationship with other people is by making a real connection with what is valuable in them. This is the beginning of conscious love.

X: Sometimes when you have made such a connection with someone, they sense it and then seem to fight against it.

MRS. POGSON: They want what they are used to. This is the only possible real relationship, although there are many possible mechanical relationships: relationship through polarity, common buffers, common false personalities, for example, disliking the same people. False personality relationships usually break up. But a relationship through personality isn't bad. It is good for partnerships.

And it can last, for there is a common motive. Mechanical man loves someone to feel comfortable with. Conscious love has nothing to do with this.

It is interesting to see what St. Paul says about conscious love.

[The thirteenth chapter of I Corinthians was read.]

MRS. POGSON: Try to forget all associations. The word "charity" has descended in scale, as has also the word "love." Go back to the original word, *agape*. How shall we think of it? Shall we think of it as conscious love? Can you see that when we are in certain conscious "I's," nothing else is necessary? Everything is in its proper place. This is school work. This is what can be achieved in a school; otherwise only isolated individuals achieve it. Where conscious love is achieved, envy and jealousy go. It is said about the Essenes that no one was above the other. There was no question of comparison among them. When ten people were gathered together, they considered themselves a group, ten being a sacred number.

What is spoken of so much in the Work is developing the inner "I's," letting them have your consciousness. You can see when people are in mechanical "I's" most of the time, and then also when they are in deeper "I's." This is not criticism: one just sees where a person is in himself.

X: To say "conscious love is not selective" means that you do not reject someone because of his mechanicalness?

MRS. POGSON: You have to accept the whole person. You see the whole when you are in inner "I's." Dr. Nicoll saw and accepted us; even after seeing our worst "I's," he didn't turn away from us. He knew a person's emotional center, and he called forth the "I's" in the inner parts of centers and saw them developing. What do you do with a person?

X: In mechanical "I's," I find out what he likes and dislikes, which either agrees or disagrees with mine.

MRS. POGSON: In a group it's different. You begin to see the whole person and become fond even of the funny mechanical reactions. Yet sometimes people go through Dorton without ever seeing others or being aware of them. But what is so wonderful about the Work is that people are always changing, and each Dorton is different.

X: Do we all have the same unpleasant manifestations, only in different degrees?

MRS. POGSON: Everyone is different. Everyone has unpleasant manifestations in mechanical "I's," when they are very mechanical. For instance, phrases people have used for years and years are repetitious and boring. But everyone has a kind of darlingness. We must see the whole. You see why we're saying all this. I was so struck by this description of the Essenes, that they were able to love one another more than any other group.

CHAPTER 8

SUMMER SESSIONS
AT DORTON HOUSE

August 4, 1958

[To illustrate the concept of inner and outer in a person's being, the following was put on the blackboard.]

> God
> Real I: under 12 Orders of Laws;
> Essence: under 24 Orders of Laws;
> Personality: under 48 Orders of Laws;
> False Personality: under 96 Orders of Laws.

MRS. POGSON: The false personality is under large numbers of quite unnecessary laws, such as the law of identifying and the law of internal considering.[1] It is even possible to die under the law of accident, and to receive many events which do not belong to one, and were not designed to further the development of consciousness. The law of cause and effect, the law normally obtaining on this planet, implies meeting the consequences of all our thoughts, words and actions.

> Real I: under the law of will;
> Essence: under the law of fate;
> Personality: under the law of cause and effect;
> False personality: under the law of accident.

MRS. POGSON: The word "fate" is derived from the Latin verb *fari*, to speak, alluding to the Word spoken at birth outlining the lessons to be learned by the Essence of the newly-born child. The parable of the Prodigal Son illustrates the various stages of the outward journey and the return. Once one has really started on the return journey

---

[1] Cf. discussion of laws in *Work Talks at the Dicker*, pp. 70–100.

one should meet only the adventures which are right for development. . . . One way of helping Essence to grow is to give less of one's time and energy to false personality. But in order to achieve this, it is necessary to see where one is in oneself. False personality can take over anything, even the Work.

During sessions at Dorton, we try to be aware of where we are in ourselves. Following the example of the Essenes, we should try to avoid mixing levels by talking about the Work while engaged in our daily activities. We should reserve such talk for times when we can give our whole attention to it. Dr. Nicoll called that sort of mixing levels, profanity.

The theme for study: what it means to become balanced. The most important quality a balanced person possesses is a permanent center of gravity. It enables one always to return to the equipoise of the Work, as a teetotum regains a vertical position however hard it is knocked. Also, balance is not just between the different centers, but between inner and outer in each center, with the inner in control.

We should make it an aim to avoid what is unnecessary, especially mechanical talking.

August 5, 1958

["Happiness means balance" (Ouspensky, *The Fourth Way*, p. 155). How would you explain to a new person what this means, giving examples?]

MRS. POGSON: Happiness is not connected with the pendulum of pleasure-pain, or elation-depression. It is in the strength to make contact with the real part of ourselves. . . . It is connected with the *center* of the pendulum-swing. The implication is that it is necessary to be able to use all functions fully. Then you can choose which to use, and not let them use you. . . . The image of the teetotum, the toy which always rights itself, is the sort of image to have. You move, but always come back to your center of gravity. Not unyielding, flexible rather, not losing equilibrium.

X: You spoke yesterday of a special task for which we come into the world; is it connected with chief feature?

MRS. POGSON: Yes. You can see the pattern. The young child is left free for a very short time before personality, under the direction of the ruler of the earth, chief feature, takes charge.

X: Is chief feature given?

MRS. POGSON: It is attracted by Essence. Outermost influences govern the outer person. The task appears for a long time as a struggle against mechanicalness. This is all one can see at that stage.

X: Then all this is a good thing, otherwise we should be unable to develop? False personality is necessary?

MRS. POGSON: It has to be seen through and deflated. Everyone is surrounded with these balloons which protect the places where one is empty. False personality is one's idea of oneself—unreal. The force taken out of this can feed Essence.

X: To be elastic, flexible, helps to soften the blow when false personality is touched.

MRS. POGSON: Yes, if one has a center of gravity, one comes back.

X: What if the center of gravity is in false personality?

MRS. POGSON: Then one is not balanced at all. One may fall down at any time.

X: Then we should ask ourselves often where our center of gravity is?

MRS. POGSON: Yes. Dr. Nicoll compared the halt, the maimed, and the blind with psychological states. People are divided into those who have no need of repentance (who think they're all right as they are and so have no aim); those who have an aim but miss the mark, the sinners; and the few who have an aim and hit the mark, saints and conscious people who leave us their instructions.

X: Those who never even have an aim often seem free from negative emotions.

MRS. POGSON: Yes. People in the Work often have a lot to work on. It may be this which brings them into a group. We are not the "best" people at all.

People often lose balance by excessive devotion, say to a cause. Where there is overenthusiasm there is lack of balance. The balanced person is often called sly; cleverness seems to belong to the balanced person. For example, he or she will economize in the use of energy. He or she does what is expedient. The correct meaning of "expedient" in the New Testament is "profitable for awakening."

X: Are those who are not trying to hit a mark the Pharisees?

MRS. POGSON: Pharisees are those who think they are hitting the mark all the time. It is in imagination, gone into false personality. This can happen to anyone, even in a group.

On the subject of balance, Ouspensky says that development of centers is only of subsidiary importance, and that it is stressed because they open to higher centers. The vital thing is development of consciousness. What is your idea of consciousness?

X: Awareness?

MRS. POGSON: That is one aspect. Remember the definition "knowing all together." Dr. Nicoll used often to refer to it as light.

To become conscious you have to make the necessary energy by self-observation and self-remembering. Some energy is there from the right work of the food octave, but we must make more by effort.

X: What brings my self-observation to a stop is getting bored with myself. Outside things seem more interesting, so I turn away.

MRS. POGSON: You have hit the point. No one wants to observe himself. We will look at this.

WHY WE DO NOT OBSERVE OURSELVES?

1) Inertia;
2) Lack of energy;
3) Dislike of effort;
4) Fear of discomfort;
5) The illusion that self-observation will be easier in the future.

X: Are there not powerful cosmic forces in the world to prevent self-observation and self-remembering?

MRS. POGSON: Yes. But there are more powerful forces above to help if we can connect with them.

X: We are nearer the lower forces.

MRS. POGSON: Yes, so they seem more powerful.

WHAT CAN HELP US TO OBSERVE OURSELVES?[2]

1) Our aim in the Work;
2) The idea that we have help;
3) Understanding that only through self-observation and self-remembering can the energy be made to increase consciousness;
4) Awareness of difficulties.

X: Shouldn't the fourth come first?

MRS. POGSON: No. There has to be some aim in the Work. Can you work from dislike before you have aim? Can you come into the Work through disliking something in yourself?

X: Do not these four points resemble the Work octave?

THE WORK OCTAVE

Fa	Level of balanced man;
—	
Mi	Realization of personal difficulties;
Re	Application of the ideas to oneself;
Do	Evaluation of the ideas of the Work.

MRS. POGSON: This is an octave of development, an ascending octave. Octaves of creation are descending. If one is searching for something, then the shock of meeting these ideas enables a strong *Do* to be sounded. *Re* is the beginning of self-observation. Now

---

[2]Tabular summaries of aspects of practical work were continued in later meetings.

notice the gap at *Mi*. Only on the other side of this gap is the level of balanced man, at which we are aiming. It is at this gap that everyone sticks. But you will never reach the note *Fa* if you get bored with self-observation! However, later on you may feel some apprehension as to what may come. Remember the two meanings of the Delphic injunction: "Know Thyself." These two words imply both self-observation and self-remembering: awareness of the unreality of the outer person, leading to cognition of the real self within.

Do you realize that self-observation takes so much energy, that we only do it for seconds at a time? Notice where you waste energy that might be saved. Then use some of that energy for self-observation.

X: Self-observation is more difficult if one is trying to observe something abstract.

MRS. POGSON: Yes. You must observe yourself as you are at the moment. Don't pick on an abstract idea—pride, for instance—and watch only for that. Take a snapshot of yourself in action just as you are.

At the note *Mi*, one comes up against oneself, one's pictures, buffers and all the rest. After seeing something of the outer person at *Re*, we come up against him at *Mi*. Here is the gap that it takes so long to cross, but if one receives a strong enough shock, one can emerge a new person, as Jonah from the whale.

WORK AT THE *MI-FA* GAP

1) Becoming aware of the pendulum—learning to say Yes *and* No;
2) Furnishing centers—balancing inner parts with outer;
3) Becoming aware of the dark side of ourselves—working against chief feature;
4) Awakening to real conscience—gradually increasing contact with higher centers.

MRS. POGSON: Furnishing the inner parts of the intellectual center entails taking in new ideas, attempting to practice psychological thinking, finding the inner relationship between esoteric writings and the Work. The inner parts of the emotional center are furnished with appreciation of truth and beauty. Both centers are fed with "B" influences. All work at this stage leads to the development of Essence.

[There was a reading from Nicoll, *Psychological Commentaries* "Notes on Lower and Higher Centres: On Balancing a Centre," Vol. V, pp. 1691–1693.]

MRS. POGSON: It is important not to be too ambitious, not to try to do marvels, but to follow humbly the Work teaching with the aim of reaching influences streaming down the Ray of Creation. Then one will have pointers and will know what to do in one's particular circumstances.

BALANCED MAN—SLY MAN

1) Has permanent center of gravity;
2) Has contact with higher centers;
3) Works for a Work reason;
4) Has real conscience awake in him;
5) Knows real aim and how to attain it;
6) Uses all his centers, and all of a center;
7) Can remember himself at essential moments.

MRS. POGSON: To achieve this state, the first essential step is self-observation.

Three Lines of Work
August 6, 1958

When someone comes to the gap in the Work octave, one of the other octaves can help bridge the gap. For example, Mr. Gurdjieff found that at a certain stage of his work he needed to form groups and to start the second and third lines, in order to bridge the gap in the first. On the second line, and at Dorton especially, it is friction that overcomes the heaviness that falls on one at the missing semi-tone. People have not enough energy; but by stopping their leaks they can save enough. The three octaves must go hand in hand, not obstructing, but complementing one another.

August 7, 1958

MRS. POGSON: A Work group can be an accumulator of force; members of the group may draw on this energy for their work. Therefore some people may receive energy that is not really their own—they are permitted to draw upon it.

Contributing in one's turn to the group accumulator is one aspect of the third line of Work; and that helps toward the general aims of the group. The aim of every esoteric group is to serve as a reservoir to attract energy from the level of Conscious Humanity. The way to contribute to this is to save energy as well as you are able; through working you create more energy. While false personality is active you will not be able to give anything; you will be drawing energy without contributing anything; in fact, you are robbing the group of force.

THIRD LINE OF WORK

1) Work for the general aim of the group itself;
2) Observation of leakage of energy;
3) Work on wrong psychic functions;
4) Economy of energy (Method of Sly Man, and inner silence);
5) Creation of energy, through effort and self-remembering.

MRS. POGSON: The last four in particular contribute to the group pool of force.

X: Why is all this the third, not the first line of Work?

MRS. POGSON: Because the motive is different. . . . The motive is to enable the group to attract forces that are there to be attracted. There should be many pools of force scattered around the Earth to receive influences from the level of the Sun, force which could redeem the world. Such powerful forces cannot reach individuals, the "voltage" would be too strong. Often people say they can work better alone. The reason is that there is no friction; but work of this kind goes on mostly in the imagination, such people are brought up short when they are confronted with the reality of themselves.

"B" influences can supply us with energy if we can receive it; but until it is prepared, the machine is not in a fit condition to digest the force that it might.

Another aspect of the third line of Work is refraining from doing anything that could harm the Work:

6) Not harming the Work.

MRS. POGSON: What does protecting the Work mean? It means, among other things, protecting it from words that lead to confusion. Protect it from wrong, careless and inaccurate talking, from half-knowledge, which could confuse others, starting a chain of distortion. Preserve esoteric truth in the ark of the school from distortion and profanity—"pitching the ark."

Questions
August 8, 1958

MRS. POGSON: Are there any questions?

X: If I have no question, does it mean that I haven't any real desire for understanding?

MRS. POGSON: X, you answer this.

X: Perhaps one reason for not having a question is that there has been no self-observation recently.

MRS. POGSON: A question should nearly always be simmering in our minds. If you live with a question, the answer will be given, perhaps when you open the *Commentaries*, or at a meeting, or from inside you. It is wise to formulate questions, and have them ready for a meeting.

X: What is the difference between being responsible for the impressions we make on people, and internally considering about the impression we make?

MRS. POGSON: The two things are quite different. You have to *act* a little to give the correct impression; this is conscious acting. Internal considering is mechanical. We should make effort to give the right impression. If the impression we make comes from the false personality, it is never received as we intend.

X: What does it mean, to come to the end of your being?

MRS. POGSON: When you are busy, and perhaps have a lot of interruptions to cope with, you may reach a stage when you say, "This
is the limit." At this point you are likely to become violent. Instead
you should be able to say, "This is it," and to try to go a little further, beyond your present being, or perhaps to get into another
center.

We should have psychological maps of ourselves and a com-
pass. We should recognize the bogs and bramble bushes which
scratched us before, and get to know the reliable paths.

X: How can we recognize by inner taste whether we are in false personality, personality, or inner parts of centers?

MRS. POGSON: In false personality we feel uneasy or glowing with
elation. In personality we feel we are doing what we know how to
do. In inner parts of centers we are more relaxed, we have time to
feel at peace.

Levels of Consciousness
August 9, 1958

MRS. POGSON: The readings we have had from *Flatland* have been to
make it clear that one level cannot understand the levels above it,
cannot even understand the next level. We were reading a description of Lineland, where it was impossible for the king of this one-
dimensional country to understand anything about other levels. He
thought Lineland was the universe. Then we go to Flatland, where it
is difficult for the people to understand a visitor from another
dimension. Here there is a great deal about scale. The author
describes how people's rank is shown by the number of sides they
possess. This is spiritual rank. As your rank increases, you have
another side, that is, you have more consciousness. You become
almost a circle at a certain stage. You can see from all sides. It is all
about scale.

> . . . an *idea* which belongs to the level above us must have
> more "reality" than any of our ordinary ideas that we
> derive from natural, three-dimensional life. It must there-

fore have the power of *drawing energy* out of our ordinary
states (*Living Time*, p. 154).

Each higher dimension has more reality; each lower dimension has
less reality.

Let us think of practical things. In this Work idea of a higher
dimension, a fourth dimension where everything exists together, we
have one technique for stopping the waste of energy in our ordinary
states. It makes our ordinary states less important, it transforms
them. In self-remembering we are conscious in another dimension
for a brief moment. Let us think how being conscious in a higher
dimension could take energy out of the various wrong psychic functions.

BEING CONSCIOUS IN A HIGHER DIMENSION CAN TRANSFORM:

Negative emotion—because we see the end, the cause and
the effect; we see the whole thing together.

Identifying—because the feeling of "I" is in a different
place and you can see that the event is not important
enough to be identified with.

Self-justifying—because you would see it as untrue, as
lying.

Inner accounts—because we would be shown that we are
not owed, but that we owe.

MRS. POGSON: Dr. Nicoll says in *Living Time* that if we could really
see in the fourth dimension, all accounts would vanish because we
should see that people do not really owe us anything, it is the other
way round. Everything depends on the place where we are in ourselves.

It is a sign of being if we will accept injustice; this is why in
schools people are sometimes treated with apparent injustice, in
order to test being. How can a person of higher being accept injustice? One way is to see that the other person is mechanical, and
another way is to see that you probably have done the thing of
which you are accused, or that at least you are capable of it.

All function is four-dimensional. The moment is not long enough. Anything you plan can only be carried out in the fourth dimension. You think it out, you have an end in view; that is the cause of the work being done; but it takes a certain time to get the result. You who have made it can think of the thing as a whole. Other people may see just the object, but we when we look at it will think always of the days that went before in making it; it will represent for us its end, its cause and its effect.

X: The end would be the first thing, wouldn't it?

MRS. POGSON: Yes, the end is what you conceive in your mind; the end comes before the beginning. Normally we only see cause and effect, but we should never forget that everything is a triad.[3]

August 10, 1958

MRS. POGSON: Everyone has flashes of being conscious in a higher dimension, but they are only flashes, they only last for a moment, they are quickly forgotten unless we do something to cherish them. These glimpses must be clearly formulated, recorded, put in the Work memory. Register them in yourself.

X: They have to be visited.

MRS. POGSON: Yes, visiting them nourishes them. Think how many glimpses are lost to us through inertia.

X: Pascal recorded his experiences during such a moment of consciousness and kept the record in a locket above his heart.

X: You may remember the moments but lose the understanding they brought.

MRS. POGSON: You must give them attention. This demands force. It is a conscious action requiring effort.

---

[3]Mrs. Pogson was referring to the construction of a glass mosaic which the group had planned and made during the session.

X: One has such a flash during the night and thinks one will get up and write it down, but then goes to sleep again. You think you will remember it.

MRS. POGSON: You must accept once and for all that you will not remember, and that you must write it down at the time. Also in a moment of consciousness, you can ask a question, and the answer may come straight through, because the door is ajar. It can connect us with a Higher cosmos.

August 12, 1958

X: We talk about an act of self-remembering and a state of self-remembering. But is there a third thing? I have heard people say, "Then I remembered myself." What do they mean?

MRS. POGSON: It is a question of degree. A state of self-remembering which may come in a flash is given as a delayed reward for work on oneself. An act of self-remembering must be a conscious act. It can be of different degrees. To lift oneself just a little is already to remember oneself. Some of us who were here at one of the meetings suggested that we make a certain small aim. When you make aim it must be made in a higher place in yourself. Then there is this aim on this level all the time. It hasn't disappeared. You remember it on a different line. During daily life we may forget it, but we can get back; every now and then we can get back to it. That is one form of self-remembering. We made the aim here not to attempt to make people like us. It was made for a certain reason. Nearly everyone mechanically tries to make themselves liked; many manifestations are an attempt to make people like us.

X: The aim wasn't quite as easy as I thought at first.

MRS. POGSON: First we had to see why—the motive for the aim.

X: Because it wastes force.

MRS. POGSON: Yes, we need force to work and all the time without us being aware, there is this continual leakage. Here this particular behavior is unnecessary; people just are.

Now can you see that there are degrees of self-remembering? We must be in a higher place. A state of negative emotion is a good place to start from. Negative emotions are $H 12$, so by a real act of self-remembering you can reach a state where this fine energy can be used for other things.

Inaccuracy
August 14, 15, 1958

MRS. POGSON: People are always passing on inaccuracies based on imagination. There are many reasons for this; we will try to gather some of them together.

CAUSES OF INACCURACY IN SPEECH

Ignorance;
Lying;
Incomplete attention (thanks to identifying);
Thinking you know already;
Thinking you ought to know, and so not daring to ask
    for further explanation;
Imagination;
Self-justification;
Misuse of language—not explaining clearly;
Exaggeration to make an impression.

MRS. POGSON: If we realized all the inaccuracies for which we are responsible in ordinary conversation, we should feel that the ground was insecure under our feet! One reason for inaccuracies is the paucity of our powers of observing impressions. We only receive impressions of part of a person. A more conscious person would receive a more objective impression.

X: The things which we see most clearly are the things which hit our attitudes.

MRS. POGSON: We go about getting partial impressions, and describing places, gardens etc., with complete confidence. When our machine is used like this, what hope is there of our achieving understanding of each other? All this is a form of mechanical lying. The worst form it can take is giving an account of the Work which is incomplete or inaccurate or disparaging, which may influence a new person to whom you are talking. If a wrong impression of the Work is given to a new person, you are responsible for it. It is a very heavy responsibility. Whenever we are talking to new people, we must be aware what we say.

There are these three foods for us; first, ordinary food, then air. The air octave goes on by itself up to a certain point. Then there is the food of impressions, which comes up against a block, our mechanicalness. We receive each impression as we have always received it.[4] Now what is the first conscious shock?

X: If you are receiving an impression in the normal way, and connect it with a Work idea, it is possible to break through the usual associations. Suppose one has got to the end of one's being, say over difficult people or letters, you can either expand in the direction of violence, or you can remember a Work idea and can use the energy which was going into violent emotions for self-remembering.

MRS. POGSON: What will happen if you carry on the octave?

X: Your breathing would be different.

MRS. POGSON: You become more relaxed, receive more from the atmosphere, and receive the event with new emotion. You are differently related to it in *H* 24. In *H* 12, if you go on, you are in a creative hydrogen, and can paint a picture or have a new relationship with somebody, because of the new energy. Is there more truth in an impression received like this?

X: More meaning.

MRS. POGSON: And more truth. You would see the whole. If you remembered yourselves there would be more truth, because if you are further back in yourself you can really see. You can see in scale.

---

[4] Cf. Diagram 6, mechanical man, p. 65.

Work on Negative Emotions

MRS. POGSON: Mr. Ouspensky said that the impressions we receive with only *H 48* we often do not remember. That is why we have hazy memories of our past.

It is useful to discover that negative emotions can be divided in scale. Some which belong to small "I's" in outer parts of centers are fleeting and can be worked on. Others are in deeper parts of centers. The small ones are in the first column. In the second column we have put personal, habitual negative emotions. How do you work on these?

X: By observing them first of all.

MRS. POGSON: Yes. Then you have to work on them through the mind. You transform them through new thinking. Let's take an example of resentment. Only the mind can cure you there, with Work ideas of justice. Justice does not belong to our level but to a higher one. Injustice is the rule on our level.

X: Is it a question of working on your attitudes?

MRS. POGSON: Yes. And you have to work beforehand and in between times of negative emotions.

X: The second column requires deeper observation.

MRS. POGSON: You have to observe what it is. Most negative emotions come from requirements.

X: We demand that the world should be perfect.

MRS. POGSON: Yes. It might be a memory from a higher world which we have transferred to this.

X: Resentment has a good memory.

MRS. POGSON: It is very interesting about memory. Emotions in the inner parts have a long memory, while the outer ones have short

TECHNIQUES FOR WORKING ON NEGATIVE EMOTIONS

1) **In outer parts of center**	2) **In middle parts**	3) **Inner parts**
Irritation	Resentment	Hatred
Impatience	Self-pity	Jealousy
Feeling of disappointment	Melancholy	Malice
Feeling hurt	Apathy	Envy
Small worries	Suspicion	Fear
Boredom—indifference	Sulkiness	Resentment
Small envies	Rage	Depression
Indignation	Habitual worry	Sense of mean-inglessness
Dissatisfaction	Dislike	Despair
Embarrassment	Guilt	Violence
Raising objections	Nostalgia	
Try not to express it	*Self-observation is needed — new thinking*	*Transformation only possible through prayer and self-remembering*

memories. We all have one or two deep-seated negative emotions. How should you work on those in the third column?

X: Try to find the cause . . . wish to be free from them. Prayer.

MRS. POGSON: Yes, you have to do all these, but you cannot change these emotions without prayer. Deep negative emotions have a very high energy which can also be used for self-remembering. If we can do this, we are lifted from the bottom right up to the top in a flash. . . . It is not that the negative emotion has gone away—we use the energy to go to a place where it *is not*. You are like a house of several storeys, in which you live mostly on the ground floor.

Upstairs there are rooms where one can have better conversations. At the top there is a small secret room where one can be alone with oneself. At the bottom there is a damp, dark cellar. This is where one is when one is depressed and so on. You can go upstairs *if* you can remember that there *are* stairs.

The Kingdom of Heaven
August 16, 1958

A Work interpretation of the Lord's Prayer:

> Give us today *Mi 12* (trans-substantial, supernatural, and
> extra force) so that we may cancel all internal accounts,
> and let it not lead us into temptation, as an access of force
> can do so easily, but let it lift us above evil. For only you
> have power to do all this. We can do nothing without
> you. So be it.

MRS. POGSON: This means that every day we should ask for the necessary force to transform the day: if the day is transformed early the
force will last.

X: If the extra force goes into negative emotions we become violent.

MRS. POGSON: Extra force goes down into violence because our
emotional center has places of leakage. It is necessary for us to see
these leaks. The great secret of the Work is that the energy used by
negative emotions can be transformed and used for self-remembering.

X: Can you store extra force?

MRS. POGSON: It is stored in the big accumulator. It can be used in a
psychological way, for thinking beyond one's ordinary thinking, or
for external considering. But you cannot "sink your treasure in the
earth" or expect it to last.

It is said in the Gospels that it is very difficult for a rich man to
enter the Kingdom of Heaven. Dr. Nicoll interprets this as meaning
a person with a rich personality. The task has been given of finding
in the Gospels examples of those who cannot enter the Kingdom at
all, of those who can enter only with difficulty, and of those who can
enter.

To seek the Kingdom of Heaven is to go on a journey. If the journey is south and people are going north, they may get experience in
other things. If they are not on that journey they will not arrive at the
journey's end.

THOSE WHO CANNOT ENTER THE KINGDOM OF HEAVEN

1) Those who blaspheme against the Holy Ghost, who love evil better than good and foster the worst in others;
2) Those who having started turn back;
3) Those who like the foolish virgins do not practice the truth;
4) Those who do not forgive;
5) Those who think they can do, like the Pharisees;
6) Those who seek to save their souls, instead of giving them up.

MRS. POGSON: There are many of these in the Work, people who want to eat their cake and have it. They want to keep their first love.

7) Those who harm new understanding, their own or that of others;
8) Those who have no wedding garment;
9) Those who bury their talent: who do not use their knowledge.

MRS. POGSON: If you are given knowledge and do not use it, it will be taken from you.

10) Those who are not born again;
11) Those who hate not their fathers, mothers, wives, and their own lives—or rather, what these represent within themselves;
12) Those who are dead;
13) Those who deny Christ—that is, who deny anything which can transform them, Christ in themselves;
14) Those who cannot go beyond themselves;
15) Those who trust in their own righteousness.

MRS. POGSON: All these are really "I's" in ourselves. They must be starved, hated, fought.

X: What is meant when it is said, "Unless you hate your father and mother you cannot enter the Kingdom of Heaven"?

MRS. POGSON: The father and mother are old "I's" in personality which come to take control of us and it is these things which must be weakened. These "I's" are formed through the influence of parents and environment in childhood.

THOSE WHO CAN ENTER ONLY WITH DIFFICULTY

1) Those who are rich in possessions and personality, like the rich young man;
2) The Prodigal Son—that is, everyone who seeks to return;
3) The critical one, the one who judges (as long as he or she criticizes, the energy goes into criticism, and he or she is delayed on the journey);
4) Those who are choked with the cares of the world;
5) Those who have not a high aim (those who do the easy thing, who love their friends and do not attempt to love their enemies. Such people have not begun to work);
6) Those who are violent;
7) Those who have little faith;
8) Those who are identified with their families;
9) Those who postpone things;
10) Those who love the praise of man more than the praise of God.

MRS. POGSON: As long as you are dependent on the praise of others, you are delayed. You can imagine such a one calling at cottages on the way. [In answer to a question about violence]: When you find your own recurring point of violence you will be close to chief feature. When you are violent, something else takes over and acts for you. Everything is taken out of your hands.

THOSE WHO CAN ENTER THE KINGDOM OF HEAVEN

1) Those who do the will of the Father, not their own will (this leads to rebirth);
2) Whosoever shall humble himself as this little child is the greatest in the Kingdom;
3) Whosoever is born of the spirit (in whom Essence is reborn);
4) Those who follow the instructions of the Sermon on the Mount;
5) Those who have faith (who have understanding of scale, and can "do" beyond their being, thanks to their faith in scale).

X: Is repentance enough?

MRS. POGSON: To repent is to change your way of thinking, and this is a necessary preparation for rebirth; but it is not enough by itself to get you into the Kingdom of Heaven. John the Baptist taught repentance and was described by Christ as the greatest outside the Kingdom of Heaven.

Your Relationship to Yourself
August 3, 1959

MRS. POGSON: We want to talk this time at Dorton about our relationship to ourselves. On this everything depends. You can only begin by seeing that a person is not related to himself or herself and has no inner harmony. It is necessary to see this first before anything else is possible. Through practical work with Dr. Nicoll it was possible to discover more quickly that one was mechanical. Can you see why? If you are among people with a common aim, then mechanicalness shows up more. Not everyone is mechanical at the same time. It is possible to take things in a new way, to talk in a new way. New people are coming to Dorton and part of our work is to take events more consciously, so that they can see what it is like to work against a different background.

Do people know what it is like to be conscious in observing "I"? It takes a lot of force to be conscious in observing "I." Usually it is possible for a few minutes only. The rest of the time you know vaguely that you are mechanical, but this is not the same as observing yourself in the moment in action.

X: When you formulate an aim, is that being conscious?

MRS. POGSON: It is not the same as being conscious in observing "I."

X: I accused someone of being stubborn as we traveled to Dorton today and after thinking about it I remembered that my family always said I was very stubborn, and I thought I must have the same stubbornness in myself.

MRS. POGSON: You and the other person have this stubbornness. I have seen it in both of you. But you have not seen through self-observation that you have this quality. It is not the same thing to believe it because someone has told you about it. Now observe it.

X: Well, I suppose it must be true.

MRS. POGSON: You cannot accept this until you have seen it for yourself. Do you all realize now why it does no good to be told things about yourself that you have not seen? You do not believe them.

This quality of stubbornness is useful in the Work when it is transformed, when it is not attached to the self-will. It becomes perseverance and can serve the Work.

X: Can you observe yourself if nothing much is happening outside?

MRS. POGSON: You can observe your inner state while nothing much is happening. You may be having an event with your thoughts.

X: Being more aware of what you say is using observing "I"?

MRS. POGSON: You must know what the feeling is like of being in observing "I." There is a special force in it.

Can people think of certain forms of mechanicalness which you have observed at other times at Dorton and are now relatively free from?

X: Internal considering.

MRS. POGSON: Yes, that form of mechanicalness is shared by almost everyone because people cannot be released from it for a long time. Try to reduce everything that is unnecessary, to save force for other things.

In the commentary "On Realizing that One is not Conscious"[5] Dr. Nicoll says that effort in the Work has to be passive—observing oneself remembering oneself being sincere with oneself, not identifying with everything, not letting negative impressions fall where they mechanically fall, not making accounts against others. This is the kind of effort to be made in the Work. There should be no strain-

---

[5]*Psychological Commentaries*, Volume III, p. 1005. Cf. Pogson, *More Work Talks*, pp. 28–33, an extended discussion of this commentary.

ing in Work effort; it is not tense effort. Try to see inner states clearly. When you have observed an inner state, you are not that state. This is the first secret of esotericism.

August 4, 1959

MRS. POGSON: The work here is to see one's mechanicalness and realize that one is not conscious. Until this stage is reached these things, such as the relationship to oneself, cannot be understood. It is necessary to know the outer person who is mechanical, who has our feeling of "I," and whom we do not know. I want you to have small shocks in which you realize that the outer man is doing things to which you have not given your consent. The outer person is sometimes called Mr. *A*. You have to get used to being aware of the presence of Mr. *A* who leads your life for you. Internal considering is done by Mr. *A*.

> In this Work you must learn to know the real from the invented and later to separate them. And to begin self-observation and self-study it is necessary to divide oneself into a real and an invented side. That is, a man must realize that he indeed consists of *two men*. All this takes time. But so long as a man takes himself as *one person he will never move from where he is* ("Commentary on Internal Considering," in *Psychological Commentaries*, Vol. I, p. 280).

MRS. POGSON: What do you substitute for *A* while this commentary is being read? Your own name? You are all at different stages, but from one point of view the early stage of the Work has to do with getting to know Mr. *A*.

X: Is *A* partly the person other people see and you don't?

MRS. POGSON: Yes, and you don't like what they see. What other people say about *A* is often true. They can see the outer person better than you can.

X: Does chief feature belong to *A*?

MRS. POGSON: Yes. *A* is in the control of chief feature.

X: It is difficult not to feel upset when one sees something about oneself.

MRS. POGSON: Yes, because you identify with yourself. You need a space in order to take a snapshot. We must try to be conscious in observing "I," and not put the feeling of "I" into what we see.

X: Isn't there a halfway point? Seeing, and still feeling, "Oh blast!"

MRS. POGSON: Then you are not conscious in observing "I." A camera doesn't say, "Oh blast!" It registers and records. This is a pure feeling of really seeing something. It is very rare.

If you are going to observe Mr. *A* you must see him in all centers, see his gestures, see him showing off, notice the tone of his voice. This is what you can photograph. Every time you speak in your familiar way, it is Mr. *A*. He is constantly changing. He is like a kaleidoscope. From about age seven Mr. *A* has taken over. And he has to be there or you wouldn't have grown up. You can't get away from him, but now you have to learn how to control him.

X: I can't seem to find anything beyond Mr. *A*.

MRS. POGSON: This is what we have to see.

X: The camera cannot see itself and yet it exists.

MRS. POGSON: There is an inner man, turned inward, who will eventually be able to take charge. But first one has to get to know the outer man. There is a place to be free from Mr. *A*, and there something can grow. You cannot talk about this abstractly. After a while *A*'s behavior has to depend on your consent. Now he has your feeling of "I"; it has to be taken out of him. *A* objects all the time, and this is what spoils life. You have to see that you can't stop it, it has gone on too long. Outer man is beyond your control. As soon as you can go further back in yourselves and see what is happening, see that you cannot stop the outer man, that it is something you carry around with you, then the inner man begins to grow. *Outer man cannot exist without your feeling of "I."* When you are able to withdraw this feeling of "I" from outer man, something can happen. But first you must see that he has your feeling of "I" most of the time.

X: Do you have to beat Mr. *A* in smaller places first? By knocking bits off?

MRS. POGSON: You don't beat him. It's all a question of who is going to have your feeling of "I." These "I's" are going on saying "I" for you: you cannot "knock them off." You cannot put it this way. Do you see how important language is? You are responsible, if you speak in the wrong way about the Work and so give the wrong impression.

You withdraw the feeling of "I" gradually from small "I's." You hear an "I" after it has spoken, then slowly you begin to recognize it. Then you hear it suddenly just as it is going to speak, and your voice trails off. Then, perhaps, you remember it next time *before* it speaks.

["Commentary on the Relationship of a Man to Himself" (*Psychological Commentaries*, Vol. I, pp. 365ff) was read.]

MRS. POGSON: Do you see how important this is? All these commentaries are the result of the work Dr. Nicoll did on himself. The material is from work on oneself. Where does one look when one feels that something is wrong with one? Does one think: "I'm unwell," and hope to be better tomorrow? Does one look to the body, or to the outer world, for the cause? Or does one look in oneself to see what is wrong? There are many possible causes: thoughts, not listening to one's intuition, and so on.

Withdrawing the feeling of "I" further and further back is long work. We begin to be conscious in observing "I," then in deeper and deeper "I's." Our aim is to be conscious in "Real I." You have to begin by seeing what is saying "I" in your name. Listen to the "I's," but do not think you are saying it. Think: *What* is tired? *what* doesn't like things? and so on. Notice in particular the "I's" that speak with emphasis.

August 5, 1959

X: You once said that one can only do the Work by wanting it, and one can only want it more by doing it. Is this not a vicious circle?

MRS. POGSON: Both things are necessary. By doing the Work you want it more, but you can't begin to work without wanting it. It is impossible to work from feeling "ought," or "must."

X: Isn't "ought" a step in the right direction?

MRS. POGSON: Yes, you do have feelings of "ought"! Wherever you feel "ought," have a look and see what it comes from. Real work comes from *desire,* not from feeling "ought." "Ought" has to do with acquired conscience, not real conscience. Our first education is necessary. We have to be given some external authority. But the Work is to give us a new authority, which is "Real I." When real conscience shows us, we work from love, there is no alternative.

X: If you want to do a thing, you do it willingly. But if you have to make an effort, there seems to be an "ought" behind it.

MRS. POGSON: Then you have to *want* to make the effort.

X: There is often a feeling of being driven.

MRS. POGSON: The feeling of being driven does not come from real conscience. If you mean the feeling of *urgency,* that is different.

> One can only do the Work by wanting it.
> One can only want it more by doing it.

On Moving about in Oneself

MRS. POGSON: I want to speak today about the middle parts of centers. You should have seen outer man more clearly since yesterday. Perhaps we can see that he isn't the companion we should wish to choose for life, but we've got him. So instead of his leading us, we must learn to lead him. At Dorton there is a chance to rest from Mr. A. This is true relaxation. And the relaxing of the outer "I's" is followed by physical relaxation. Then "I's" in the middle parts of centers, which have potential, can develop. These "I's" use attracted attention. They are "I's" that feel wonder at the beautiful, delight in new discoveries, reverence for the higher. They can look upward and inward as well as outward. All the new activities at Dorton are designed to feed these "I's," for instance, painting the flower patterns, or trying to hear new sounds that are usually shut out. These "I's," when they become strong and developed, will nourish Essence.

Dr. Nicoll used to talk a great deal about the journey through ourselves, about how new truth, when it is established in memory, will help memory to travel to the inner divisions of centers. Outer "I's" have only poor memory. New truth falls on the middle parts of centers; it connects with Work memory. As memory moves inward it develops and becomes stronger. This is one way of preparing the lower centers for higher centers. During the last year of his life, Dr. Nicoll spoke very much about the middle divisions of centers, because this is where reversal takes place, where we can turn around in ourselves.

[For illustration of the three qualities of attention see diagram 9 on page 77.]

X: When they are developed, can these "I's" in the middle parts of centers look both ways?

MRS. POGSON: Yes. The middle parts of centers are emotional. Here it is possible to see and hear and do new things. Until your attention is attracted, it is in small "I's" which do not hear very much, but wander off into associative thinking. Supposing people come to a meeting and the feeling of "I" is in small "I's." What happens?

X: Today I was watching others who were watching a wasp.

X: I was in small "I's" thinking of hanging up dresses.

MRS. POGSON: It is necessary to know all the time where you are in yourselves. Do you all recognize the feeling of being scattered? At the beginning of every meeting this happens. You are in scattered attention. But this shouldn't happen. Do you realize that you are not present at a meeting until you are at least in attracted attention? And yet people forget they're not here. They think: "I wonder what we are going to talk about," or "What was the meeting about last time?" You cannot connect with the last meeting or with a Work idea in the outer part of a center. Outer "I's" don't remember. It is necessary to be already in attracted attention at the beginning of the meeting. You can be holding a thought or an idea from the previous meeting. Then I am talking to a few people who are in the same place. But where are all of you? Where have you been? What we want are people who can connect with the meeting, connect with my thoughts. During the meeting some thought may register in the middle part of a center, and then you can go on thinking about it with directed attention after the meeting. This is the way to make it your own.

X: Are outer "I's" of no use at all? I find it restful sometimes, for instance on a train, to be in outer "I's."

MRS. POGSON: Real rest is only possible in inner "I's." At Dorton we have the chance to rest from Mr. *A*. This is true relaxation, resting from the wish to make an impression, for instance.

X: I find it very restful to paint, but it needs a great effort to start.

MRS. POGSON: Yes, it is the initial effort required to get into deeper "I's" that makes you think it more restful to be in outer "I's." The outer "I's" see only the effort; but once you are in inner "I's," real rest becomes possible. Did you not find this in painting flower centers?

X: There seems to be a judge in me sitting at the door, who sorts out everything that comes in from the meeting.

MRS. POGSON: Judging is in outer man, in small "I's." Logical mind is the judge. Outer man is not in the Work until he is in the control of inner man. Listening takes place in the middle part of a center, without judging or comment.

If you really listen, you know what you've heard. It falls on a place of greater memory. Then, after the meeting, you see what can be incorporated into your own structure, the Work structure each of you is building. What is important will be recalled after the meeting. The people who have done the most practical work on themselves will connect with the most in a meeting. We must ask ourselves: What "I's" do we listen with?

X: There is always a feeling of magic in directed attention. If it's heavy, where would you be?

MRS. POGSON: You might be distracted by certain "I's" objecting, or in some kind of negative emotion, or between centers. If you're really in directed attention, interruptions can come and you are able to go back. In attracted attention you don't like interruptions, but you can't be put off in directed attention. In directed attention *you* have control. Small "I's" have certain ways of imitating attention, such as frowning or leaning forward.

I'll read a sentence from *Waiting on God,* by Simone Weil: "Every time we really concentrate we destroy evil in ourselves."

August 8, 1959

MRS. POGSON: We are going to read the play, *Zeal of Thy House,* and see the film of Job. I want no one to discuss the play. If you begin to talk about something immediately after seeing it, you are too close to it. Both in oneself and in the group, *the level drops unless something is holding it.* We are drawn into attracted attention by plays or works of art, but we are being taken in, aren't we? We don't of ourselves go into that state. Suppose the play were not being read, would you be able to go to that place? You wouldn't know how to do it, because you can't walk about in yourselves. This is what we are learning. It needs practice. You can't stay in this place because you are not used to it. Someone approaching balanced man should be able to hold the level in himself for a time.

X: It would seem here to be a question of having received so much force that one doesn't know what to do with it.

On Feeling Special
August 7, 1959

MRS. POGSON: About being special: this feeling they are special prevents many people from coming into a group. They cannot accept that they are the same as others. Then others want to be special *within* a group. This is a thing which just has to be sacrificed! You have every opportunity to work against this at Dorton. In real group work, people work together, they share. It is not a question of one person doing especially well, but of each doing what he or she can to help group effort. You will find that you have to let go of phrases like, "I ought to be doing that job, I can do it better," and on the other hand, "I can't." There is not time here for, "I'm no good at this," and, "What's the point when others can do it so much better?"

That is all just internal considering. In these activities you can relax from false personality.

X: In a choir, a boy with a specially good voice which *will* keep coming through the others is sometimes asked to leave for the good of the choir as a whole.

Mrs. Pogson: That is a good analogy. In any form of collective work, you have to be serving something bigger than the self.

X: When I lost the feeling of being better, I observed that I was losing my incentive to work; I began to slow down.

Mrs. Pogson: In group work there is opportunity to see more clearly what you feel yourself through. A group can use people with special gifts (and there are many with these) only so long as people don't feel themselves through these gifts, don't feel they are special. You are not really in the Work until you see that you are like everybody else.

[The record was read of a discussion with Dr. Nicoll at Amwell at a meeting based on a commentary on self-love. In the discussion, Dr. Nicoll had used the phrase, "The self-love wishes to be its own architect."]

Mrs. Pogson: *This* is the core of the conversation. Self-love wants to build itself into the Work. What each of you needs to be is your own demolition company! This was a real strong conversation with Dr. Nicoll.

If you have "I's" that resist the Work, then you can be sure that there is something behind them which hates the Work and would destroy its influence over you. If you come to Dorton at all, it must be because other "I's" in you want to be changed, not because you wish to be your own architect.

X: One wants to choose certain ideas and to reject others.

Mrs. Pogson: You have to accept all the ideas. The system can fulfill its function only if it is complete.

X: Why is it said that we only have fragments of a teaching?

MRS. POGSON: The Work becomes a complete structure only when one has built it up in himself or herself. Then it is all there in the inner world.

Have you all understood what we have been talking about? When for a moment you feel just the same as other people, then you are really in the Work, in an inner part of yourself. When you feel separate from others, whether superior, or inferior, or incapable, you are in the outer man. That part of you is not in the Work.

Taking Events as Tests
August 10, 1959

X: I like to think of people leaving Dorton as knights going out into life.

MRS. POGSON: The times of festival were the times for tests, when there was special force available. Certain knights, who were ready for a test, would be sent out at Christmas and Easter and Whitsun after a feast, with the force of the whole court behind them. Then some adventure would arise, an adventure whose inner meaning was a psychological test. Some would come back renewed through having conquered something; with others it took longer.

X: And they realized that the court was waiting.

MRS. POGSON: Yes. We must remember that there is always someone in a group having some kind of test.

X: There is the wonderful feeling of the group here; that laughter is not against the person but with him.

MRS. POGSON: When there is a loud burst of laughter from the group it means that someone has said something typical. It may be that he or she has spoken from chief feature. The thing to remember in connection with all this is that events are specially arranged for each person by an inner force.

X: It seems to me that after practicing self-remembering for some time, there is something that remembers.

MRS. POGSON: You see if you can raise yourself up to a place of self-remembering, you are in a place where things are related and linked, where you have made connections before.

X: Do tests become more and more difficult?

MRS. POGSON: Things in life are an image of what is true in the psychological world. Everything becomes harder in life; examinations become harder, for example, but the pupil knows more. And so, psychologically, you have more to meet the tests with because you have grown.

I always liked the adventure of Sir Lancelot where he had to approach the castle in a cart that was used for taking malefactors to the gallows or pillory. It was the greatest disgrace for an ordinary person to be seen in such a cart. After this adventure he was called the knight of the cart. This was his event. This was a test which he could only approach if he felt himself no better than anyone else. Some people have had their adventure before coming to Dorton and so have been unable to come. This may be their test. It could be taken wrongly, someone might think: "If only I could be at Dorton!" The event may be to miss something. What will help more than anything else will be to recognize the event. Everyone may expect a kind of test event after leaving. But no one should say: "If only I were having a different sort of journey I could remember the meetings at Dorton!"

[A passage was read from *In Search of the Miraculous* where Mr. Ouspensky is recalling what he said to a friend with regard to the change which had taken place in him after he had been in the Work for four years. He speaks of the "strange confidence" he has acquired: ". . . a confidence in the unimportance and the insignificance of *self* that self which we usually know. But what I am confident about is that if something terrible happened to me like things that have happened to many of my friends during the past year, then it would be *not I* who would meet it, not this ordinary I, but another I within me who would be equal to the occasion. . . . All the ordinary life goes on in the ordinary way. . . . But if something big were to happen . . . then I know that this big thing would be met not by the ordinary small I . . . but by another, a big I, which nothing can frighten and which would be equal to everything that happened. . . . I know, for myself, that this new confidence has not come simply as a result of a great experience of life. It is the result of that work on myself which I began four years ago."[6]]

MRS. POGSON: This is something to remember, that ordinary "I's" have to go on for a long time. But there is something else, and sometimes it is possible to be conscious in this new place. Mr. Ouspensky recognizes that this self we talk about is unimportant; it cannot meet a real event. So when a big event occurs the consciousness is shifted inward, and the event is met in a different way.

X: What has helped me so much is the idea you gave us once of "This is": This is called negative emotion, this is being angry.

MRS. POGSON: Yes. Dr. Nicoll often said this. He also said that there are only a certain number of possible events in the world, and one attracts only a certain number of events. It is good just to have a look at them and describe them, remembering they are only events.

X: Does one look at the pleasurable events as well as the unpleasurable?

MRS. POGSON: Yes. But they are not as important to work on because they usually take less force. But a pleasurable event might be the swing of the pendulum starting.

August 11, 1959

MRS. POGSON: What I want is to awaken everybody to the recognition of events, and I hope that the people going away have taken this new thinking about events with them. Most events are people. If you can see an event as one in a series which has happened many times before, you are almost ready to take a photograph of yourself

---

[6]*In Search of the Miraculous*, p. 380.

in action. Then next time the event comes you may be able to stop your reaction to it. In fact, you almost freeze and cannot go on with it. But usually a person is wound up by an event like a clock-work.

Time and Memory

Mrs. Pogson: I want to talk about memory and time. (See diagram 16.)

[The chapter "Time in the Invisible Worlds," pp. 48ff in *The Theory of Eternal Life* by Rodney Collin, was read.]

> Now Plato, in the *Politicus* myth, seemed to develop the idea of time running alternately backwards and forwards as referring to different ages of the larger cosmos of the earth. But at the same time he indicated that this principle must refer to all cosmoses, including the microcosm of man. For this was the way God arranged his creation— first, the winding of a spring by a higher agency, then the running of the clock-work by mechanical laws.[7]

Mrs. Pogson: Do you understand this? A law like this must be true in every cosmos, on every scale. In the ancient Indian religion all creation is described as a breathing out, a big breath in which all worlds are born on different levels. But there cannot be a breathing out forever. At a certain time everything will be drawn in. Rodney Collin is applying this principle everywhere. He applies it to our memory. In the invisible worlds our memory goes backward, whereas our lives go forward.

All modern inventions are representations of inner processes in the invisible worlds. A tape-recorder, for example, unwinds much faster than it winds up. So we seem to live our lives slowly. At death we see our lives, which are still there wound round us, and we see them much faster and more intensely.

Rodney Collin goes on to play with the idea of what time would be like if it went backward. He relates it to this diagram. The two circles look like a tape-recorder. In the cellular world, time goes forward, whereas in the invisible world time goes the other way. It is suggested that this also happens in dreams. So in the invisible

---

[7]*The Theory of Eternal Life*, p. 50.

world, where there is a reversal of our usual conception of time, *man sees himself as the cause of his life.*

[The reading was continued.]

MRS. POGSON: In a moment of self-remembering it is one's experience that time does not exist. The "long body" is all one's consciousness seen as one: how one's life would appear to a higher power, on a higher level of being. What will be left at the end will be our relation to events, how we have taken our lives. This is our thread. After we come into the Work, we recognize and separate from events so the thread becomes different. A being at the highest level of consciousness, that of "Real I," can be aware of the whole life as a solid. Can you now see how important it is to raise our level of consciousness? As long as we are in life, in the events, in time, we are confused and we do not know what to do. It is only when the consciousness is raised that our lives can be seen as a whole. It is only "Real I" in us

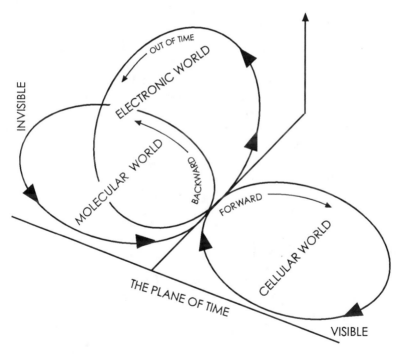

Diagram 16. Dimensions of Time.

that can see our lives as a whole. But we don't have contact with "Real I" until the door to the higher centers is opened. The only thing we can do, then, is to ask for a vision from this higher level.

The consciousness of "Real I" cannot take notice of the mechanical reactions of outer man. Beings on this higher plane go on existing—we cannot visualize this—and they may try to contact us at times if we are more awake or look up. If the person is asleep, the higher being just goes on waiting. This happens life after life. This is why self-remembering is the most important thing in the Work: when we are self-remembering is the only time when we can be reached. Only then can you see how you usually go along in time, from moment to moment. . . .

Let us talk about memory. We will read from Rodney Collin's *Theory of Celestial Influence*.

> Ordinary memory is an impulse which travels round the circle of man's life *only in the direction of time*. It arises from a moment of greater consciousness; if there is no consciousness no memory is created. Memory is the trace of potential self-remembering.
>
> Our ordinary sensation of living is, as it were, a point of slight warmth passing forward round the circle. But suppose a moment of consciousness, say at the age of fifteen. At this point the wire becomes hot. Heat impulses pass along the wire in both directions from this point. But naturally to a perception passing forward along the wire from the point in question, as we are accustomed to move in time, they will always appear to come from *behind*, that is, from the past. The conduction of heat or memory backwards, that is, towards an earlier age, will be unknown to us because of our method of perception. And again, the further we get away from the moment of consciousness, the heated point, the fainter will the impulses appear. Memory, as we all know, will gradually fade.
>
> At the same time, though memory of conscious moments does show a tendency to fade, it is important to understand that this fading does not follow from the passage of time. Our chief illusion about memory is that it decays with time, like clothes or buildings. This is not so. It

decays from lack of nourishment. Memory is generated
by consciousness, and it must be nourished by consciousness, that is, it must be nourished consciously.[8]

MRS. POGSON: One can nourish memory by visiting it. It is as if you
had a room where special treasures are kept. If you do not visit the
room, you forget what is there. You must bring out the jewels and
wear them. Certain efforts are required for this. If you don't want to
forget things, you can remember, because there is then desire.

> . . . the most usual reason for loss of memory is simply
> negligence and starvation. The ordinary man in ordinary
> circumstances makes no effort whatsoever to keep mem-
> ories alive, to feed them, recall them or pay attention to
> them. Unless they are so pleasant or painful that the emo-
> tion itself bites them into his consciousness, naturally
> they disappear. This is passive loss of memory.
>
> But there is also an active destruction of memory. This
> lies in replacing memory by imagination, or more sim-
> ply by lying. For example, I take a walk in the street,
> where I meet an acquaintance. At first the encounter
> may be quite clear in my mind—what I said, what he
> said, how he looked, and so on. But when I get home I
> recount the incident to my family. In doing so, I make
> the whole thing rather more amusing and dramatic than
> it actually was—I make my own remarks a little clev-
> erer, his a little more stupid; I hint something about his
> habits; maybe I introduce another character, or adapt
> the conversation to include a joke I heard yesterday.
> Afterwards I no longer remember the scene as it was,
> *but only as I recounted it.* Imagination and lying have
> destroyed memory.
>
> And if I spend my whole life in this way, then certainly
> after some years it will be quite impossible for me to dis-
> tinguish what has actually happened to me from what I
> wanted to happen, or feared would happen, or from
> what happened to others or what I merely read about. In

---

[8]*The Theory of Celestial Influence*, pp. 216, 217.

this way memory is actively destroyed. The difference lies in the fact that while memory lost by negligence still lies intact, though buried, and with hard work may be recovered, memory destroyed by lying is permanently damaged, if not annihilated altogether.

Yet . . . free circulation of memory throughout the long body of man's life is necessary for health and growth of Essence. . . . In the temporal sequence of life. Those years, months, incidents or relationships which we do not wish to remember begin to fester for lack of understanding. A blockage forms, a 'complex' develops, and without our recognising what is happening, the whole present may become poisoned *by that which we will not remember*.[9]

MRS. POGSON: This is why we go back over our day, recording and reconstructing it and so seeing what really happened. This exercise is taught in esoteric schools, the point of it being that we can record the truth now, and so work on and change our lives, rather than being shocked by the revelation of our lives as a whole at death. What we see at death, when our lives are shown us, will not be what we remember unless we work on them now. Just as one example, the negative part of the emotional center has a long memory, especially the inner part, but it is a most inaccurate one.

X: Do different centers have different memories?

MRS. POGSON: Yes. The outer part of the emotional center distorts. You can have a literal memory in the outer part of the intellectual center which can connect you with the ideas of the Work, but then the emotional center can interfere and Self-justify.

[Some modern psychologists] have claimed that the flow of memory may be restored even back into the time before birth. Patients under hypnosis have seemed to describe the sensations of the embryo in the womb. And one reported by Dr. Denys Kelsey even spoke of a state before that: "It was dark, yet filled with colours of inde-

---

[9]*The Theory of Celestial Influence*, pp. 217, 218.

scribable beauty; there was complete silence, yet the place was filled with heavenly music; it was still, yet everything was quivering."[10]

MRS. POGSON: Dr. Nicoll spoke of two memories. How we really took things is recorded, but we didn't know where.

X: Can one correct the inner record?

MRS. POGSON: Yes, you can, but it needs a certain conscious work. Herein is our hope. A good deal of the Work has to do with seeing the false memory and working on it, so that the memory is no longer so twisted.

X: We really know when we are not telling the truth.

MRS. POGSON: Yes, we have this double memory. . . . We are *taught* lying, but Essence is truthful. Lying slightly alters the truth to conform to something in the self.

X: Mechanical "I's" are inaccurate even when there is no reason for them to be.

MRS. POGSON: Yes, inaccuracy goes on all the time. We must see that whenever we speak, particularly when we tell stories, we lie.

X: Isn't it internal considering that leads us to lie and justify? We see and accept if left alone, but begin to lie when someone else challenges us.

MRS. POGSON: Yes. This is why it is important to record conversations as they really happened, in order to take out the distortions. When you tell stories with yourself in the center, there is always an event waiting around the corner in the form of someone who was there and who tells a different version! But does even this change you? No. It just takes the force out of that story for the moment. Lying is called the destruction of memory, so that real memory is no longer accessible.

---

[10]*The Theory of Celestial Influence*, p. 218.

Experiment in Mindfulness
August 13, 1959

MRS. POGSON: People are always asking what the Work teaches about meditation. No meditation is possible unless one is able to give directed attention in the inner part of a center, where it is possible to turn an idea over. Contemplation can only be achieved in the highest part of oneself, when one's consciousness is in "Real I." Only here is vision possible. So think what you mean when you refer to "meditation."

X: I mean concentrating on something.

MRS. POGSON: That is the beginning.

X: I mean contemplation.

MRS. POGSON: But from where? From what place? Contemplation is only possible from the deepest place in yourself which can only be reached through the process of meditation. Then there is a space, and you can have a vision.

Two basic exercises were given to Admiral Shattock at a Burmese meditation center. One had to do with observing the movement of walking, the other the slight rising and falling of the abdomen that accompanied breathing. First the intention in the mind was to be observed and then the carrying of it out. These are two separate mental processes. These exercises were given to train the attention. It doesn't matter what you give your attention to.

X: Isn't it rather like learning a musical instrument? At first you do it with the intellectual center and then moving center takes over, which can do it much better?

MRS. POGSON: But this is not an exercise in moving center, it has another purpose. This is a perfectly straightforward exercise, within the reach of everyone. Yet, although the instructions are simple, it is very difficult to do. It is like the Work in this. Such exercises show us our helplessness. We have to learn, beginning on very small scale, to move about in ourselves. They show that we cannot "do," since we cannot choose where we will be in ourselves.

X: Attempting something like this one sees the resistances and the great inertia. Something in one asks, "What's the point of it?"

X: It is impossible to keep the attention on anything for any length of time.

MRS. POGSON: After a certain time in the Work this is the chief thing that is studied. Anything that gives us more control over the attention is like treasure. What would you tell your self-will that resists and asks what the point is? You have to see that attention is going to be of value in the Work.

X: We can't give attention because we are scattered in so many "I's."

MRS. POGSON: This is a way of gathering yourself together, of gaining force if it has been lost.

[There was a reading from *An Experiment in Mindfulness* by E. H. Shattock, pp. 38–45.]

MRS. POGSON: [referring to the fact that Admiral Shattock tried to alter one of the exercises] You see, the self-will still tries to choose what it will do.

Relationship to the Work
August 14, 1959

MRS. POGSON: I wonder how much you see of the principle of working here at Dorton? In connection with the subject of one's relationship to oneself, the relationship to the Work is very important. Do you see how important it is to protect the Work from small "I's"? If you practice this here, it is easier to protect the Work when you are in life. We speak of the Work at meetings; we make connections between the Work and plays we are reading; we read books with certain Work ideas in them. At all such times the Work is protected because we are doing this in the group, which is protected by the

canopy of the Work. It is possible in the group to gain more understanding. If people are drawn into an inner place in themselves, you
have a group of inner people rather than a group of outer ones.
When inner people are together they listen. There is an energy in the
ideas that are spoken of. Even with only slightly raised consciousness, it is possible to see something in a meeting, in the presence of
the Work. This has always been the method of the second line of the
Work. It is not a method where there is a lot of personal conversation. Personal conversation is the exception. Do you see why? I will
give an example.

One person asked about the meaning of a symbol before
lunch. Can you see why it couldn't be answered? Because a small
"I" had asked it, one which thought such a question could be
asked at any time. Had it been an "I" in the middle part of a center,
it would have wondered at the symbol. The symbol would be carried around for a long time and pondered on, and then, one day,
the answer would be given. I can remember carrying a symbol
about with me for a week and pondering on it. You can't ask about
this and that from a small "I." The Work has to be protected from
small "I's." Do you see that this is the principle? This is what Dr.
Nicoll did. He always got people together into a certain place
before saying anything serious. Questions can be from curiosity,
but they can become deeper. Then you are given the answer
inwardly or, if you are almost ready for it, I might give it to you.
Many questions are unnecessary. You have to ask the question at
the right time.

In personal conversations you cannot use the Work language.
Someone who is no longer here told another person that he was
identified. This is an outer "I" speaking that had heard the term and
used it. It was really a substitute for something like: "You are irrita-
ble!" Say that instead, if you must say something. The Work language is to enable us to understand. If you see someone is
identified—*just see it.* Be in an inner place, and perhaps the person
will be less identified.

[There was a reading of several passages about Zen Buddhism from
Buddhist Scriptures, a new translation by Edward Conze.]

MRS. POGSON: This has to do with Zen, where we find so many connections with the Work teaching.

Peopie these days have their heads boiling with thought and are ever turned outwards as if searching for something. They have forgotten how to still the heart and turn within for the inward vision.[11]

MRS. POGSON: Now in these passages the word "heart" is used for the emotional center. Both the unregenerate and the regenerate emotional center are mentioned.

In fact, they know the way of going forward, but not how to withdraw . . . By paying attention to how to withdraw, by turning within and reflecting, one can reach the inexhaustible treasure there.[12]

MRS. POGSON: Outer "I's" know only how to go forward, not how to withdraw.

One has sometimes heard that to practice meditation it is necessary to retire to a mountain away from society, or perhaps to bury oneself in some old temple, to discard humanity and become a so-called hermit. Of course, it may be that for the final training in seeing one's own nature and attaining enlightenment it would in some cases be necessary for a time, but this is not one's objective. Zen must be to use that power which grips the Zen meditation and to bring it directly to bear upon and vivify our present daily life.[13]

MRS. POGSON: The purpose is to use the power of attention in daily life. This is also the Work teaching.

Withdrawing into meditation, and then advancing and handling affairs—this advancing and withdrawing, movement and rest together, must be Zen.

The Taoist book 'Saikondan' says: 'The rest in rest is not the real rest; there can be rest even in movement.' An

---

[11]Edward Conze, *Buddhist Scriptures* (London: Penguin Books, 1943), p. 135. Reproduced by permission of Penquin Books, Ltd.
[12]Edward Conze, *Buddhist Scriptures*, pp. 135–136.
[13]Edward Conze, *Buddhist Scriptures*, p. 136.

ancient worthy says: 'Meditation in movement is a hundred, a thousand, a million times superior to meditation at rest.' In this way he teaches the importance of meditation in activity.[14]

MRS. POGSON: Do you connect this with self-remembering in the Work? We are taught to remember ourselves the moment *before* doing something important. Then we can go into it, and it won't entangle us. This is the Zen way of living. Christ was not in the mountain all the tune. He was able to be down among the people teaching them, because he was able to talk from the place of withdrawal in Himself.

The Sutra teaches that by the practice of meditation the lake of the heart becomes pure and calm; and when the lake of the ordinary man's heart becomes pure, it is the reflection of a Bodhisattva which appears within it . . . The world of light, of virtue, appears, and now our daily life has a changed meaning. In fact, for the first time our ordinary life becomes radiant with real meaning.[15]

MRS. POGSON: This is the room in oneself where there is stillness and where meaning can be received. Then he speaks of Buddhist instructions:

What was it that Buddha wished to teach? . . . He simply wished to show all living beings how to set in order body and mind . . . 'Think of not thinking of anything at all. How is one to think of not thinking of anything at all? Be without thoughts—this is the secret of meditation.' Being without thoughts is the object of Zen meditation; the control of body and mind is only a method of reaching it. . . . The living *Samadhi* of all the Buddhas is no other than that state of absolute absence of thoughts.[16]

MRS. POGSON: This is described in Admiral Shattock's book. Where would a person be in that state? In the deepest part of a center and beyond all thought, where there is a space that can

---

[14]Edward Conze, *Buddhist Scriptures*, p. 136.
[15]Edward Conze, *Buddhist Scriptures*, p. 137.
[16]Edward Conze, *Buddhist Scriptures*, p. 138.

receive from higher centers. This space is between the centers and higher centers.

> An ancient says: 'In Zen the important thing is to stop the course of the heart.' It means to stop the workings of our empirical consciousness, the mass of thoughts, ideas, and perceptions . . .

> Buddha was about to die. In the final teachings to his disciples, the last phrase of the warnings about mind and senses is: 'you must subjugate the mind'. This does not mean the Buddha mind or Buddha heart, but it means the egoistic heart of the ordinary man who employs his mind actively all the time. Was there ever any chameleon comparable to the human heart? Just now it was happy and laughing, but all at once it is sad, then in a rage about something or other; or it wants to eat, or to sleep, to praise or to slander . . . This is why in the Consciousness Only school of Buddhism, all changes are called transformations of consciousness.

> As to whether the heart in itself is good or bad, some say good and some say bad, and there was also a view among the ancients that it is neither. However that may be, what is clear is that our hearts from morning to evening in their ceaseless activity undergo thousands and millions of changes and transformations, good or bad.[17]

MRS. POGSON: This is Mr. Ouspensky's doctrine of "I's." This is what happens in us.

> Buddhism teaches that the human heart has two aspects. They are, the pure heart and the impure heart. But the heart in itself is not two; it is only classified in these two ways according to its workings. The pure heart is the pure heart of our own nature, our natural heart which is not a whit different from the Buddha heart.

> Opposed to this is the impure heart which gives us no peace from morning till night, the egoistic heart of illu-

[17]Edward Conze, *Buddhist Scriptures*, pp. 139–140.

sions, the passion-ridden heart. Because the selfish pas-
sionate heart is not natural, we are always affiliated with
sufferings; endlessly this heart, absolutely careless, leads
men astray.[18]

MRS. POGSON: Isn't it so? Isn't our emotional center called the "rogue
elephant" that cannot be controlled? That goes its own way?

Fundamentally our true heart, our true nature, is pure
and infinite, like the moon clear in the blue sky. At some
distant time past our knowing, it was tainted by passion
and became the impure heart, something not our real
selves but which came afterwards.[19]

MRS. POGSON: This is what the Work teaches: that Essence was born
pure.

But this which came afterwards becomes predominant
and sets at naught the true heart, just as the concubine
sets at naught the real wife . . . Just in this way we entrust
ourselves to the operations of the deluded and passion-
ridden heart, so that the real master, the Buddha heart,
cannot even show its face. The thoughts of the impure
heart are topsy-turvy, for it sees reality as upside-down.
The villains who act as chief contributors to the delusion
are what the World-honoured One called "the brigands of
the five senses."[20]

MRS. POGSON: We know it is through being turned to the senses that
all this has arisen. . . . Then he describes the method of cutting off
associations:

Now the delusions which are the impure heart come up
without ceasing. We should make these fancies, coming
one after another, the 'Koan' (theme) of our meditation.[21]

---

[18]Edward Conze, *Buddhist Scriptures*, pp. 140–141.
[19]Edward Conze, *Buddhist Scriptures*, p. 141.
[20]Edward Conze, *Buddhist Scriptures*, p. 141.
[21]Edward Conze, *Buddhist Scriptures*, p. 142.

MRS. POGSON: You begin by giving attention to one action. Then associations come. Well, give your attention to them. You are still giving attention. Let the association go on and give attention to it.

Now here we study one system that becomes our touchstone to all other systems. When you have the Work system complete in yourselves and are sure of the language, then you can study and relate it to other systems. But it is necessary always to name a system or tradition if you quote its language. It is necessary not to confuse the languages. Some people, when they first come into the Work, confuse the Christian terminology with the Work language. They must be kept separate. It is valuable to use parallels. Dr. Nicoll was interested in other systems. But you must always be sure of which language you are using. If you mix them up, it is a sign of a weak intelligence, and I'm not sure that anyone who mixes up the languages of different systems would be able to learn the Work system. *It is necessary to keep things clear and to discriminate.* Just realize that these are parallels which can be used for the purpose of illustration.

August 16, 1959

MRS. POGSON: We began by discussing outer man. We have to discover, first of all, our outermost man and the things of which we are most unconscious. Then we worked inward, discussing the middle parts of centers and the awakening of inner "I's," which can feel wonder. We tried listening and looking more from the middle parts of centers. Here is the place of reversal, of turning around. Then we talked about attention, its importance, and the methods of giving attention. Directed attention takes us into the inner parts of centers. Then we spoke about self-remembering. In this way we have gone through the center.

All this has to do with moving about in ourselves. Have you begun a little to have a taste of this? First you have to see that you cannot move about in yourselves. We have also seen the effort required to be in bigger "I's" and how, after one has been there, one so easily falls back into small "I's." Here at Dorton you can go into a different place in yourselves more easily because the force of the group makes this possible. But you can slip back because you have not created the opportunity yourself; you have not *chosen* to go into this place. But you can have a taste of what it is like. This is why directed attention is so important; because it comes *from you*, and enables you to control your stay in that place.

[There was a reading from *Psychological Commentaries*, "Observation of Attitude to the Work," Vol. V, pp. 1737–1738.]

> Now the Three Lines of Work, which are work on yourself, work in conjunction with others, and work for the Work itself, require three different attitudes. It is true that you can get something for yourself in each case, but your aim will not be only to get something for yourself in each case. If it is, you will probably get nothing. If you do not work with others, you do not see them in yourself and yourself in them. Lacking this indescribably important development of consciousness, you get a distorted view of your own value. Again, if you do nothing for the Work, it will not do anything for you. If we could work without expecting to get an immediate reward and losing any faith that we had in the Work if we do not get a reward, we would have gone a considerable way in making False Personality passive. It may strike some of you as extraordinary that a person should ever make effort unless a reward were given him. But here lies a mystery which I do not attempt to explain. . . . It is possible to make effort even although one does not expect a reward. There is such a thing as love of doing a thing for its own sake. There is such a thing as being free from making internal accounts and no longer looking at life with a jealous eye, asking where one comes in oneself, or how much one will make out of it. . . . To work for the necessity of working on yourself, from the understanding of its necessity in view of your gradual dawning consciousness of what you are really like, is not to work for immediate reward but to work from understanding that this is what you have to do with yourself, and this is the scheme, and this is why you are on this planet which is so far down in the Scale of Being.

MRS. POGSON: You see, we always have self-love on the left-hand side in the diagrams. Every time you want something for yourself—

except understanding—you are working from the wrong place. Dr. Nicoll suggests another possible attitude, and that is working from *necessity*. I am going to read to you from a talk given after the paper.

> DR. NICOLL: We do not usually do things except for reward. For instance, if I say to you, "How well you asked that question, and how you helped me," that is getting a reward, but supposing I just look at you in a certain way, then you will say, "I wonder why he does not praise me, I am always trying to do my best." We live very much on praise and blame. If you employ people do you not have to give them a word of praise?
>
> Now, there is such a thing as *gratification of your conceit,* and such a thing as going against your conceit, which has quite a different taste, quite a different happiness. . . . To work on oneself is to go against the gratification of one's conceit.
>
> About this inner and outer happiness. The gratification of your conceits gives you outer happiness, and going against your conceits gives you inner happiness—that is called work on yourself. To go against the gratification of your conceits would be to go against your mechanicalness, and to go against the satisfaction of your conceits would be work.[22]

MRS. POGSON: You can't bring yourself down to be the same as everybody else. This is what he was always saying. You just can't bring yourself down to be an ordinary person. Yet this is the only place to start from.

> DR. NICOLL: You think that making effort is just like: "We must roll up our sleeves and get the washing up done."

MRS. POGSON: Now this is something simple. Can you see why this is true? It is a feeling of *doing.* His feeling of "I" is here. "It would be

---

[22]These quotations are from unpublished notes of a meeting at Great Amwell House on August 16th, 1953.

work not to do that." You don't actively gather people together to go down to the site: "Come along!" If you did you would be feeling yourself through this.

> DR. NICOLL: We do not understand where the Work lies. . . . We take a very stereotyped view of the Work, and think that rolling up our sleeves, etc., is making effort, but it is showing off most of the time. You can tell from inner taste. A careful trap has been laid, and you fall right into it. What am I supposed to do—save you? Some of you are supposed to be able to steer yourselves a bit. Someone says about your friend Mr. Smith, "I cannot think what he sees in Mr. Smith; I suppose he knows best." You get very indignant. Is it easy to protect yourself against these things? But supposing you were sealed in the old Hermetic sense, you would be invulnerable to anything said against Mr. Smith. I am trying to show you where the Work lies.

MRS. POGSON: Instead of getting indignant, you'd just see that someone was being mechanical, criticizing Mr. Smith. Dr. Nicoll is talking about two kinds of happiness here. It's strange how the second kind of happiness can come to us when we've done nothing. After you've seen something it comes, maybe much later, and then you feel conjoined with the Work.

> DR. NICOLL: You have a map in your own psychological country and you will know that you should not go down that road because you know what will happen, so after a time you will avoid going down certain roads.

MRS. POGSON: But to do this, you will have to be able to move about a little in yourselves, so that you do not go into a certain place. There is always a direction in which you shouldn't go. Who has been able to do this? To see a chain of associations and then save himself or herself from going with it?

X: I can see—but still I go.

MRS. POGSON: Seeing is a beginning. At least there's a little pause.

DR. NICOLL: Some people think they have not much to do in this work, that there is no special task. But of course you have, you have chief feature for one thing; there is always something to work at. I think it becomes plain that there are some things that if you had started working on earlier, it would have been a good thing. I am speaking to those who know there is something wrong with them. . . . If we do some work on ourselves and have valuation for the Work (but not if we value ourselves more than the Work) the force that we create by our Work-effort will be preserved for us according to our valuation.

MRS. POGSON: But if our valuation is for ourselves, it won't be preserved. If anyone works for any kind of reward, he or she gets that reward. If he or she works for false personality, false personality gets it.

DR. NICOLL: If you work on yourself, you give force to others, not only to yourself. When people are not working, it is a very great drag on me and Mrs. Nicoll. But when anyone works on himself or herself, it gives force to everyone. That is why it is important to remember that. . .

One of the causes why the Work seems some distance from you is that you are resenting something. You make accounts about everything, some of you, very quickly. . . . Some of you even think it is good of you to be here. If you are going to *serve the Work* it is no use standing on your rights. . . . You have to have a big background for this Work, not a little mean background.

Paul has a good way of describing what we must do. He said: ". . . the inward man is renewed day by day" (II Corinthians, 4.16). We must renew the inner man, not the outer man. But if everything to do with my conceit of myself is so great that there is no room for anything else, I cannot take in that there is anything greater than myself, and I cannot take in that in comparison to myself this Work is so great that I am just nothing.

MRS. POGSON: Now these are some of Dr. Nicoll's words. They still hold good. What he is saying all the time is that you don't always see where the Work lies.

When we come into the Work, we say we want self-knowledge. So we set out on our adventure, and it is like going through the forest seeking treasure. But then when people pick up a precious stone, they don't want it. It looks uncut and perhaps dirty. They think this was not what they were looking for, yet it is what they want. So you should be very careful to know what you are seeking. You should formulate clearly what you want. The path to unity with yourself is through self-knowledge. *There is no other way.* You must be clear about this.

You have to discover what you trip over most. If you really ask to be shown, then you will be shown. If you see too many things, then you are only generally aware of these things, you do not really see. Do you understand the difference? If you see several things, you must decide what you want to work on most.

Tasks suggested in group work are not the same as your personal aims. When the group works on small weekly or fortnightly aims, people are able to help each other. Someone will observe something in particular which the others can learn from.

X: In formulating an aim should one make a small aim in order that it may lead you to realize what larger aim may be made?

MRS. POGSON: Yes. You must be sure you are in a deeper place in yourself when you make aim, so that you can really know what you want and make your aim from a place where there is valuation and memory of the Work. Small aims are included in the large aim.[23]

A Man's Relationship with Himself
August 8, 1960

MRS. POGSON: I think it would be good if at the end of this period people were able to develop some small skill in withdrawing their feeling of "I" from certain "I's" and putting it into a deeper place if necessary. You see, unless we are able to do this, we cannot be relied on in the Work. Can you see why? People who can be dragged down into negative emotions, self-pity, or justifying, or can be upset by a remark someone makes or by circumstances, cannot be relied on.

---

[23]For another discussion about aim and practical work cf. chapter 9, page 237.

You don't have a point in the Work until you are always able to come back to this place in yourselves. I think we all need to have this toy that doesn't topple over, but always returns to its own center of gravity.

Many of you have "I's" formed in Deputy Steward, but it is incomplete and once outer "I's" have taken your feeling of "I," it may be several days before you get back to this place in yourselves.

X: Does this have to do with sealing yourself from life?

MRS. POGSON: That comes later. First there are some "I's" and then later there is a place in yourself where you are inviolate.

X: This was where the gap comes in between knowing and willing the Work. There is not sufficient strength in the emotional center to get back to the place of the Work in oneself.

MRS. POGSON: Yes, that's the trouble with so many of you. Emotional center is not developed. So many of you can think about the Work and make good connections with it, but the emotional center won't cooperate.

X: Some people act more in the intellectual center, their center of gravity is more there. Are these people less prone to negative emotions?

MRS. POGSON: Not necessarily. If you have a good intellectual center, you may have to work on negative emotions and on developing "I's" in inner parts; that is the Work for you.

X: In that way you develop the right part of the emotional center?

MRS. POGSON: Yes, because you can't work on the emotional center unless you want to and develop the "I's" in it that want to work; so in this way will is developed toward the Work.

But this is only descriptive of one type of person whose center of gravity is in the intellectual center. With another type of person, whose center of gravity is in the emotional center, there may be some "I's" already formed in the middle part of the center, but not developed enough. Their emotional center is then inadequate.

X: And how does that person do the Work?

MRS. POGSON: It is always the same answer which Dr. Nicoll gives: By doing the Work! And the same answer is given to the question of how to form the second body, the emotional body: Do the Work. The second body is in chaos in most people, although the mental body may be partly organized. Doesn't this seem a strange answer?

X: The question is how to want the Work more.

MRS. POGSON: By doing it. I have been looking back to see what Dr. Nicoll was talking about on roughly this same day. In 1952, he was talking about self-love and the inner man—a conversation we've read at Dorton before, because it always fits in during August. In 1953, he was talking about the growth of Essence. This applies to what we are talking about.

[Passages were read from *Psychological Commentaries*, "Growth of Essence," Vol. V, pp. 1735, 1736.]

> The Work moves inwards. It falls first on the outer psychology, on the Outer Man in yourself. If it is received and appreciated, its action is to penetrate inwards to the Inner Man and transform him. When you will not abstain from stealing, say, because you fear being found out, but because you dislike stealing. . . . At each inward movement of the Work—at each deepening of the Work in your understanding—it is as if you had to begin again. You become aware that you had got things wrong—the Work and yourself—and mixed it up with this amazing conceit common to all of us sub-humans. The stages of the Work are as if at intervals you had to be put under another—and sterner—master, as if you had moved up from one form at school to another where things were no longer play but beginning to be real. . . .
>
> Now the Work goes in stages or levels—layer by layer. It certainly is difficult to take the Work more deeply into oneself without a great deal of perplexity and thought and sincerity. It is just here that people stick. They begin to see that they have been doing the Work from self-love

and not from love of the Work. And unless they are capable of great honesty with themselves they may not be able to find deeper reasons and emotions for continuing to work on themselves. . . . However, everything that you have done genuinely as far as you can will come to help you in these moments of temptation which are bound to occur when the necessity of deepening your understanding of the Work is encountered. This is where Work-memory especially comes in. *'I's that wish the Work in you together form your Work-Will, whereas 'I's that do not wish to work form your Life-Will.*

MRS. POGSON: These are in the emotional center—the "I's" that have to be developed. Which "I's" get the most time? If it's the life "I's" in you, then they're the Stronger.

X: In a later stage would the Work "I's" manage the life "I's"?

MRS. POGSON: Yes, you walk on Earth as if in Heaven.

X: It's sometimes easier to be alone.

MRS. POGSON: There mustn't be this distinction between life and the Work. The idea is that people establish the system in themselves, and they then live in life from the Work. It may seem much nicer, perhaps, to be alone at home without interruptions, as long as one isn't going through some accounts! But it is not so profitable.

X: If the Work Will were strongly formed in us, we shouldn't have to stop and think about what to do.

MRS. POGSON: No, but there is a long period in which there is a series of choices. It is important that the day become a series of choices, for this is the friction.

X: If one were conscious there would no longer be a choice.

MRS. POGSON: No—that's what I said. After a time there would not need to be this choice.

Some 'I's are on the wrong side. Never make the mistake of thinking that only stupid 'I's can be Work-'I's. We are told to be wise as serpents and harmless as doves.[24]

MRS. POGSON: You see, some of your cleverest "I's" are on the other side. Do you see what would happen if they were drawn onto the side of the Work? Now, they are in the wrong place, but you don't know this until you've observed it. Have a look at your more clever "I's" and see what they're working for.

If you never really think about this Work, of course, nothing is possible. You must remember also that what is thought about but is not in your will is not yet real in you, because it leads to no action, and therefore cannot affect Essence.[25]

MRS. POGSON: Many things you think about but don't yet will.

X: A person who feels himself through the emotional center has first of all to work on the intellectual center?

MRS. POGSON: The work in this system begins in the intellectual center, but valuation is in the emotional center. The two things have to go on together. One sometimes finds that a person has studied the whole system but has not yet begun to work on his or her emotions.

X: What does it mean—number two man?

MRS. POGSON: A number two man approaches life through like and dislike. He (or she) may have a good valuation of the Work and valuable "I's" in the middle parts. If your center of gravity is in the emotional center, what you dislike may arouse you and what you like excite you, and you are easily upset.

X: Is it the same as wanting?

---

[24]*Psychological Commentaries*, Vol. V, p. 1736.
[25]*Psychological Commentaries*, Vol. V, p. 1736.

MRS. POGSON: Yes, small desires. But there is no use comparing people with centers of gravity in different centers. They are both equally bad, because they are both mechanical, and they both have difficulties to work on.

X: Isn't it easier for an emotional person at first?

MRS. POGSON: It is easier for an intellectual person at first because he or she can take in the ideas of the Work more easily.

X: But he or she has difficulty in interpreting these ideas to the emotional center.

The Absolute
August 10, 1960

Absolute	DO	1	
All Possible Worlds	SI	3	
Our Galaxy (Milky Way)	LA	6	
Our Sun	SOL	12	Do
Planets	FA	24	Si
	Fa Sol La		
Earth	MI	48	Mi
Moon	RE	96	Re

[The First section on "*The Absolute*," from *The Theory of Celestial Influence*, by Rodney Collin was read.]

Philosophically, man can suppose an Absolute. Such an Absolute would include all possible dimensions both of time and space. That is to say:

It would include not only the whole universe which man can perceive or imagine, but all other such universes which may lie beyond the power of his perception.

It would include not only the present moment of all such universes, but also their past and their future, whatever past and future may mean on their scale.

It would include not only everything actualised in all the past, present and future of all universes, but also everything that potentially could be actualised in them.

It would include not only all possibilities for all existing universes, but also all potential universes, even though they do not exist, nor ever have.

Such a conception is philosophical for us. Logically it must be like that, but our mind is unable to come to grips with the formula or make any sense of it.[26]

MRS. POGSON: Did you hear what was read? It's difficult to talk about the Absolute. It is what contains everything within itself, the source of the Ray of Creation. If you want to have some conception of this, you have to stretch your mind very much. All religions have their own ways of describing the Absolute. The Absolute is the creator and source of everything, the first cause: this is the principle of creation, that *everything created is within the Creator*. We can understand the principle by looking at ourselves. What do people create— a painting or something? The idea comes first, doesn't it, containing all that is created.

We cannot communicate with the Absolute, nor can we give it any personal attributes. Think of the cells in your body which are much lower in scale than man: can you have any communication with a cell in your body? Not in any direct way. (Although, with self-remembering, a kind of communication from Higher to lower is established, for in self-remembering the chemistry of every cell is in some way altered. So something can be received by the cell from a higher level, and this must be true of everything in creation even though what is received may not be understood by the lower.) On the next level are the three forces of creation. Now, can we communicate with a galaxy? You can lift up your heart to it in a way. If you are sensitive to your relationship to it, something is communicated, but it can be nothing personal. You are within the galaxy. (I don't know if a cell could feel aware that it is within a human being.) Then we come to the solar system. We have to remember that man doesn't appear in the Ray of Creation. We have to understand that the Ray is a descending octave, as all creative octaves are. In the descending ray, the details are further and farther away from the source.

---

[26]*The Theory of Celestial Influence*, p. 1.

We are part of the film of life which was created on earth to link Earth and the Sun. The link is firstly by way of nature. What effect could the Sun have on a hard crust, if Earth had remained a hard crust? It could have none. So the film of life was created which contains something which can receive from the Sun. The Sun sends heat, and organic life grows up toward it.

X: Does the idea of a personal God come in here, in the relation of man to the Sun?

MRS. POGSON: Yes, and this is something we can begin to understand. In the primitive religions, the Sun was often made the symbol of God.

X: Does a kind of personal-ness come in here?

MRS. POGSON: Yes, it does—in the side ray which was created by the sun, and in the creation of man with his double destiny. For we see how man can grow up toward the Sun in an inner way, corresponding to the way in which nature grows upward to the Sun. The whole flower is within the seed. We have seen how it can be photographed in the seed, and so also what we might become is contained in the seed which was sown on Earth.

X: How do we connect psychologically with this?

MRS. POGSON: All creation has inner bodies. There is such a thing as the spiritual sun in and behind the physical Sun, and all great religions know this.

Now, each individual has his or her own creator like the Sun, on the level of the Sun, called sometimes the "solar angel" or God. . . . Everything has its long body. We are contained in the long body of the Sun, we are within the being of the Sun, as is also the whole solar system. We know that all the planets are different organs in the being of the Sun. But here again there cannot be any communication—only worship. But the spark is sown on Earth which can become a complete man, and if it grows, it will return to its creator. Here is the God with whom we can communicate, called in this teaching "Real I." We are within this being. If we could only remember this! So we come down to our personal scale, to something we can understand. From the divine intelligence on the level of the Sun come the divine sparks, so that people can grow as individuals. We are sown, if you like, as in the parable of the sower; and sometimes there is increase and return to the place of origin. There are two influences: the downward influence of nature which is all right for living on this planet, and under which we eat and drink and multiply; and then the influence that can draw us upward.

Then comes the question of prayer. In prayer we can think of the Creator of the whole, but we cannot be personal, except to express gratitude and worship. But on another level, in relation to what is God for us, we *can* be personal.

[Mrs. Pogson then read from *The Fourth Way* what Mr. Ouspensky has to say about prayer.]

> Q. One cannot help thinking that the Absolute is one name for God.
>
> A. [Mr. Ouspensky]: "No, you are quite wrong. The Absolute is the principle that lies in the beginning of things and behind everything. I never connected the Absolute with God in the religious sense. God in religion can do many things for you, but the Absolute can do nothing for you (p. 404).

MRS. POGSON: The Absolute can do nothing for you, can it? It's the origin of the principle of creation, with all its laws which are part of the principle.

[Mrs. Pogson then went on to read what Mr. Ouspensky has to say about the Lord's Prayer, for example that it is divided into three times three, and about the meaning of some of the petitions. (See *The Fourth Way*, p. 408ff.)]

MRS. POGSON: What do "Our Father" and "Heaven" mean according to the Work? Our Father is "Real I" for us and heaven is the higher level for us, the level of Conscious Humanity, of Greater Mind. And it is possible to communicate with greater minds if we raise our consciousness to that level above us. We begin to see that we can do nothing, but that something can be done on a higher level. Laws Operating from a higher onto a lower level are called miracles.

The word "our" in the Lord's Prayer is used because it is a prayer for all of us to pray together.

"Thy Kingdom come." This is praying for a higher will to be done on Earth. There are two scales here. It is possible to think of the higher will being done through humanity—which we say is not possible as things are now because humanity is not conscious enough. But then there is also the scale on which the will of God can be done on the Earth of each person; Earth being "mechanical man," and God being one's "Real I." That is why this teaching is designed to make it possible for us to cleanse our centers and create second and third bodies, the emotional and mental bodies, to do the will of God instead of being only a hindrance.

X: We have to learn to receive it.

MRS. POGSON: Hear and receive it. How much work is necessary here, preparing for this! "Daily bread" refers to the higher energy which belongs to us and which will make it possible to awaken. Mr. Ouspensky says we can't really forgive at our level until we have will. But we can cancel through *metanoia*.

X: Can you interpret "lead us not into temptation"?

MRS. POGSON: We have to have trials in order to grow. I take the two petitions together as meaning: "Lead us not into temptation *except* we be delivered from evil."

X: Could it mean "Do not give us trials greater than we can bear"?

MRS. POGSON: It's the same thing really. Prayer must be directed to the highest level of oneself before anything can happen. We pray for contact with this level in us, and then we can possibly contact someone else. Possibly we could reach "Real I" in another person.

X: It gives real feeling to think that there are greater minds who once were mortal and are waiting for us to develop.

MRS. POGSON: Yes, and what is their work? To raise other people. It is easier for them to contact groups. A few individuals are sensitive, such as poets and others, and can receive; but many people working together make a greater focus to receive these influences from Conscious Humanity. The thinking of a group is a different kind of thinking, it thinks together; otherwise there are only flashes from Conscious Humanity. This is the reason for united prayer in churches.

For the next time: *remember to listen*—to anything, to people, to sounds, to birds, and inwardly too.

August 11, 1960

MRS. POGSON: Let us think a little further about the Sun octave and the planets. Do you see the relation of good and evil to the Ray of Creation? In the Work, good is what awakens us and evil puts us to sleep. Now, any influence coming downward is what brings things outward into manifestation; but it is only evil if you no longer want to be under its influence. To go downward is to go outward into creation, to multiply. This is good for the Ray and good for the Earth; so don't think of good and evil in the old way, but only in this connection. For us, anything that helps us to ascend the Sun octave is good for us, although it might appear evil from the old acquired conscience. Can anyone think of an example?

X: Losing one's money?

MRS. POGSON: Yes, one might have to lose one's money if one were identified with it. When one is in the Work, one does lose things one is identified with; I've found that.

X: *Failures* might be considered bad from the life point of view, yet good for the Work.

MRS. POGSON: Yes. Now, a reconciling force is needed to relate us to the ascending octave. And it is said that Christ is this relating force.

X: Can you say more about the idea of being sown on Earth?

MRS. POGSON: Yes—we used as illustration the parable of the sower, and some of the seed grows and some does not.

X: The Ray is an environment for man rather than part of man?

MRS. POGSON: We have to be aware of where man is in the Ray of Creation: he is within the solar system, within the milky way.

X: He is not a stage but part of the being of all creation? That is what I meant.

MRS. POGSON: Yes. And the mystery of this lies in the relationship of the cosmos and in the possibility of moving from one cosmos to another. Think, for instance, of the cosmos of man, and then of the cosmos of the Sun, and then of the cell, and what a difference there is between the cosmos of man and the cosmos of the Sun, and then between the cosmos of the cell and the cosmos of man. You would think it impossible for the two to be related at all.

X: Are the multiple cosmos' physical?

MRS. POGSON: Each cosmos has a visible and an invisible part. It's so simple. Some of the sex cells which are within a man can develop into a man, which is another cosmos; and so a man (the species) also can develop and become part of Conscious Humanity. Out of millions, one or two cells may develop and become a man. And if a man ascends the side octave think how far that cell has come!
I'll remind you of a kind of gap which Mr. Ouspensky speaks about in *In Search of the Miraculous*. There is the Way; but before one is really on the Way, there is a stairway to climb. This is a stairway between life and the way.

[The passage from *In Search of the Miraculous* relating to this was read (pp. 201–202).]

X: Does one have to become "balanced man" first?

MRS. POGSON: In a sense, but a person may have some gaps and imperfections and still be on the Way. I think he'd have to have seen his chief feature. But we can't be specific. Many old tales and fairy stories represent these truths about the Way.

X: Would Steward have to be operating before one was on the Way?

MRS. POGSON: Yes. When you have Steward operating, then you also have Deputy Steward formed in you, a group of "I's" through which Steward can act. Then you can receive instructions from within.

X: Is Steward the same as real conscience?

MRS. POGSON: They are connected. One might say that real conscience has to be operating before Steward can give instructions.

There's something else. At the level of "Real I," the time-body can be seen as one thing; just as when we look at things below us in scale, we see them as one. So "Real I," at that level, can see our life as a whole. There is one moment at death when we can see our lives as a whole.

Coming back to the question of cosmos—or would you rather call it worlds on certain scales?—can you direct your imagination to something small, for example, to the cosmos of cells? They only live a few days of our time; and yet, although their lifetime is different, there is the mystery that all lifetimes are the same. There is really only one lifetime, which in each corresponds to the world to which it belongs. Then the cells have, in their own world, their own hierarchy: there are the brain cells, which are immortal on their scale, having the lifetime of a person, and the sex cells, which have another possibility; and then the ordinary cells which have the lifetime of their own cosmos. Then there is the higher cosmos of stars, and the cosmos of electrons. But can we really think about this?

X: There is emptiness as well—so Mr. Reyner said.

MRS. POGSON: Yes, Mr. Reyner reminded us of the empty spaces within the atom; and this is true within the solar system between the planets. It seems to be true on every scale. And there seems to be something in the empty spaces which makes the link possible. But we get on better if we direct our imagination upward instead of downward in scale.

CHAPTER 9

NUTLEY TERRACE, MICHAELMAS

Psychological Exercises
August 18, 1959

MRS. POGSON: Most of the people here were at Dorton, where all these ideas come alive. What could you say about Dorton?

X: The thing that became clearest to me this time was the fact that we must see the opposites in ourselves. You can't say anything about a tangible self because you see an opposite at the same time. It's very concentrated psychological work at Dorton, and it takes a long time after Dorton to digest and assimilate the self-knowledge one gains at this period.

X: One thing that became more real to me at Dorton was the importance of being in deeper "I's," and being able to move about in oneself.

X: I think at Dorton one can accept oneself more easily because one is more transparent to others.

X: During the time at Dorton I realized how difficult it was even there to stay in deeper "I's." I saw how weak I was.

MRS. POGSON: You see, it's because people haven't practiced this moving about in themselves. One has gone with outer "I's" for so long. It's like trying to get someone in a club out of the armchair he's always sat in. So with the "I's": it requires long work to undermine them.

X: Is it attitudes that keep us from turning around?

MRS. POGSON: Habitual attitudes. And we don't see the need to turn. Many of these small "I's" are "I's" that object. Inner talking is going on all the time. We have an attitude that everything should be perfect and our lives should run smoothly. If anything falls below this standard of perfection, we object to it. We expect people to be patient, respectful, civil, understanding, grateful, and so on. When they are not, these small "I's" object. But the Work doesn't say that life should run smoothly. A different attitude, from the Work, would change all this objecting.

X: When a day begins badly, if we don't do something about it right away, it will continue that way. And then we justify by saying it's that kind of day.

MRS. POGSON: Dr. Nicoll told us how we can conjoin with a day. If we try to relate to a day thinking it is our enemy, then there is no relationship. But if one takes the day from another place in oneself, one can go through it without being affected by it. It is good to see that you are going through the day and not being dragged through it, as if you were being dragged through a hedge backwards! You have your knife and can cut a way through the day, as the prince did in Sleeping Beauty.

MRS. POGSON: Only very strong people can do the Work. It can become dangerous for people who are not strong—but mercifully these people usually leave early, before they are really in the Work. You are usually shown only gradually what you have to work on, no more than you can bear. What is the definition of a strong and a weak person?

X: You once referred to a strong person as being like water (cf. p. 140).

MRS. POGSON: Yes, a person has to be able to yield like water; you have to be able to yield in yourself to the power of the Work and not be brittle. A person with a strong false personality is brittle. *The strongest person is the one who is capable of great humility.* A Strong person is one who has Self-knowledge. Humility comes with self-knowledge.

There is a series of exercises taught in the Work in order to gain agility in being conscious in more than one part of oneself simultaneously. I have been thinking recently about the fact that the children of Mammon have more skill than the children of Light in this. People are able to do many things at once for life reasons. Yet we in the Work need this skill. We have to be able to work in different parts of ourselves at the same time, to be in a deeper part of ourselves and still let the outer "I's" carry on with what they are doing. Eventually we have to have this double consciousness.

How many of you are able to conduct two or more conversations at the same time, or dictate two letters? It is possible to keep two clear trains of thought going at the same time. People become wonderfully capable in life of being conscious in several "I's" at the same time, even though they are only small "I's." Dr. Nicoll used to say it was a sign of under-development to be able to do only one thing at a time. I'd like you to try something like this as an exercise. You see, psychologically we are coming to it.

X: gave a good example of it when she said she was able to go on thinking about the meeting while she was reading a detective story. Dr. Nicoll used to work with a detective story in front of him. And I have worked in this way. It goes better if your attention in front is a little engaged. This is a kind of in-between stage. When you are deeply thinking, you don't need this. How many people do you think Dr. Nicoll could talk to at once? We could all be around him in a group, and he would be carrying on many conversations at the same time, although we didn't realize it.

X: I get muddled and tired when I try to do that.

MRS. POGSON: When the conversations are all separate, nothing is tiring. They are only tiring if they overlap. Something should be there, on guard, watching while your conversation is going on. Then you no longer identify.

X: Would you explain "inner stop"? Sometimes one is reading and then suddenly realizes that one has not taken anything in but has gone off with some association.

MRS. POGSON: When you see the train of thought which has taken you off, you say STOP. And it does stop for a moment. But then it comes again. And you say STOP again. Then maybe next time you don't go so far away. But you have to keep bringing your attention back. Saying STOP gives you a space, but you can't stay thinking of nothing. If you become interested in this and try to stop associations, in time they stay further back.

X: With regard to this exercise, do you mean us to give attention to two different things on the same level, or on two different levels?

MRS. POGSON: No, give attention on two different levels. I have told you how Dr. Nicoll was thinking out his paper for the week while reading a detective story.

Pride and Humility
September 22, 1959

MRS. POGSON: There is an opportunity for studying self-love in the film, *The Nun's Story*. What was her chief feature?

X: Pride. I saw myself in her.

MRS. POGSON: There are many kinds of pride. She was certain she knew what was right, she was set on doing everything in her own way. It was her way of being special. She couldn't be an ordinary nun. This is what we always come back to. Later, when you have learned something, you can be used. But you can't choose your own kind of specialness.

X: Do we all feel unique in some way?

MRS. POGSON: This is a double kind of thing. Essence knows it's unique, but it doesn't feel it's better than other people. But we want to be special for the wrong things.

We gather from this story that the nun was not helped psychologically to see these two things in herself as we in the Work are taught the difference between the inner and the outer. She seemed to have to wrestle with things alone. She was asked to fail her examinations on purpose in order to learn humility. But that is not the way you learn humility. Had she done so—unless she were to have done it from herself and not because someone else had asked her to—it would have led not to humility but to spiritual pride. I wonder if anyone knows how humility comes? It comes through seeing the truth about yourself and through a recognition of scale. . . . The thing is to love something higher, then everything is rightly arranged for you.

We thought about this in seeing the film: that what the nun found difficult was having to break off what she was doing five times a day for prayers. In the Work this wouldn't happen because everything is inner. We do not need to break off what we are doing; we can go on with what we are doing and still, in another part of ourselves, think of the Work. This is inner work; it is double consciousness again. Nothing is jarring, nothing is breaking off. But these mechanical aids—the Angelus and other forms—must be there too.

X: Does being with others, in church for example, give more force?

MRS. POGSON: In the Work you have the group within you.

X: In the beginning in the Work, we set aside a specific time for working, reading *The Commentaries*, and so on. Then interruptions come and, because we are identified with this set time, we are very annoyed. Then slowly we learn that the Work has to go on inside us all the time, not at set moments of the day.

MRS. POGSON: Yes. You can use these interruptions for working. But the other person must not say: "Where have you gone?" This is using the Work intelligently.

In *The Nun's Story*, it is supreme self-love, obeying the commands of chief feature, that takes her out of the community. This is the place of greatest separateness, of feeling special or different from others. Where you feel the same as other people, you are safe. In Essence there is no feeling of difference. Try to see where you feel separate and begin to work there.

X: As personality has to feel special and better than others, it would help to do the things you can't do well.

MRS. POGSON: I found it very restful to do something I couldn't do at all—for example, plastering or lathing at Tyeponds. It was almost an essential feeling. In such things one can rest.

The Tea-Man and the Ruffian
October 6, 1959

MRS. POGSON: I want to read a Japanese story to you, called "The Tea-Man and the Ruffian." During the past year we have talked a lot about not being distracted by associations: in thinking, feeling, seeing, or hearing. A swordsman is also trained to wield a sword without any distracting thoughts about winning or losing, or the quality of his sword. This is a good image. The sword is like the mind. Can you see how every time the swordsman has any personal thought about whether he will win or die he is weakened? And the swordsman fighting an adversary represents someone whose mind is trained or not trained enough. When the mind is trained, something else can come through and use the sword, and you do not interfere.

> The story concerns a tea-man, challenged by a Samurai ruffian to a sword duel. The tea-man takes his dilemma to his master, who instead of counselling him, asks him to make tea. After sharing with his master in the tea ceremony, the tea-man goes to meet his adversary. But on taking a close look at his intended victim, the Samurai declines the fight.

MRS. POGSON: Do you see how wise the master was when he asked the tea-man to make him a cup of tea? By the time he had made the tea he was a different kind of man through having got into attention. He was then a man who could contain himself. This was all the master could do for him. The tea-man, by giving his attention to the one thing he knew how to do, got into a deeper place in himself so that his superficial manifestations disappeared and he appeared a different man to the samurai.

Dr. Nicoll did the same thing with us. Suppose some person went into his room identified with some so-called problem (and people were always coming down to see him on the weekends, all agog and tense and bursting to pour out the details) Dr. Nicoll would say: "We are making this birdbath outside the window." And then he would describe the plan of it and maybe ask the person to get a hammer and nails and come and help him. If it wasn't a birdbath, it would be something else. It might be something to do with wine, or a new book, or a painting that he wanted to consult the person about. People might be asked to frame a picture or mend something, or there might be something to do in the garden. Do you see the technique in this? In the state of being identified people cannot listen, they only want to talk. The only thing to do is to draw the person out of these "I's" by arousing interest in something, by attracting attention elsewhere, by asking the person to do something. And after a while the person would be talking about something else in a reasonable, interested way. Dr. Nicoll would bring the person into a quite different state, where the problem didn't seem the same any more. And he or she might even go home without having talked about the problem. For when he or she was no longer on the opposites, the event could be seen differently and the person could see what to do. So the tea-man, when it came to the time to fight, was able to be in a place where there was no fear.

X: The key to the story was his willingness to die.

MRS. POGSON: Yes. But he changed after he had been to the master, for then he was in an inner place where the fear of death did not exist. Can you see how this is with your inner enemy?

Life and Work
October 1, 1960

MRS. POGSON: You agreed to spend one day differently, with more of a sense of urgency than usual, and to be present. The day we decided on turned out to be sunny and beautifully still. We had been reading the commentary in which Dr. Nicoll says the day is the epitome of the life; the day is the lifetime in miniature. The year is, too. If we can spend one day more awake and remember our aim, it may be a way of transforming the life. If you have no sense of urgency about the day, then you will never have it. This is Mr. Gurdjieff's most striking message.

There is no need to do anything special, just to live the day differently. The way to live was well-expressed in a dream of one of the group. The dreamer was with a party of people in a ship on a lake or inland sea. People lived in the ship, and were allowed to go ashore, but when on shore, they were asked not to eat anything and not to go to sleep, but to return by nightfall. They could do as they liked as long as they didn't eat or sleep and returned at night. The ship is our real home, it is the innermost part of ourselves where we really belong, and can be present. Here we gain our nourishment and rest. As long as we are aboard ship, we are safe. We can go on shore, into life's events, but what happens is, we go to sleep and forget the ship. We become identified. The events become more important than the ship. The chief thing was that she shouldn't eat ashore, she shouldn't get nourishment from life things. It doesn't matter what you do as long as the outer man is not nourished. Nourishment on the ship is daily bread.

[Another parable about a ship and an island was read. It concerns a cast of actors who land on an island to rehearse a play (*Psychological Commentaries*, Vol. II, p. 74).]

MRS. POGSON: This is simply an allegorical representation of what happens in our lives; whatever we have to do in life is our part. Younger people say that they haven't yet found their part, but you have to have many small parts to play. Through the Work you find what is to be your real meaning, but meanwhile you have to accept any situation as your part. It may not be a permanent situation. People tend not to count what they are doing now, but they are gaining experience, it is all counted. When you look back, you see now how the small parts were important. People always want to go on to the next thing. Remember it is said that we always come into the Work at the right time. The influence of the Work doesn't want you to move immediately. Perhaps you will have journeys; there is always some snag at the start.

X: If one has a rôle that one doesn't believe in from a life point of view, how should one connect with doing it well, except from a life motive?

MRS. POGSON: Before, the rôle was probably playing you, but now you can see that this is just a part to play. People act on the stage all the better if they are not lost in their parts. You can do it as a Work task. This happens to businessmen in the Work. Their task is then to go with it until they are shown very clearly that the stage is over. To gain this experience is the purpose of our descent to this earth; this is shown in fairy stories and in the Gospels, treasure which is distilled experience. One *could* go out the same door by which one came in, go out unchanged.

At one time we were told to enjoy ourselves—one of the most difficult things. The dream of the ship applies here. If you are lost in this enjoyment it is like having food ashore. It is the taste of identification—not a good taste. If you could enjoy yourself and remember! You remember the next week when it is dull; when things are pleasant we are inclined to sleep. But the cards are dealt to us, it is all the same.

In the paper Dr. Nicoll says we should remember ourselves once a day. It is as if an actor on the stage forgets he is acting; you must remember just as much when you are enjoying your part as when you are not. You have to practice, then when you come to a part that is really difficult, you will remember. It is the difficult parts that give you the most reward. Keep this vision in mind, and you will never say: "Why does this happen to me?" Why does it? Perhaps because you attract it. It is the stage that your being has reached that decides on the scheme of your life. That is the deepest meaning of the statement, your being attracts your life. But false personality attracts things which don't belong to you.

Sometimes people we know move to a different place, and when they write it is always the same letter. Things are happening, but they are always the same. Now Work ideas are dynamic. Once this idea has gone into your heart, something can change, you have a basis from which to act. If you have something in your life which is very difficult, you have to look at it in more than one way. Have you attracted it? If not, perhaps Essence wants it for gaining experience. We have to keep on falling asleep, because we cannot yet stay awake. We just have to keep trying, then eventually we learn how.

August 15, 1960

X: If our being attracts our lives, how does this square with what we want?

MRS. POGSON: *What* wants? What wants a cup of tea? Praise—anybody want any praise? False personality wants praise, it doesn't mind what it is for, it will believe anything. What does personality want? It likes to do a job well, and rather objects to flattery. The people with more false personality are weaker and need more encouragement. What does Essence want? Eventually it wants to find its real task. It wants to give, it loves beauty and truth, nature, animals, the good in people, children, but not in a sentimental way. It needs affection. At the level of "Real I" what is wanted? One is only conscious for a moment at the level of "Real I," but then we know what we want. The only want is to do the will of "Real I," to do what we have come here to do. Essence knows, but it is weak and young and childish, it has to grow, then it will be possible for the will of what is God for us to be done on Earth. Chief feature, the most external part, also has a will; it is the self-will. This keeps us asleep, shows us material things, whereas Essence wants spiritual things. According to the things you want, you can know where you are. Where your treasure is there will your heart be also.

Aim and Payment
October 20, 1959

X: This being in the middle: it is a different state and very rare.

MRS. POGSON: Yes, you are on a higher level. It is psychological thinking in the middle, where you can see both sides. First of all, in the Work we are asked to get to know our own opposites. And the first pair of opposites, which we usually don't observe, is that known as elation-and-depression. You have all experienced this. Knowing this pair of opposites you can remember that it is better to beware a little when you feel elated. The period in which to work, and to remember, is when the pendulum is rushing down toward the middle. Dr. Nicoll said that there is a point in the middle of the swing of the pendulum where utterly new meaning enters. It is important to remember this and never make a decision at one end of the pendulum, but always wait until you can see both sides, both yes and no.

I found an interesting connection with this in a book which arrived this afternoon, called *Symbol and Image of William Blake* by G. Digby. I opened it first at a picture showing a young child being snatched away from the opposites. Here was represented the living moment between the opposites, where the new meaning is to be found which yes-*and*-no can give you. This is especially true with regard to people—I'm always coming back to people! Can you see why? And how it is necessary to see both sides of a person?

Today I want to speak about basic things—about aim in connection with what we really want. But people don't know what they want. From the point of view of the Work it doesn't matter what we are or have been: *we are what we want.*

You are not only your understanding but what you want. As your understanding grows, so your idea of what you want grows. To begin with it is a muddle, with different "I's" wanting different things, and you cannot see what it is you really want. But after a time you begin to see that there are two things, two different "wants" in you. Then friction develops between these two things, and out of this something new can grow.

X: Then the states of elation and depression do not last so long.

Mrs. Pogson: No. But what do they come from? You have to see this. When do you feel elated, when depressed? It is your self-love that feels elated, and you are depressed when someone has pricked your balloon.

X: It's such a small thing that can cast you down.

Mrs. Pogson: Yes. Everyone should see this for themselves. It is the small meanings which are pricked. Everyone should see this. Where can you be pricked or cast down? Eventually there should be no such place. It is the false personality from which these states of elation and depression come. If you feel elated, it is so easy to collapse. Everyone should be awake, so that when someone makes a disparaging remark you are not cast down. How many of you can do this? . . . This is how we begin to become balanced. When there is something in the inner parts of the centers, we have something to fall back on.

Let's come back to the question of what we want. If you want to be free from the demands of the false personality, then you are shown. You are directed, and the observations link up.

[The last paragraph of the "Commentary on Aim" (*Psychological Commentaries*, Vol. III, p. 1098) was read.]

> This personal work of self-observation is for *all one's life.*
> Out of it comes the dawning of real aim which is in its
> greatest formulation the desire to awaken. . . . Then peo-
> ple find, specifically, what particular features in them-

selves keep them identified with themselves and so prevent any awakening from taking place. Then they can begin to see where their aim really lies. Then indeed they can pray—that is, ask for help intelligently. They may get it, but only by paying for it—that is, by the sacrifice of something hitherto precious to them.

MRS. POGSON: I want to talk about this question of payment. You get help through paying, through sacrificing something. Do people know what is meant? In ordinary life you pay *afterwards*. In fact, most people's lives consist in paying for the mistakes they have made. This is cause-and-result. It is said that the Work releases us from the law of cause and effect. You are able in the Work to travel along a higher line where cause and effect don't operate, *because you pay first*. How do we pay? All processes are said in the Work to be a reflection of the invisible world. So buying and selling is a reflection of what happens psychologically. That is why you have the term used in the parables: a man goes and sells everything he has in order to buy the field. In the Work we pay gradually. What is paying? We have to give energy and attention. Dr. Nicoll always said that *effort* was our money. We need energy to buy the field.

[The following was put on the board as different members of the group suggested forms of payment.]

PAYMENT IN THE WORK

1) By sacrificing our suffering;
2) By making the effort of self-observation;
3) Giving up grievances;
4) Giving up blaming;
5) Giving up the pleasure of wrong imagination about oneself;
6) Giving up feeling frustrated;
7) Giving up habits;
8) By living with myself, once I know what I am like.

MRS. POGSON: Giving up grievances is one of the hardest things to do. Nearly everyone feels he is owed in some way. When we write this on the board, does everyone visualize a grievance which can be given up? Nobody owes us anything, really. All we get we have attracted. The nagging torment of a grievance can go on for years.

X: This is why I think we have to pay in self-observation, because we are gradually stripped of illusions about ourselves.

MRS. POGSON: Yes, but not until a place is prepared for us and we are able to inhabit deeper "I's." The two things happen together.

How does Essence grow? Chiefly through truth, truth about oneself; through new ideas, new understanding. What does the idea that false personality feeds Essence mean to you? Do you see that the energy which till now was fuel for false personality goes to nourish Essence? If we use energy in grievances, we don't have it to nourish Essence. Now real suffering gives us great energy, because it is seeing the truth about ourselves.

People ask what to work on. It is whatever is there every day, whatever wastes our energy every day. You pay expensively through frustration. Dr. Nicoll was always angry when people asked him what they should work on next.

> ". . . all that we study here is how to pay in advance" (*The Fourth Way*, p. 281). There was a reading of questions and answers on *payment* (*The Fourth Way*, p. 282).

MRS. POGSON: For a long time we want something for nothing. People want all the blessings of the Work without having to pay. They do not think about giving up their grievances for a long time. They think the Work is just given. . . . At first people think: what a wonderful laboratory—so wonderfully equipped! Now my life will change! But then they have to make the effort to learn how to use it. False personality cannot make effort. It is utterly mechanical. It cannot pay. Something deeper has to pay, a deeper level. And you do not know what you will get when you have paid. It is a new experience when you are freed from some of these things. All that we pay is unreal, imaginary. It is all our suffering. To think about changing one must think about what has to go before there is change. One wants to remain the same, and add a little more. But first of all you have to see that you do not want to change. You don't want to do all this work. Until you see this, nothing can happen. You get a shock when you really see that you don't want to change. You have to have many shocks before you want to change.

X: I've observed myself thinking that I've taken a lot of trouble to make myself what I am, and I don't want to waste anything.

MRS. POGSON: Yes—but then you see that what is of value is real and is in you and will not be lost.

Mr. Ouspensky talks about school work: for some people the Work is a school, for others not—and yet the others are there. One may be a person who is not in a school, and yet one day may be in a school, because there is a time when it is possible for the Work to begin to work on a person. It depends on what you want, and what part of you wants it, whether it is a school or not. This is always true. Also, time comes into it. Some people may be working on themselves to begin with; some people may be the material of which the school is made, from which the accumulator is formed, and on whom the Work is working.

Aim—To Live in the Presence of the Work
September 20, 1960

MRS. POGSON: Dr. Nicoll said that the Work looks on one not as what one has been or what one is now, but what one wants. How many of you can believe this? It is this that makes all the difference. You are not judged for what you are or have been, but for what you want. How many can say that it's our past, or even our present lives, that make us valuable to the Work? No, it's what you want. After a time, people in the Work will begin to appear to you as what they want. Some of you will have seen this.

About *aim*. You remember the parable of the rich young man who asked what he should do to inherit eternal life. Our aims are really too vast, too much in imagination. Eternal life! Who can really say that he wants this? We've discussed it before and connected its meaning with the meaning of Aeonian life, of being conscious at the level of "Real I." In flashes of self-remembering, we can remember and connect with this, then the flashes go. Who can say that we want this in ordinary life? We have difficulty in expressing in words what we do want, what our ultimate aim is. In order to attain this ultimate aim, payment has to be made, and we have to think what is necessary in this connection. In their imagination or on occasions, people think they want eternal life or to enter the Kingdom of Heaven, as it is expressed in Christian terminology. But do they think what is meant practically, what is practically necessary? The Work gives us the means for understanding this in a practical way.

Most people want to increase themselves *as they are* and also to attain this level of the Kingdom of Heaven—which will take many lives. They do not see that these two things are incompatible. In the story of the rich young man, he was told to take from the rich and give to the poor, which means to take from the outer man and give to the inner man. The outer "I's" don't know about this aim. What do they want? A piece of chocolate or a cup of coffee? If you look at yourselves at any odd moment during the day, you will see that it is like this. This is how we're constituted.

Now I want somehow to come through tonight to some understanding of what the possibilities of this other way of life mean. You see, people have some understanding of this parable, but they can't apply it. You have to see that it's only a question of changing your attitude to life, not of changing life itself. How shall I put it? You can still do the same job, have the same pleasures, but *in the presence of the Work. . . .* We can formulate our big aim like this—to live in the presence of the Work. Don't you think if we say something like this, the aim comes a little nearer? Isn't this your aim, if we put it like this? To be present in the Work. Then your small aims can be related to this. You can then see that the small aim must be connected with whatever makes you forget your big aim.

It was once said that when the Work is planted in one, it cannot be dislodged. Once a seed begins to grow, it is there; once it becomes a tree, it cannot be removed. Then it doesn't matter what you do, for you do it in the presence of the Work and it is blessed. You see, *life and the Work are not opposites but levels.* You can live on the level of life and then you serve life, a hard taskmaster. If you serve the Work it is different, a hard taskmaster, but different. This means having an ark in yourself, a safe place. The question is how to reach this place.

We've spoken about the narrow way, about the place between *Mi* and *Fa*. People now know about this intellectually, but they don't understand it in themselves. They don't understand what has to become smaller. It's one's feeling of oneself that has to become smaller. Dr. Nicoll used to say: You have to get rid of Mr. *A*, or you have to get rid of Miss *B*, and so on. At first we didn't understand what he meant. It takes very great intelligence to see what he meant.

X: In his commentary on the Work Octave, he says that if the Driver awakens and sees the state of his horse and carriage, he has to think from the Driver and not from Nicoll (*Psychological Commentaries*, Vol. III, p. 1076–1077).

MRS. POGSON: It means you can't do the Work in your usual way. It must be in a different way. *Your payment is what you usually feel yourself through,* whatever that may be. Here we come to a kind of deadlock, because we don't see what it is. We see what it is in other people, but not in ourselves.

X: It means having to lose Mr. *A* completely. Once Dr. Nicoll put a diagram on the board which helped me very much. It was a diagram of a U-tube, down which one has to go and lose oneself completely.

MRS. POGSON: And who comes up? We can't call him Mr. *A*. Someone quite simple, who goes on with whatever he is doing. You see, people don't have to throw away gifts and faculties. Dr. Nicoll used to be quite annoyed if people thought that. It's the way of approach that has to change.

Talking about becoming smaller in the feeling of oneself, I received an example from someone in the Brighton group, someone who was originally very bombastic and took up a lot of room and a lot of time. Now he fits into a very small space and doesn't take up much time. The person stopped at his usual tearoom on his walk and was received in an unusually rude manner by the proprietress. He then recalled that the same event had occurred many years before and he had walked out in a huff, and only later, after he had come into the Work, returned to the tearoom and made it up. This time he decided to take the event differently, so he sat down quietly and waited. After a while the woman returned and said: "So, you're still here! I thought you wouldn't go away." He saw that she had been disturbed by the sudden rush of people into the tearoom and hadn't known what she was saying. This is changing a recurring pattern. You all have a pattern of recurring events which you have to learn to recognize. When certain events recur, then you have choice. No longer does this person have to have in his memory a moment when someone was rude. The change could happen because the person had become smaller; he took up less space, less room. Everyone has such possibilities of choice in his or her pattern.

The important thing in this group is to connect knowledge and being. X writes about this in her letter from India. She has been having Work discussions, and she writes that all this discussion about knowledge made her lose sight of the discipline of the Work. She was then able to see why knowledge can never get us anywhere by itself. She spoke of knowledge as bringing restlessness. You see, she saw that knowledge not put into practice leads nowhere.

What can you say about this ultimate aim and bringing it closer—being present in the Work—whether we are mechanically happy or in trouble?

X: It's a new idea to me that the Work doesn't take us as we are.

MRS. POGSON: Yes. You see, it's a kind of seed in us—what we want. Where would we be if the Work took us as we are, or were? *What we want* is the beginning of realizing our possibilities, if we want it from the right place, if the inner man is strong enough.

X: After a while we are no longer in the extremes of wanting something very much. Then we could become lukewarm about the Work.

MRS. POGSON: It is just a stage. You have to see it. After wanting something very much, then there has to be a calmer stage.

How much of the knowledge have you been able to act from? Or has it all gone into a "haze, a daze, and a maze," as Dr. Nicoll used to say? Try to think about what is the most practical way of coming toward this aim of being longer in the presence of the Work. . . . In looking back over some past meetings I found that we were also talking about aim after the Easter Dorton. We connected it with the hindrance in ourselves that keeps us from working. So *observe* what it is that prevents us from being in the presence of the Work. This is the beginning of a new formulation of aim.

X: If you recall the aims you've had at meetings and personal aims, you find a large list of aims that have been important to you. It's quite easy to connect any of these with big aim intellectually, but more difficult to make the connection emotionally.

MRS. POGSON: These small aims form a kind of acquired conscience. You have to be connected with your big aim, then the small aims connect with it. Any small aim serves its purpose for a time and then gives way to something else. When it comes round again you don't start from where you were before.

[Mrs. Pogson then read from the "Commentary on the Relationship of a Man to Himself" (Vol. I, pp. 365ff.) in which Dr. Nicoll speaks of the "third relationship which is really the subject of this teaching—namely, the relationship of a man to himself."]

> We miss many opportunities for work because we forget about this third relationship. We may be depressed by illness or by the external situation in life to which we happen to be related at the time and, finding no particular comfort in either of them, we may feel at a loss. But over and above both these relationships lies the possibility of the third relationship. We forget to summon the Work just at the very time when we should summon it. Our ordinary thoughts connected with our ordinary daily affairs do not lead into the ideas of the Work. We have to jump: we have deliberately to make a connection with the Work and we must all find different ways of doing this. You all realize how life puts us to sleep, how our pre-occupation with our life-problems cuts us off from the influences of this Work. I would define two different conditions in which anyone in this Work can find himself. One is simply that a man finds himself in the condition in which he feels immersed in things; he feels rather depressed . . . and being as it were, unable to lift his head up, he views life along the vistas of his own negative feelings. The second condition occurs when a man *knows* he is in a bad state from the Work point of view and cannot find out how to get rid of it. I think it is this second state that is most interesting to study in oneself. One knows one is asleep, one recognizes that there is something all wrong, but one does nothing to help oneself. It is just here that some of the worst negative thoughts about the Work can arise.[1]

---

[1]*Psychological Commentaries*, Vol. I, pp. 366, 367.

Mrs. Pogson: This is one of the hindrances that cut us off from the influences of the Work. Who will remember this? If you did, everything would change. People don't hear.

> Here one of the many aspects of sly man comes in. . . . if you feel that you have lost contact with yourself, if you feel that this third relationship which the Work is about has gone wrong and wish to re-connect yourself, you may find some way to do it and deliberately apply it without spending time in being miserable. . . . Recently observing myself under such a condition I began quite deliberately to think of the Ten Commandments. I tried to repeat the first five Commandments from memory and found I did not know them distinctly enough. . . . And just by thinking of these references to following the Will of Higher Beings from which the teaching of this Work comes, I felt a complete transformation taking place in me which was like a shock, and suddenly everything looked different . . .[2]

Mrs. Pogson: Here is his own experience for you, and this is possible for everyone. He devised his own technique. Dr. Nicoll was so practical. He tried something. And the Ten Commandments are so dynamic. They are from C influences. Just to say them was enough. These sources of power are all around us.

Aim and I's
October 4, 1960

Mrs. Pogson: We have the diagram of the cage of "I's" on the board (see diagram 17 on page 256). Mr. Ouspensky said that there were thousands of "I's." At last we have this diagram drawn with enough "I's" in it! Now, it's these "I's" that meet events. They have been engendered in us since the time we were born. There are all kinds. Some are childish, some are educated. Here is man the multiplicity. The Work "I's"—where are they? There are "I's" among these that can hear the Work, that can discriminate and can eventually form Deputy Steward. They have to come together. The hostile "I's"—the

---

[2]*Psychological Commentaries*, Vol. I, p. 367.

ones hostile to the Work—we have to get to know. These are the ones that prevent us from being in the presence of the Work.

[The commentary "Efforts against certain 'I's'" (*Psychological Commentaries*, Vol. III, pp. 974ff) was read.]

MRS. POGSON: You see, if everyone could act from what is said in this paper, there would be a great change. To like what you dislike: not to dislike anything that happens to you. Do you all know what "I's" in you dislike? Do you have a list of your "I's"? You should have a list of ten phrases of dislike that occur during the day. You should see this clearly—but we dream in the Work. Some of these "I's" have only one phrase. It doesn't help what you're doing to let them speak. If someone dislikes you, notice what he dislikes, see what it is. It is most illuminating, what you see. He may have good grounds for disliking you. But he doesn't dislike the whole of you; he dislikes certain "I's."

Can you begin to see the "I's" which have led your life for you? You see that you have not chosen these "I's," and your life is in such

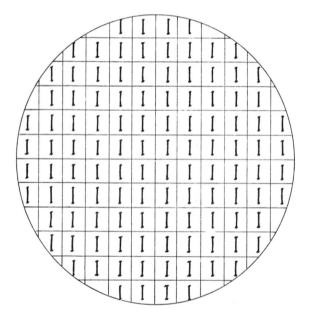

Diagram 17. *The cage of "I's."*

a muddle because of them. Then there are some "I's" that don't want it like this, and they can gradually come together and form a nucleus. This paper was suggested in connection with the aim from last time. Certain groups of "I's" want their own way. They are from the self-will and they can be very strong. When they get their own way, the Work is furthest away. But when you are under the aegis of the Work, you may not get your own way all the time, because something else is drawing you slowly away. When you are checked or frustrated, it is necessary to see whether you want these "I's" to lead your life for you. If not, then you have to work from another place. . . . Can all of you see this motley crowd in yourself? We first thought that Mr. Ouspensky was greatly exaggerating when he said there were hundreds and thousands of these small "I's." But it isn't an exaggeration.

Now people are always asking about decisions. It is usually the small "I's" that make decisions. You'll find this, that you are making decisions from the small "I's," each of which has its own self-will. If we make an aim in the group, it must be made from a deeper place. You have always to think from what place you decide.

[Some passages were read from the "Commentary on Making Decisions in the Work" (*Psychological Commentaries*, Vol. III, pp. 784ff).]

MRS. POGSON: The real Work lies in *remembering,* remembering that there is this place where the Work can make decisions for us.

X: The difficulty is in wanting the Work to make the decisions for us.

MRS. POGSON: Yes, because most of your "I's" don't want the Work to make decisions. The small decisions of a life nature can be left to the small "I's," to the personality "I's" which are capable of deciding such matters. But don't think they are important; don't identify with them; don't allow them to live the whole of your life. What about the rest of your life? *What do you want?*

You have to know what will appear as second force in yourselves if you make an aim in the Work. You have to know what your enemy is when you make an aim, according to your stage and level of being.

[People gave examples of external things which they thought would prevent them from following the way of the Work, such as activities, being too busy, weather, other people, etc.]

MRS. POGSON: Yes, people often think that such things are second force, external things, but second force is within us. It exists in the form of inertia—which is also a cosmic force—or ambition, or wanting other things.

X: It is also wanting to work in your own way and not on what is served up to you.

Mrs. Pogson: Yes . . .

X: There are religious systems which are designed to keep people in the presence of God, or of the Work, all through the day.

MRS. POGSON: Yes. This is what we also speak of in the Work, this is our aim: to be where, as Mother Julian said, we know that all manner of things is well. To be where we know that what is Higher will take over our lives and guide them. This is called being in the presence of a Higher Will. This is also a technique in the Work. Like Brother Lawrence. If we can withdraw our consciousness from these small "I's," the Higher Will can come through and we can see that it is good. But we can only remain in the presence of this Higher Will when this level can be maintained. But is this what you want? Have you thought about this as being the aim of the Work? Sometimes, when you are at a meeting and are in attracted attention, you may want this—but not all the time.

We've spoken so much about being flexible and being able to withdraw consciousness and be further back in ourselves. Now who has been able to do this? Who has found that through *wanting* to very much, he was able to? Because that is how it happens, through wanting to . . .

[A passage was read from the "Commentary on Second Force in Oneself" (*Psychological Commentaries*, Vol. II, p. 543).]

> There are two lives that you can lead. After a time you begin to know what the other life means that you can lead in yourself which the Work can form in you, and you can distinguish it from the life of the ordinary affairs of the day. Eventually you should be living in both. They gradually should cease to be in opposition to each other.

MRS. POGSON: We should be leading two lives, and they are not in opposition to each other. This may sound like theory to some people, but I assure you it is true. People talk about life and the Work as if they should be in opposition. They are not in opposition, but on different levels.

X: It is what we don't know about ourselves which can take us by surprise and put us to sleep.

MRS. POGSON: Yes, that's a good remark. It is something we haven't discovered about ourselves that puts us to sleep. Also, the second force of inertia keeps us from remembering ourselves.

X: The friction we experience makes us think of life and the Work as opposed to each other.

MRS. POGSON: I am glad you reminded us of this. Yes, it has to be like that for a time: that there is friction and a series of choices.

After death we meet our "I's." If they haven't been observed and known, our negative emotions and "I's" appear to us, as in dreams—and some of them in a terrifying way. The Work shows us how to get to know them now so that they cannot terrify us and cannot appear as externalized enemies after death. If we see our "I's," they can no longer harm us. The dying are always reminded, as for example in the *Tibetan Book of the Dead*, that what they are meeting is themselves. We have to see ourselves now, so that this work is over. Once the inner man is in charge of the outer man, once we are integrated, we do not have to go through this experience which someone in whom the outer man is still in control has to meet.

Teachings of Jung
November 3, 1959

> Whatever we neglect or avoid, whatever we dislike or fear, whatever disgusts or irritates us, tends to pass out of consciousness (Nicoll, *Dream Psychology*, p. 176).

> Nothing changes permanently so long as it remains unconscious, except to grow in strength by attracting

energy to itself (Dr. Jung in an interview, *Listener*, October 29, 1959).

MRS. POGSON: I couldn't help thinking how interested Dr. Nicoll would have been that such a talk should have been televised, with so many ideas close to the Work.

X: It is interesting what he says about his father, and about the violence in himself.

MRS. POGSON: Yes. Dr. Nicoll learned from Dr. Jung that one had to learn about one's dark side, that it becomes one's enemy because it has slipped away out of one's consciousness. We haven't deliberately done this, but things we haven't accepted slip down. And they are dangerous because they are still there in us. That is why the Work leads us very gently to see where we can become violent.

X: As long as you are aware of something, you can keep your hand on it and control it. But if you forget about it even for a minute, it pops up.

MRS. POGSON: Isn't it like this? It is this thing which can spoil our lives.

Self-knowledge includes the dark side. This is what Dr. Jung made clear to Dr. Nicoll. Dr. Nicoll's knowledge of this dark side enabled him to lead us toward our own chief features, and to show us how we projected this dark side onto others. . . . In dreams this shadow self can appear in the form of anyone of the same sex, as a younger brother or a colleague.

Dr. Jung spoke of the deep unconscious, below the personal unconscious, where we had knowledge that was common to the race and where there are archetypal images also common to the race. These images appear in myths and also in dreams. The higher centers use what is in the deep unconscious.

X: Is it related to real conscience?

MRS. POGSON: Yes. It is possible to have dreams in which these images are used, and they relate to no part of one's conscious experience. I once had a Mithraic dream of this kind. Dr. Nicoll found it interesting to compare the dreams of patients and to see that they used the same symbols. Here also in the deep unconscious is the violence, the racial violence. Here is the primeval man who may, if the circumstances are right, be stirred to violence. In order to become non-violent, one has to learn about one's own forms of violence.

In the daytime our centers work together; in sleep, they are gradually disconnected. There are different stages of sleep, and dreams can come from every stage. Dreams also come from different centers and different levels. They may come from the instinctive center or the moving center, the emotional center in the form of small anxieties, or the lower mental center. You know that you dream about an examination before you have to take it. Dreams can also come from higher centers. When what is Higher in us wishes to send messages, they are sent through the higher centers, which are like doors. They use the symbols in us. The higher emotional center shows us visions, the higher mental center may show us things in an extraordinary way, in geometric forms. The dream can tell you something you don't know in your waking moments. Where does it come from? We think it comes from something higher in us that is trying to teach us. The dream has to use the material available. The material consists of impressions the person has had. So the dream is dressed up. The same message may be conveyed differently to different people, according to the material available in each of them.

X: But sometimes it uses material which is not in one, or at least of which one has never been conscious. I am thinking of a Sanskrit word which appeared in one of my dreams. It required a great deal of research to discover its meaning.

MRS. POGSON: When one asks a question and receives the answer on awakening, this also comes from higher centers.

Dr. Nicoll's dream of crossing the prehistoric ditch is very significant. The ditch represented the deep unconscious, filled with prehistoric bones, with violence. Beyond violence, on the other side of the ditch, was a man who was able to teach new recruits without being impatient, without being identified (*Psychological Commentaries*, Vol. V, pp. 1595–1597). It was shown to Dr. Nicoll so that he could see how he was to teach. But in order to do this, in order to reach this place, you have first to cross the ditch; and before that you must see it in yourself. You have to see where you get violent and what makes you violent. Then possibly you can meet a situation which would usually make you violent without violence. But this requires preparation.

Can you see the reason why, now that we are in the Work, we think it expedient to review the day? Because now we do not want to let things go down and be repressed. Do you see that this is our reason for wanting to recall the day accurately, especially when we have had an argument or given in to negative emotions or had what we call an unpleasant experience?

X: What should we remember?

MRS. POGSON: We should record how we react. Just look at it truthfully and record what happened. This is what life leads us to: to go to psychiatrists and talk it out. Now we don't need to do this. You can look at unpleasant events and see and record them.

Meaning

MRS. POGSON: We spoke recently about the need to be in the presence of the Work during the day, and then we spoke of what it was that prevented us. It is necessary to know this, so that we can know where to work.

Meaning is important in this connection. The outer man has one sort of meaning, and the inner man has another.

[The commentary, "Further Notes on Meaning" (*Psychological Commentaries*, Vol. II, pp. 469ff) was read.]

MRS. POGSON: When I get to know anybody new in the Work, the chief thing I want to know is where the person finds meaning. This is what one needs to know about a person.

X: You get meaning in a new way by seeing that it is more important to transform a recurring event than to go on doing the same thing.

MRS. POGSON: Yes. You may have got meaning from getting negative about a certain event. Or when you speak with emphasis or with gestures, there you find meaning. For a long time people find meaning in negative emotions. This is what Dr. Nicoll called "poor meaning."

X: What really happens is that a small group of "I's," with your consciousness which they have robbed, gets meaning, but it doesn't give meaning to the whole of you.

MRS. POGSON: This has to do with being ill in the world of meaning. Dr. Nicoll sometimes told us about people who had come to him having had a nervous breakdown. He said it was because they had lost their meaning, and what he did was to give them new meaning. He didn't always tell them about the Work, but showed them other kinds of meaning.

X: Often the event changes when you take it differently.

MRS. POGSON: Yes, but you can't work for this result. It happens particularly in relation to people, because in the invisible world one emotion affects another, and your transformed emotion will affect the other person.
 It is necessary in the Work to nourish this growth of new meaning. When you have been some time in the Work, you will find there is new meaning around you on all sides. Essence grows from this new meaning. The outer man can grow up to a certain point from old meanings, but new meaning nourishes Essence, and this we can take with us from life to life.

[A further passage from the commentary was read.]

MRS. POGSON: Dr. Nicoll says that what may be possible now may not be possible later. We always talked about things in a new way with him, from different points of view. One time we would talk about the Parables, another time we would see it from the point of view of dance. You notice also at Dorton how we are always changing the way we talk about ideas. There always has to be this change. We have to be flexible, and not go on too long in any one way. We find new meaning, then we leave it for a time, and later it will return.

X: I re-read the story of Lazarus, after thinking I understood it. I found several passages I didn't understand.

Mrs. Pogson: When we read it at Dorton, it conducted more meaning; it is not always possible to reconnect with this later. People also find that in re-reading the Dorton notes. At one time, you may begin to discover the Enneagram and have thoughts about it, and then you think you've forgotten what you once understood. But it's not quite forgotten. It will come back. Things go on underground.

With Dr. Nicoll we also frequently changed aims, and it would sometimes seem that we'd leave an aim half-finished. But you find when you come back to the original aim that it is stronger. There is a kind of turning circle. This is how the Work works.

X: This shows the unity of the Work.

Mrs. Pogson: Yes. Everything is connected. Anything not understood can be laid aside for a while, and in the end it has its place. I remember how this was myself.

Self-Love and Freedom
October 18, 1960

Mrs. Pogson: One of the group, sending in her observations, has referred to the commentary on the Seal of Solomon as appropriate to our aim for the past fortnight. She writes: If only we could keep this symbol in mind always, seeing in it that we are in everything presented with a choice (see diagram 18).

In this commentary ("Commentary on Self-Love, II," Vol. II, pp. 474ff) the symbol is referred to in a way I like very much, as "a sky

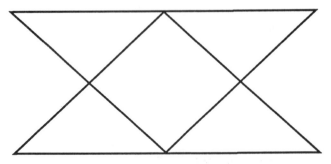

Diagram 18. The sky fitted over the Earth of ourselves.

fitted over the Earth of ourselves." It is a dimension we are not aware of always. You see how broad this "earth of ourselves" is, where the small "I's" are on the ground. But whenever we are aware of the new dimension of ourselves, like an umbrella over us, we can be under its protection. This is the meaning of the canopy as it appears in many ways, over our Queen, over a Bishop, and so on. It means that for the time being the person is acting from a higher law, and the person is protected. To remember this higher dimension is a form of self-remembering. The canopy represents the level of the Kingdom of Heaven.

X: This is how many mythologies begin—with the marriage of Earth and Sky.

MRS. POGSON: Yes, and so we do, too. Essence knows about this canopy, for it is the child, and so is protected. But the false personality doesn't think there is a need of anything else. That is why this commentary is called a commentary on self-love. For the self-love says: "What on Earth has it got to do with me?" No—nothing *on Earth!*

[Several passages from this commentary were read.]

MRS. POGSON: You see, new meaning gives freedom and old meanings are what keep us in prison. I wonder if you can see it like this. Old meanings are some of the bars that keep us in prison. You have to see what you really want to be free from. Most people will say immediately negative emotions or something else, but these are often just words.

X: I want to be free from having my life lived for me.

MRS. POGSON: If you have really seen this and want to be free from it, then it is something real. But people don't very quickly come to see this. They prefer to go on in the ordinary way. People like prison, in a way. It's easier than the unknown. But it is possible to be freed from it.

X: I want to be free from accounts.

MRS. POGSON: Do you really want to be free from accounts? You all say this, and yet, on the way home, you may get out an old account and look at it. People are always going over their accounts, again and again. Yet we know there is a way of canceling accounts.

X: I want to be free from inner talking.

MRS. POGSON: How do you stop inner talking? By making inner stop and then giving your attention to something, to a definite train of thought.

X: I want to be free from fear of other people, in particular other people's opinions.

MRS. POGSON: Who is free from that? Only the Work can make you free. Here is a man, well-dressed and so on, but he is terrified of what other people think. But the inner man—is he afraid of other people? No. He has nothing to lose.

X: The outer man gets his meaning from what other people think.

MRS. POGSON: Yes, he very often does.

X: Does he know he's hollow? [X refers to the wooden doll—a Russian doll balanced on the table—that Mrs. Pogson had just been speaking about.]

MRS. POGSON: Yes—maybe he's protecting it. The inner man has some humility. The outer man asserts himself the more he sees he's hollow—so that others won't see, and partly so that he won't see it himself. How do you think to become a bit freer from this? By knowing yourself, knowing that the outer man is imagination anyway.

X: And that many times the other person isn't thinking of you at all when you're wondering what he is thinking.

X: One can have moments in a group when one feels it isn't necessary to worry about what others think.

MRS. POGSON: Yes, at Dorton this is possible. It is possible to become freer from worry about other people's opinions when one loses some coats of the false personality.

X: I want to be free from the need to be right.

MRS. POGSON: Who is free from this? Some of you are gradually beginning to be free from this. It is almost like coming out of prison to admit you're wrong. It is a terrible effort to be right all the time.

X: I want to be free from identification with people and things.

MRS. POGSON: Yes. Identification with people is the greatest. How do you become free from this? By thinking from the Work; by inhabiting "I's" in the inner part of the emotional center, where one has understanding and can release the other person and so release oneself. This has to do with work on the emotional center, work against the self-love to begin with. In the outer part of the center are the "I's" of the self-love and in the inner part, charity and love. It is a question of withdrawing our consciousness into a deeper part of ourselves.

X: I want to be free from comparing.

MRS. POGSON: The ideas of the Work can free us from this: the idea that everyone is unique, that where we are is what we've earned, that another person is at a different stage, that everyone has a different task to do, and so on. All the ideas of the Work can help. I wish I could make you all understand this. Now, give examples of comparing.

X: Comparing when you're doing a job—someone else is doing it better.

MRS. POGSON: We are under a higher form of justice, and yet we tend to judge as if we were all on the same level of being. We are not all the same. What are you like inside, that's what matters. In everything you do, you show your being. But you can, at different times, be in different places in your being. A person could ask a question from the false personality—or from Essence, and a real place. You just have to see this. If only this could be clear to you. If you hear a real question, there is no need to compare. Be glad, because all real questions help the group.

X: Comparison comes from seeing that someone else has more of something.

MRS. POGSON: We are under this law of inequality.

X: But people bring things off better than you do.

MRS. POGSON: You are all at a certain stage of being; try to see others like this. How can I help you to see people as I do? Do you see how people are, how each person in Essence is unique? I see people as the possibilities they may grow into. A person is what he wants. That is what's interesting. If you see a person is asking a question from false personality, you just see that it is so. See where a person is. There is no question of comparing qualities in any way. There are infinite possibilities for everyone.

X: I wish to be free from the feeling of being owed.

MRS. POGSON: Yes, this is the greatest prison. This is an account. Dr. Nicoll used to show us our account books, and how they were fuller on one side than on the other. For example, someone owes me an apology, or understanding, or a book he's borrowed, and so on. But what about the other side? What do we owe? We owe so much; once we begin to fill in this other side, we see it. On bigger scale, we owe consideration and listening to people we've never listened to.

All Saints' Day
November 1, 1960

MRS. POGSON: We have spoken before of the cosmic principle that when anything dies energy is released. When an account dies, when we die to anything in ourselves, energy is released for future work. This is a day, All Saints' Day as it is called in the Church, when we think of what we owe to Conscious Humanity, to all those saints and teachers who have gone before, opened the door and shown us the way. They have released a great deal of energy into the world. We owe them a great deal for this. In the lives of the saints there is a series of deaths in which energy is released. This is why more conscious people are able to give so much to other people, because they are able to die to something. We saw this in our teachers. And this is true of Christ on very big scale. Today is the day to think of them. They form a nucleus who can eventually contribute to the raising of the level of being of the whole.

The Guy—which Dr. Nicoll used to love to act—we carry about in front of us. We carry him before us through the crowds. But how much easier we could walk through the crowds without this guy. Eventually the guy has to be burned. We have a fine guy enacted for us in the streets at this time of year. This is at the time of an old Celtic festival when people used to make their own guys or masks representing symbolically the "I's" in themselves they wished to discard. Then the masks or guys would be burned, and on the principle of sympathetic magic they would be freed from something. These festivals go on, as this one has, if they are based on a truth.

X: The same festival can be found in Asia Minor and Greece.

MRS. POGSON: Yes. This one is based on a Druid festival. It is interesting how this festival was revived by Guy Fawkes![3] This belongs to the process of inner development: what is unreal, the mask, can be thrown on the fire so that the person can be free.

It would be interesting to see what it is that is always getting caught on something, that is always getting offended. Can you see what it is? . . . As we are now, we feel ourselves through pictures, but if we could lose our pictures, our requirements would be reduced and we should become more simple and less vulnerable. It was wonderful to see how Dr. Nicoll became more simple.

It would be good if you could let one requirement go each week! In Essence there are no requirements.

Last time we took one thing we wanted to be free from, namely accounts. Now how would you set about being free from the fear of other people's opinions or criticism? This is something that can happen in the Work if you want to be free, because you go back into your own center of gravity and don't work for approval. . . . The inner man is not vulnerable to all that happens around us. If we live in external parts of ourselves, we live with half-meanings. "The external man . . . is open to the ambitions, cares, and worries of life." The external man is worried in different ways, about other people's opinions, and so on; but the inner man is turned the other way, he is cherishing his own thoughts; and if circumstances change he still has his thoughts and his meaning. He is not vulnerable.

---

[3]American readers may not know about the English celebration of Guy Fawkes Day. More information is in *Unforgettable Fragments*, in "The Fires of Scorpio," p. 251.

"Self-esteem, self-liking, self-approbation keep the external man active." And this includes the esteem and liking of others; for some people, if this is withdrawn, they collapse.

X: Does the inner man take meaning with him through the periods of darkness and difficulty?

Mrs. Pogson: He takes with him the meaning of what he has heard when he was listening. If you take one idea, for example the idea that we owe more than we are owed, that idea is pregnant with meaning. You can take it with you and ponder on it when waiting for a bus. It is an idea that can make Essence grow.

Then it is necessary to recognize when to act from it. It is possible to hold it in the middle part of a center for a fortnight and not see where to apply it. You have to be practical. You have to see the picture of yourself, see the requirements you no longer need, and then act without a requirement.

What plans do people have for making ideas practical? Do you write down the aim so that you won't forget it? If you want to carry out an aim you find that something almost immediately presents you with an opportunity. But some people will say: "Oh, I didn't mean to begin so soon." And others will recognize the opportunity when it comes.

BIBLIOGRAPHY

Blofeld, John. *The Wheel of Life*. London: Rider, 1959; Boston: Shambhala, 1988.

Collin, Rodney. *The Theory of Celestial Influence*. London: Vincent Stuart, 1954; New York: Samuel Weiser, 1973.

———. *The Theory of Eternal Life*. London: Vincent Stuart, 1956; New York: Samuel Weiser, 1974.

Conze, Edward. *Buddhist Scriptures*. London: Penguin Books, 1943.

Digby, G. *Symbol and Image of William Blake*.

Guillaumont, A., Puech, H-CH., Quispel, G., Till, W., Yassah 'Abd Al Masih. *The Gospel According to Thomas*. Leiden: E. J. Brill, 1959.

Grant, Robert M. *Secret Sayings of Jesus*. New York: Doubleday, 1960.

Graves, Robert. *The White Goddess*. Magnolia, MA: Peter Smith, 1983; London: Faber, 1952.

Lost Books of the Bible and The Forgotten Books of Eden, translated from the original tongues. New York: Meridian, 1974.

Mead, G. R. S. *Thrice Greatest Hermes*. Reprint: York Beach, ME: Samuel Weiser, 1992. Originally published in London in 1906.

Nicoll, Maurice. *Dream Psychology*. Originally published by Hodder & Stroughton in 1917. Reprinted by Samuel Weiser, York Beach, ME, 1979.

———. *Living Time and the Integration of Life*. London: Vincent Stuart, 1952.

———. *The Mark*. London: Vincent Stuart, 1954.

———. *Psychological Commentaries on the Teaching of Gurdjieff and Ouspensky*, five volumes. London: Vincent Stuart, 1952.

———. *Simple Explanation of Work Ideas*. London: Privately printed limited edition, 1994. This previously unpublished manuscript was discovered among Beryl Pogson's papers.

Nott, C. S. *Teachings of Gurdjieff*. London: Routledge & Kegan Paul, 1961; New York: Samuel Weiser, 1961.

Oldham, Muriel and Ronald. *Short Talk on Work Teaching—Work Poems*. London: Privately printed limited edition, 1993.

Ouspensky, P. D. *The Fourth Way: A Record of Talks and Answers to Questions based on the Teaching of G. I. Gurdjieff*. London: Routledge & Kegan Paul, 1957; New York: Random, 1971.

———. *In Search of the Miraculous: Fragments of an Unknown Teaching*. London: Routledge & Kegan Paul, 1950; New York: Harvest, Harcourt Brace, 1965.

———. *The Strange Life of Ivan Osokin*. New York & London: Holme Press, 1947; New York: Viking Penguin, 1988.

Pogson, Beryl. *Commentary on the Fourth Gospel*. London: Privately printed limited edition, 1993.

———. *In the East My Pleasure Lies*. Privately printed limited edition, 1994.

———. *Maurice Nicoll: A Portrait*. London: Vincent Stuart, 1961. Reprinted by Fourth Way Books, New York, 1987.

———. *More Work Talks*. London: Privately printed limited edition, 1966, 1994.

———. *Unforgotten Fragments*. Privately printed limited edition, 1994.

———. *Work Talks at Brighton*. London: Privately printed limited edition, 1966, 1993.

———. *Work Talks at the Dicker*. London: Privately printed limited edition, 1966, 1993.

Reyner, J. H. *God Beyond Time*. New York and London: Regency Press, 1965.

———. *Universe of Relationships*. London: Vincent Stuart Publishers, 1960.

Shattock, E. H. *An Experiment in Mindfulness*. London: Rider, 1958.

Schonfield, Hugh J. *The Authentic New Testament*. London: Dobson, 1956.

The Talmud. Translated by H. Polano. New York: Federich Warne & Co., n.d.

Watts, Alan W. *Myth and Ritual in Christianity*. London & New York: Thames & Hudson, 1953; Boston: Beacon, 1968.

Weil, Simone. *Waiting on God*. New York: HarperCollins, 1973.

Wouk, Herman. *This is My God*. London: Fontana, 1976; New York: Touchstone, Simon & Schuster, 1986.

Index

Beryl Pogson was a pupil of Dr. Maurice Nicoll for nineteen years and his secretary for fourteen, during which period she was one of a small group who lived with him and Mrs. Nicoll at the houses where "The Work" was carried on: Typeponds, Birdlip, Quaremead and Great Amwell House. Before his death in 1953, Dr. Nicoll authorized Beryl Pogson to teach "The Work." Her biography *Maurice Nicoll: A Portrait* was originally published in England by Vincent Stuart in 1961 and reprinted in the United States in 1987 by Fourth Way Books, New York. She is also the author of *In the East My Pleasure Lies, Work Talks at the Dicker, More Work Talks, Commentary on the Fourth Gospel, Three Plays by Shakespeare* and *The Royalty of Nature.*